Spacematrix

SPACEMATRIX

Space, Density and Urban Form

Meta Berghauser Pont
Per Haupt

NAi Publishers, Rotterdam 2010

FOREWORD

This book is the result of the cooperation between two architects and researchers with very different geographical origins; Meta Berghauser Pont, who was born in Cameroun and grew up in the east of the Netherlands, and Per Haupt, who gradually moved from rural Sweden to more populated areas in the south of that country. We met in Delft and for the last one and a half decades have combined living in the Randstad with frequent visits to the north, and in so doing experienced both personally and professionally the pros and cons of physical concentration and desolation.

The Netherlands, with almost 500 inhabitants per km^2, has one of the highest overall population densities in the world, while Sweden has slightly more than 20 inhabitants per km^2 and represents a country with one of the lowest overall densities.[1] The capital cities Amsterdam and Stockholm, however, have about the same population density, between 4,000 and 4,500 inhabitants per km^2. It is worth noting, though, that Stockholm offers its inhabitants three times more urban green open space per city dweller, which means that the density of the built up areas in general is slightly higher there.

1
UN, National Statistical
Offices/UN/Euromonitor
International, 2009

In our practice as architects and urbanists, we have been studying the potential of urban density as a tool for urban planning and design ever since 2000, when we executed a commission for Bureau Parkstad in Amsterdam. Even before that, in 1997, density played an important role in the graduation project of Meta Berghauser Pont. *Pink is Beautiful* proposed to rearrange and relocate pork farms in relation to population densities in order to minimize transport and disease risks.

Our fascination with density is not primarily normative. We do not claim to know which density is the best, but are driven by the wish to understand the relational logic between density and different spatial and non-spatial properties. In our opinion this is a prerequisite to understand and successfully predict the effects of specific design and planning proposals. The relation between the visual image and the spatial characteristics present in that image, and numbers such as amount, size, physical properties and economic values are the focus of our attention. Thus we are interested in demystifying the use of image-based references and concepts such as 'urbanity' by challenging the reliability of such concepts and critically examining the possibility of partially redefining them through density.

The aim is not to turn architects and urban designers into technocratic number fetishists, or to provide developers and bureaucrats with shortcuts to making the role of the designer irrelevant. Quite the opposite is true. Equipped with structural understanding of the nature of urban density, the skills of architects and urbanists needed in their daily trade-offs between quantitative requirements, physical constraints and qualitative preferences will be expanded. And it should also empower us as professionals in our cooperation and confrontation with economists, engineers and politicians.

The inconsistency of three recent newspaper articles illustrates the need to better understand the relation between density and urban form.

Former minister Jacqueline Cramer (Ministry of Housing, Spatial Planning and the Environment) and former minister Ronald Plasterk (Ministry of Education, Culture and Science) discuss the necessity to densify our cities and claim that high-rise buildings will solve the problem;[2] architect Rudy Uytenhaak, however, states that 'towers are not the best way to build a lot of dwellings on a small area of land';[3] and Friso de Zeeuw claims that 'with smart low-rise solutions there is plenty of space'.[4] All three opinions underestimate the inherent spatial logic of density, ignore the importance of scale, and end up in discussions about architectural solutions. We hope that our research can contribute to a more fundamental and factual discussion concerning space consumption, density and urban form.

2
Anonymous, 'Nota tegen rommelig bouwen', NRC Handelsblad 28 June 2008.
3
Hulsman, B., 'Die domme steden', NRC Handelsblad 28 February/1 March 2009, 4-5.
4
Schreuder, A., 'Wat goed in Breda past, past niet overal in de Randstad', NRC Handelsblad 13/14 September 2008, 5.

This book is based on research done by the authors at the Department of Urbanism of Delft University of Technology. The dissertation titled *Space, Density and Urban Form*, defended in November 2009, forms the basis for this book. As already mentioned, the product is the result of a close cooperation. Each of us has contributed to the final result with his/her specific knowledge, capability and fascination. The synergetic effect of this specific working process has resulted in the present book. The search for a method that can convey simultaneous information about quantity (density) and quality (properties), and can serve both planners, designers and scientists was made more efficient and innovative through our close cooperation. The method that is presented has been developed through synchronicity and iteration – jumps between different scales, simultaneous awareness of generic abstractions and contingent, material cases – and can be described as a bridging construction that spans the gap between image-concerned designers and commissioners, and number fetishists among engineers, economists and commissioners. The interaction between abstract modelling and empirical analysis, between isolated innovation and reality check has not only been central to the research, but has been strengthened by the difference in expertise between the two researchers.

Besides thanking each other for the constructive comments, the critical notes and the firm discussions that were central to the process of thinking and writing, we would like to thank Han Meyer and John Westrik for their conviction of the importance of the subject and their unshaken faith in our abilities to explore it. Special thanks are due to Eric van der Kooij who has been a true believer in Spacemate since 2000 and has given us the opportunity to test the results in different projects in Amsterdam ever since. Further, we would like to thank Håkan Ericsson, Hanneke Rolden and Eric Dorsman who have helped us with parts of the fieldwork. Håkan especially has been a true 'space mate' through all these years, travelling with us to, among many places, Achterbos, Dwarsgracht, Barcelona and Berlin, always providing us with both excellent photo material and exciting discussions on village and city life. In Delft we have had the opportunity to work with Rudy Uytenhaak, Truus de Bruin-Hordijk and Marjolein van Esch during our investigation of daylight performance in relation to density. During joint workshops with Master students in Delft, and on many other occasions, we have enjoyed the intense discussions with Rudy Uytenhaak about density and the 'best' way to densify our cities. We would also like to thank everybody who made the publication of this book possible; Marcel Witvoet (NAi publisher); D'Laine Camp (editor), Studio Joost Grootens, the Ministry of Spatial Planning and the Environment (VROM), the Municipality of Amsterdam (dRO), EFL Stichting, and the Department of Urbanism (TU Delft). Of course our two children, Kajsa and Elis, must be thanked for keeping us from working now and then. And, last but not least, we would like to thank our parents and friends, who after periods of optimistic time management were always willing to watch the children so we could work.

To our great sorrow, during the writing of this book we lost the world's best father and a dear friend. We will miss him forever.

Meta Berghauser Pont and Per Haupt
May 2010

Concentrated high-rise development in Hong Kong, China.

Low-rise development in Phoenix, Arizona, USA.

1
THE CONCEPT OF DENSITY

How humans have come to use space over time – in some cases judged as too intensely, in others as not intensely enough – and the problems connected to this, have resulted in discussions concerning the application of the concept of density in urbanism.[1] The use of the concept has varied greatly through modern planning and design. At the beginning of the twentieth century, Raymond Unwin claimed that nothing was to be gained from overcrowding in cities; he proposed a standard density of 12 houses per net acre *maximum*, or 30 houses per hectare.[2] Fifty years later, Jane Jacobs warned that American slums were not only an issue faced in the inner cities, but also in the low-density, dull areas on the fringes. She suggested that a *minimum* of 100 dwellings per net acre (250 dwellings per hectare) was a necessary condition for a vital and participatory city life.[3] Today high densities and the compact city are often seen as prerequisites for sustainable urbanization and economic growth.[4]

The concept of density in urbanism is frequently used to describe the relationship between a given area and the number of certain entities in that area. These entities might be people, dwellings, services, or floor space. However, the simple fact that density is used in, for instance, design requirements, plan descriptions and communication between parties, does not mean that it is used correctly or to its full potential. In the following chapters, we describe the origins and the contents of existing density concepts, the way these concepts have been used to guide the use of space, and their limitations in doing so. We also present an alternative, multivariable approach, and the results it has achieved. Before doing so, this chapter defines the main research questions and the structure of the book.

It is important to make a distinction between urban density used to describe a built environment (*descriptive* use); and urban density used as a norm in the process of planning and designing the city (*prescriptive*, or normative, use). Prior to the twentieth century, density in cities was merely a result of the complex process of city development. Building techniques, legal constraints, traditions, the requirements for economic profitability, etcetera determined the possible resulting densities. However, no conscious use was made of density. As a matter of fact, density as a concept in urban analysis and planning probably did not exist until the second half of the nineteenth century. During this period, high densities in industrializing cities were argued to be one of the major causes of fires, disease and social disorder. Mainly through critical publications in England and Germany, the awareness of the problem grew among legislators and urban planners. As a result, planning controls were developed that prescribed *maximum* allowable densities.[5] The legislative developments were paralleled by the introduction of a scientific approach to the large city expansions that took place during the economic and demographic boom of the second half of the nineteenth century. In works by Reinhard Baumeister and Joseph Stübben in Germany, density played a role in the discussions of the preferred urban form. At first, the regulation of density was more indirect through prescribed maximum building heights

1
With the term 'urbanism' we refer to the intentional ordering and designing of settlements, from the smallest towns to the world's largest cities. Also referred to as urban planning and urban design.
2
Unwin, R., *Town Planning in Practice* (London: T. Fisher Unwin, 1909), 320. 1 acre = 0.405 hectare.
3
Jacobs, J., *The Death and Life of Great American Cities* (New York: Random House, 1992), originally published in 1961, 211.
4
For example: Hall, P., *Cities in Civilization* (London: Phoenix, 1999); Florida, R., *Cities and the Creative Class* (New York: Routledge, 2005); Jenks, M., E. Burton and K. Williams (eds.), *The Compact City: A Sustainable Urban Form?* (London: E&FN Spoon, 1996); Lozano, E., 'Density in Communities, or the Most Important Factor in Building Urbanity', in: M. Larice and E. Macdonald (eds.), *The Urban Design Reader* (Oxon: Routledge, 2007), 312–327; Newman, P. and J. Kenworthy, *Sustainability and Cities: Overcoming Automobile Dependence* (Chicago: University of Chicago Press, 1999).

5
Churchman, A., 'Disentangling the Concept of Density', *Journal of Planning Literature*, 13 (4) 1999, 389–411.

and minimal street widths. Later, mainly through building ordinances, maximum densities were explicitly used to regulate the urban plan.[6]

If the 'regularism' of the second half of the nineteenth century was a means to facilitate the expansions of the industrializing cities by shaving off its most gruesome edges, the later Garden City Movement suggested a totally different urban model. Critics and designers such as Unwin and Ebenezer Howard in England used density to propagate the advantages of decentralized and self-contained smaller cities.

Taking off in the 1960s, extensive discussions took place concerning the issue of urban sprawl and its negative effects on the liveliness of cities, on transportation and the environment. The criticism was not only directed towards the privatized forms of suburban sprawl (low-rise) but also against the relatively low-density, high-rise expansions of the Modern Movement that were built after the Second World War. Compact cities were judged by many to be the best response to counter these developments. In many parts of the world, the affluence of societies has been manifested through increased space consumption. In some cases this has led to calls for regulating the *minimum* densities of redevelopments and city expansions.

> During the last century, density has thus been used both to describe the problems of the city (as too dense a century ago, and as too dispersed today) and, based on such diagnoses, as a norm to prescribe alternatives, at times formulated as maximum densities, at other moments as minimum densities.

In spite of the practical advantages of the concept of urban density in urban planning, critics have argued – especially since the revolt in the 1970s against the quantitative methods of modernist planning – that the use of density for anything but statistical purposes is questionable, as it is perceived as a too elastic concept that poorly reflects the spatial properties of an urban area. Professionals, as well as researchers, hold the opinion that measured density and other physical properties are independent of each other:

> Very different physical layouts can have similar measured densities. Previous analyses . . . show that measured density and other physical factors are quite independent of each other.[7]

> Often people confuse density with building type and assume, for example, that detached houses are lower density than attached housing types. While this is generally true it is not always the case. A high-rise tower with large units set on a park-like site may have a lower density than a set of detached houses on small lots.[8]

> One of the problems of defining density in operational terms is the relatively weak relationship between density and building type. The same density can be obtained with radically different building types, and the same type can be used to obtain different densities.[9]

Besides the argued lack of relationship between density and form, density is also considered with suspicion because of the confusion regarding the definition of plan boundaries and the scale at which these are measured.

6
Rådberg, J., *Doktrin och täthet i svenskt stadsbyggande 1875–1975* (Stockholm: Statens råd för byggnadsforskning, 1988).

7
Alexander, E.R., 'Density Measures: A Review and Analysis', *Journal of Architectural and Planning Research* 10 (3) 1993, 181–202, 184.

8
Forsyth, A., 'Measuring Density: Working Definitions for Residential Density and Building Density', *Design Brief*, 8 2003, Design Center for American Urban Landscape, University of Minnesota, 4.

9
Lozano, 'Density in Communities', op. cit. (note 4), 325.

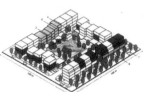

Three areas with 75 dwellings per hectare (Fernandez Per & Mozas 2004: 206–207).

Although it is common to distinguish between net and gross density, the definitions vary from place to place:[10] parcel density, net-net density, net and gross residential density, general density and community density are some of the units of measure used. For instance, the population density of the municipality of Amsterdam was 44 inhabitants per hectare in 2000 (excluding water). The density of its urbanized areas, however, was 63 inhabitants per hectare, and the gross residential density – excluding large-scale working areas and green areas[11] – was almost three times higher: 125 inhabitants per hectare.[12]

Notwithstanding the described shortcomings of the existing density concepts, there is a pragmatic need to continue to use density during the process of city building. In general, however, the use of density seems to create some discomfort. For one, we continue to use and require the concept for planning, programming and in the evaluation of urban environments. On the other hand, we are told that the concept of density has very little relevance for the resulting urban form. It is disturbing that the concept comes with a large 'warning disclaimer'. However, what if the definitions and methods that have been used to argue against a relation between density and form have just been ineffective in establishing such a relation?

After an apparent lack of interest in density in urbanism, the concept recently received attention in a series of Dutch polemical designs: *Point City* and the publications *Farmax* and *Metacity/Datatown*.[13] Other examples of the (re)introduction of density in Dutch urbanism are the works of Gert Urhahn and Milos Bobic; Meta Berghauser Pont and Per Haupt; and Rudy Uytenhaak. In two publications, *A Pattern Image* and *Strategie voor stedelijkheid*, Urhahn and Bobic describe density as one important element of urban quality.[14] Of more recent date is *Spacemate: The Spatial Logic of Urban Density*, in which the first results of the research at hand were published,[15] and *Cities full of Space: Qualities of Density* which investigates the possibilities of designing and living in more compact cities.[16] Also, attempts were recently made internationally to grasp the relation between density and built form: *Visualizing Density*; *Densité et Formes urbaines dans la métropole marseillaise*; *DBOOK: Density, Data, Diagrams, Dwellings*; and *Indicateurs morphologiques pour l'amenagement: Analyse de 50 périmètres batis situés sur le canton de Genève*.[17] The number of detailed descriptions in these publications of all facets of the built environment is impressive and useful, but a basic interpretative framework and in-depth research are often lacking. Publications mostly result in an elaborate series of examples.

10
Churchman, 'Disentangling', op. cit. (note 5).

11
'Green areas' include parks, sports fields, garden allotments and graveyards.

12
Calculations are based on maps drawn by the authors using historical maps from Amsterdam and population data. For a detailed account of the data and sources, see Berghauser Pont, M. and P. Haupt, *Space, Density and Urban Form* (Delft: 2009), 235–271.

13
Koolhaas, R., *S,M,L,XL* (Rotterdam: 010 Publishers, 1995), 888–893; MVRDV, *Metacity/Datatown* (Rotterdam: 010 Publishers, 1999); MVRDV, *Farmax* (Rotterdam: 010 Publishers, 1998).

14
Urhahn, G.B. and M. Bobic, *A Pattern Image* (Bussum: Uitgeverij THOTH, 1994); Urhahn, G.B. and M. Bobic, *Strategie voor stedelijkheid* (Bussum: Uitgeverij THOTH, 1996).

15
Berghauser Pont, M. And P. Haupt, *Spacemate: The Spatial Logic of Urban Density* (Delft: DUP Science, 2004).

16
Uytenhaak, R., *Cities Full of Space: Qualities of Density* (Rotterdam: 010 Publishers, 2008).

17
Campoli, J. and A.S. MacLean, *Visualizing Density* (Cambridge, MA: Lincoln Institute of Land Policy, 2007); Fernandez Per, A., and J. Mozas, *DBOOK: Density, Data, Diagrams, Dwellings* (Vitoria-Gasteiz: a+tediciones, 2007); Brunner, C., *Densité et formes urbaines dans la métropole marseillaise* (Marseilles: Edition Imbernon, 2005); CETAT, *Indicateurs morphologiques pour l'amenagement: Analyse de 50 périmetres batis situes sur le canton de Geneve* (Geneva: Departement des traveaux publics, 1986).

There is clearly a need for further fundamental research on density. Systematic development of work dealing with the relation between the quantitative and qualitative aspects of space consumption has yet to occur. The concept of density as such cannot be blamed for explanatory shortcomings; this is caused more by the formulation of specific definitions and their applications. Formulating another definition of density might help to establish an effective relation to urban form. This book presents such a definition in the form of a multivariable density concept, the Spacematrix, and promotes the establishment of a science of density.

THE BROADER CONTEXT

Besides the mentioned arguments for a revaluation of density, there are presently two general developments in the process of urbanization which can be identified that further legitimize the study of density. First, recent changes in how city building is organized have created a greater need to relate development programmes to spatial qualities. Second, the trend in the increase in space consumption and the environmental, economic and social effects associated with this trend point to the need for research into the relationship between the quality and capacity of space.

Since the 1970s, the traditional hierarchical sequence of the planning process, starting from national, regional and urban planning, continuing on to urban design and architecture, has largely been reversed. Architecture is no longer an extension of planning, but is now often employed to trigger the planning process. In other words, city development has shifted away from normative master and blueprint planning to more strategic and project-based approaches. This has resulted in a process of city development that mainly occurs through negotiations between private and public actors. This shift is often described as a gradual ideological and practical shift from government to governance, implying a growing role for private actors in public policymaking. The government at both national and local levels no longer takes an arm's-length role, but through a new approach to governance has become one of many market parties.[18]

In addition, a greater demand for selling projects that focus on branding and seductive images, something deemed necessary in the current competitive climate, has caused a shift to a project-based design approach driven by aesthetic values.[19] Critics address the superficiality of such a project-based design approach, arguing that the urban development has evolved into little more than large-scale architecture. They posit that to deal with this, instruments are needed to link the instrumentally rational to the image, and projects to a strategy for the city or city region as a whole.[20]

The New Map of the Netherlands, launched in 1997, shows the enormous scale of new projects that the country faces.[21] From 2,650 projects in 1997, the inventory now contains almost 6,500 plans and projects and it is not surprising that the epithet 'Projectland the Netherlands' was introduced.[22] However, long-term centralized planning still plays a central role in the Netherlands. In 2008 three National Planning Reports were presented.[23] It is evident that despite the increase of more bottom-up

18
See, for example, Harvey, D., 'From Managerialism to Entrepreneurialism: The Transformation in Urban Governance in Late Capitalism', Geografiska Annaler 71B 1989, 3–17; Cammen, H. van der, and L. de Klerk, Ruimtelijke Ordening: Van grachten-gordel tot Vinex-wijk (Utrecht: Het Spectrum, 2003); Wigmans, G., 'Maatschappelijke trends en gebiedsontwikkeling: Een probleemschets', in: I. Bruil et al. (eds.), Integrale gebiedsontwikkeling: Het stationsgebied 's-Hertogen-bosch (Amsterdam: SUN, 2004), 30–49; Claessens, F. and E. van Velzen, 'De actualiteit van het stedelijk project', Stedebouw & Ruimtelijke Ordening, 87 (4) 2006, 32–37; Musch, M., 'Polder Ground', OASE 52 (1999), 16–31; Meijsmans, N., 'The Urban Project on a Regional Scale?', paper presented at the conference The Urban Project (Delft, the Netherlands 4–7 June 2008).
19
Cammen and de Klerk, Ruimtelijke Ordening, op. cit. (note 18).
20
Claessens and Van Velzen, 'De actualiteit', op. cit. (note 18); Meijsmans, 'The Urban Project', op. cit. (note 18); Meyer, H., 'In dienst van de stad onder postmoderne condities/ Working for the City under Post-modern Conditions', in: H. Meyer and L. van den Burg (eds.), In dienst van de stad/Working for the City (Amsterdam: SUN, 2005), 64–68.
21
Available at www.nieuwekaart.nl (last accessed on 19 May 2008).
22
Metz, T. and M. Pflug, Atlas van Nederland in 2005: De Nieuwe Kaart (Rotterdam: NAi Publishers, 1997).
23
The report Samen Werken met Water by the Delta-commissie describes how the Netherlands could become more resistant to flooding. VROM, Structuur-visie Randstad 2040: Naar een duurzame en concur-rerende Europese topregio (The Hague: Ministry of Housing, Spatial Planning and the Environment, 2008),

and project-based approaches, the Dutch government still produces planning documents on a macro scale. How these relate to the micro-scale solutions remains unclear. The report *Structuurvisie Randstad 2040*, presented in September 2008, foresees a need for half a million new dwellings in the Randstad, 40 per cent to be realized through densification in cities. At the same time the city of Rotterdam, in *Stadsvisie Rotterdam: Spatial Development Strategy 2030*, proposes projects which focus mainly on the realization of low-rise neighbourhoods to attract middle-class families.[24] To be able to relate the densification goals from the planning report to the proposed low-rise projects in Rotterdam, professionals need new instruments that are able to bridge the gap between the micro-scale level of urban *design* and the macro-scale level of urban *planning*. Such instruments should prevent mismatches between the spatial qualities desired and the development programme foreseen at national, regional and local scale – a mismatch that can have severe qualitative, programmatic and financial consequences. Furthermore, such instruments should facilitate the negotiation process between private and public actors and enable all actors simultaneously to assess programme and urban form. We claim that urban density could play a significant role in doing so.

Another reason why density needs to achieve a more central role in urbanism is that urban space consumption has increased dramatically during the last century.[25] The average population density of Amsterdam fell a factor of 9, from almost 570 inhabitants per hectare in 1880 to around 65 in the year 2000.[26] ❧ During this period, the urbanized territory of Amsterdam grew from approximately 560 to 11,500 hectares (a factor of 20), while the population grew from 317,000 to 727,100 inhabitants (a factor of 2.3). The growth of Amsterdam can largely be explained by the increased spatial demands per person, but only marginally by the growth of the population. This seems to be a general trend in wealthy societies; the number of inhabitants per dwelling unit decreases, dwellings become larger, and the city is less densely built. The causes of such sprawl of people and activities are complex and the effects multifaceted, but many of the effects are quite generally acknowledged. They include such factors as the increase in car and goods transport, the association of this with the increase in energy consumption, air pollution, noise pollution and the fragmentation in the ecosystems, accompanied by a reduction in the viability of public transport, local amenities and public services, and so forth.[27]

This trend of increase in consumption of space calls for further research on the relationship between the capacity and the quality of space. How can more compact approaches accommodate growth? What qualitative measures (technical and design solutions) can be used to compensate for and counteract the negative effects of higher densities? To answer these questions, instruments are needed that make explicit the macro-scale consequences of spatial choices made on project level, and vice versa, instruments that assist in predicting and visualizing the impacts of macro-scale programmes on the micro scale of a project. We claim that urban density can play a significant role in facing this challenge.

presented by the Dutch cabinet on 5 September 2008, aims to make the Randstad an (even more) internationally competitive environment, and proposes, among other things, an addition of 500,000 houses. The third document is not an official Policy Document, but expresses the intentions of the former minister of transport, Camiel Eurlings, for example to invest 4.5 billion euros in the rail network.

24
Municipality of Rotterdam, *Stadsvisie Rotterdam: Spatial Development Strategy 2030* (Rotterdam: dS+V, 2007).

25
In a general approach to this problem, one should consider the total human space consumption (ecological footprint) that is all the cultivated surface needed to satisfy our increasing demands of energy, foodstuff and other natural resources (See Rees, W., 'Ecological Footprint and Appreciated Carrying Capacity: What Urban Economics Leave Out', *Environment and Urbanisation* 4 (2) 1992, 121–130). Accepting the limitations of our discipline, however, we look at this problem only from the perspective of urbanized occupation. The larger context is, of course, always circumscribing this one aspect of the problem.

26
Including housing, green and working areas. Calculations are based on maps drawn by the authors using historical maps of Amsterdam. The sources of maps and population data as well as calculations can be found in Berghauser Pont and Haupt, *Space, Density,* op. cit. (note 12).

27
Couch, C., L. Leontidou and G. Petschel-Held, *Urban Sprawl in Europe: Landscapes, Land-Use Change & Policy* (Oxford: Blackwell Publishing, 2007).

RESEARCH STRATEGY

This book suggests a *definition* of density capable of reducing the confusion surrounding the concept of density and making it a productive concept in design and planning practice and research. Such a definition should relate density to potential urban form (type of urban environment) and other performances. By performances we here refer to the ability or capacity of the built environment to deliver different results. Examples of performances that to a varying extent are conditioned by density are daylight access, parking, privacy and potential buildings types. Through these performances we are able to temporarily suspend our judgements concerning appropriate densities. In addition, the definition of density should enable the development of a *method* that can deal with the current challenges being faced in urbanism. Examples hereof – as sketched earlier in the introduction – are the general trend from government to governance, and from blueprint planning to a more project-based approach, but also the dilemmas of increased urban space consumption. The method should help to develop a simultaneous understanding of how macro-scale planning ambitions (quantitative and qualitative) relate to micro-scale design projects and vice versa; it should make explicit the macro-scale results of a multitude of micro-scale decisions and spatial developments. Central to all this is the understanding of the variation in density throughout the scales.

This book claims to deliver such a definition and method, the Spacematrix, which can be used to uncover the conditionality of density to urban form and performances. The Spacematrix, together with definitions of scale, demarcation of plan areas and derived indicators, offers a solid basis for a method that can be used both in planning and design practice, and for scientific research. The possibilities and specific areas of application will be suggested in the coming chapters. The book aims at reviving the concept of density. This doesn't mean that an old instrument is just taken out of the basement, dusted off and reignited. No, the shortcomings of the existing density-measurement methods in conveying information about urban form and performance are certainly very real, as others have pointed out, and which we will demonstrate further on. Those shortcomings, however, have led many to the conclusion that the concept *as such* is flawed and even dangerous. We insist, though, that the problem with the most commonly used density-measurement methods is rather one of representation and resolution. A too rough a resolution, that is a method that relies on too few variables, turns the concept into a predominately statistical tool. This 'roughness' means that the capacity to differentiate is far too small to make it useful in relation to urban form and performance. At the other extreme of the spectrum, detailed descriptions (or representations) of the built environment tend to be dependent on a large amount of variables and data. Descriptions that are too specific not only make a method complex, but also quickly limit the possibilities to distil generic conclusions. Our research shows that the presented Spacematrix method contains a proper amount and sort of variables, and engages with the suitable levels of scale, to make productive conclusions about urban form and performance. But before unfolding the argument, we will put forward the central hypothesis, formulate a series of questions that need to be answered, and describe the research methods that have structured and guided our search.

The hypothesis central to this book is that urban density does contain valuable information about urban form and the performance of the built environment. If this can be shown to be the case, then urban density has the potential to be effective in developing a method capable of simultaneously articulating quantity and quality, or, expressed in a less abstract way, a method that can relate built programme to urban form and other performances. Such a method should, through its application, be able to contribute to achieving the aims mentioned above, and thus play an important role in current urban practice. To arrive at a significant and productive correlation between urban density on the one hand and urban form and performance on the other, a series of sub-questions needs to be formulated and confronted. The two parts of the hypothesis, quantity and quality, or, more fitting in the present discourse, 'urban density' and 'urban form and performance', both have to be critically examined and (re)defined before being related. For the first part of the assumed correlation – urban density – questions about demarcation of areas, entities of measurement, and levels of scale have to be articulated to arrive at an effective definition of urban density that can be used to make plausible the correlation between density and form: What is measured, how are geographical areas circumscribed, and which levels of scale need to be defined? In this research, to answer these questions we have critically examined and judged the definitions of urban density that have been developed and applied in the past, and more specifically, the indicators that have been, and still are, commonly used to measure urban density. Finally, their capacity to convey information on urban form and performance has been tested.

If the first part of the correlation – urban density – is a complex subject matter, then the second part – qualities of the built environment, in this case understood as urban form and performance – constitutes a challenge of gargantuan proportions. The aim of this research, however, has not been to develop an exhaustive and detailed definition of urban form, but to uncover a general correlation between density and built form, and, with enough precision, suggest conditional dependencies for specific urban types and performances on urban density. To this aim, the description of urban types and the choices of studied performances have sprung out of a mixed process of a relatively autonomous construction of urban types, an inventory of commonsense naming of urban types and their constituent features, and the use of existing formal analytical reductions into basic layout types. All these together combine into a workable (that is, not too detailed, but also not too inclusive) classification of urban form that later, in the final step of the research, is mirrored in the density data, producing clusterings and regularities that can support the hypothesis.

Before taking on the central challenge of relating urban density to form, the book starts with a sweeping description of the historical context of city development. This reconstruction of the history of city building in the Netherlands, since the late Middle Ages, is made to underpin the developments signalled as central to the research problem and aim (changes in the city building process and increased space consumption); to trace density developments through urban history; and to reconstruct the wider context in which density evolved from being a result

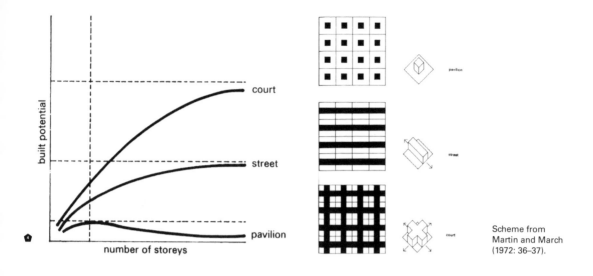

built potential

number of storeys

court

street

pavilion

pavilion

street

court

Scheme from
Martin and March
(1972: 36–37).

of circumstances to a practically applied, normative concept in city development. The historical context also serves as a source for making an inventory of the definitions and practical applications of density in city development, and it has further served to distinguish some of the differing positions on density in relation to, for instance, sustainability and urbanity. It is by no means an exhaustive reconstruction but intends to capture some decisive transformations. Its brief character makes it vulnerable to criticism for presenting a Eurocentric perspective, or even a 'Dutchcentric' one. This would be a just observation, but in our opinion not a great problem to the later developed method. We would even go so far as to ascribe the developed density method universal aspirations: a universal structure filled with content and applied in ways that differ due to specific contextual circumstances. The historical sketch serves as an illustration of the specific temporal developments in a specific geographical context, namely that of the Netherlands. At times these Dutch density developments are put into a larger context, and planning doctrines, political developments, and density methods and variables from abroad are used to balance the risk of interpreting the Dutch situation in a kind of vacuum. This wider contextualization further serves as a scan of the most commonly used definitions of density and related measurement methods.

In addition to the historical outline, the spatial and demographic developments of Amsterdam were registered to chart the density developments of the city. Different historical maps were used and measured for this purpose, as well as sources on the population development of the city.

Besides unravelling the different historical doctrines and common definitions of density, the research has also relied on knowledge in the field of typomorphology to identify the basic components of the built environment. The work of geographer M.R.G. Conzen, founder of the English school of morphology, was used as a framework. Conzen developed a methodological and theoretical manual to analyse the physical urban plan on different levels of scale.[28] This approach is in contrast to

28
Moudon, A.V., 'Getting to Know the Built Landscape: Typomorphology', in: K. Franck and L. Schneekloth (eds.), *Ordering Space: Types in Architecture and Design* (New York: Van Nostrand Reinhold, 1994), 289–311.

Basic typomorphological entities of settlements (Conzen 1960).

the other morphological schools that are more concerned with architecture (Italian school) and sociocultural aspects of city forming (French school). The studies of typomorphology were combined in the current research with a more deductive, quantitative research approach to come to understand the relationship between urban programmes and spatial properties. The research carried out by Leslie Martin and Lionel March at the Centre for Land Use and Built Form Studies in Cambridge is an example of such a deductive, quantitative approach.[29] Central to their work is the recognition of certain related factors, such as the land available, the buildings located on this land and the roads required to serve them. Rather than a separate 'school' that has little association with the detailed graphical mapping techniques of typomorphology, we see the deductive, quantitative approach as an extension of typomorphology, expanding on the opportunities provided here. The analytical techniques differ, but the research aims coincide: describing and explaining urban form.

The critical examination of the issues mentioned above – the level of scale, the bordering of areas, the definition of entities, the composition of indicators, basic urban form, urban types, performances – has led to a new, multivariable definition of density and a package of practically applicable definitions. The investigation undertaken to make the correlation

29
An institute established at the School of Architecture in Cambridge in 1963.

between density, urban form and other performances plausible has relied on two research methods: empirical and explorative research. We analysed a wide range of samples, from the Netherlands and abroad, and used these to formulate density-based urban types. This analysis of existing built environments was combined with design and calculation experiments to explore the limits of the possible design solutions under specific density conditions, and to investigate how different built environments perform in relation to density. Both the empirical and the explorative research have been guided and inspired by the two research traditions already mentioned, typomorphology and deductive, quantitative research.

STRUCTURE OF THE BOOK

The second chapter, 'City Development and Space Consumption', sketches the historical background to the development and use of the concept of density. To understand the circumstances in which the concepts of density were developed and applied in the past, a brief historical account of the developments in Dutch city building and the organization of the planning process is given. A larger international context is used at times to situate the national and local developments. The different concepts developed are discussed as well as the justification for the use of density in urban settings. In some cases the concepts were based on practical experiences gained from urban projects, in other cases, new concepts were developed for a more polemic and social purpose. This chapter also includes an account of the specific density developments of the city of Amsterdam between 1400 and 2000.

The third chapter, 'Multivariable Density: Spacematrix', looks critically at different density definitions and judges them on the basis of their ability to relate density to urban form. Apart from describing the different concepts employed, such as population density or spaciousness, the chapter also assesses measurement techniques. Issues discussed include the scale of measurement and demarcation of areas. As none of the concepts were assessed as appropriate to describe potential form, we propose a new, multivariable definition of density called the Spacematrix. The three core indicators applied are Floor Space Index (FSI), Ground Space Index (GSI), and Network density (N). The second portion of this chapter then defines the necessary measurement techniques and introduces additional, useful (derived) indicators.

In the fourth chapter, 'Density and Urban Form', the definitions from the previous chapter are used to demonstrate the relation between density and urban form. This chapter illustrates that the conditions defined by Spacematrix density, combined with real constraints present at a certain place and moment in history, limit the potential urban form to such an extent that it becomes possible to define urban types most likely to emerge under these density conditions. Besides characterizing the main formal performance of urban types, other kinds of performance relate to the conditions created by density. We discuss three of them in 'The Performance of Density', the fifth chapter: daylight, parking and 'urbanity'. Chapter six, 'Projects from Practice' describes some early applications of density in practice that have been central to the development of the Spacematrix method.

The last chapter, 'Qualities of Density', draws conclusions that offer answers to the questions and problems posed in the first two chapters, based on the results discussed in the third, fourth and fifth chapters. Besides the development of Spacematrix, which defines density as a multivariable and multi-scalar phenomenon, the research addresses the effectiveness of density in the urban planning practice, its academic relevance, and its potential to assist in the efforts to understand and tackle runaway urban space consumption.

1400

1450

(Predominately) Housing fabrics

1544

1585

1612

1626

(Predominately) Housing fabrics

1795

1900

1918

1939

■	Industrial and office areas
■	Cemeteries
■	Garden allotments
■	Sports facilities
■	Parks
■	(Predominately) Housing fabrics

1958

1984

2000

Industrial and office areas

Cemeteries

Garden allotments

Sports facilities

Parks

(Predominately) Housing fabrics

AMSTERDAM 1400–2000

1400

1450

1585

1612

1900

1918

1544

6

1795

1939   1958   1984   2000

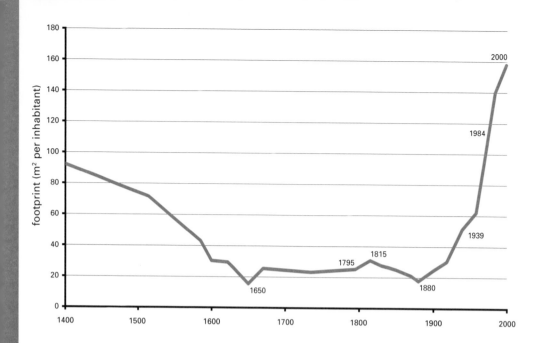

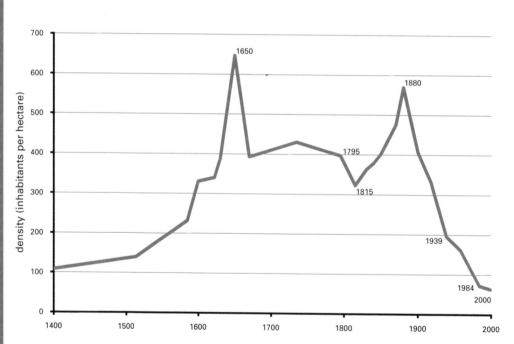

MERCANTILE CAPITALISM (1400–1815)

The majority of Dutch towns were established during this period. Feudal rulers created new towns while, at the same time, other cities arose as a result of economic growth. In the latter case, population growth forced city councils to adopt urban expansion plans. In Amsterdam, population density increased from 110 inhabitants per hectare in 1400 to almost 650 inhabitants per hectare during the Golden Age. At the height of the Golden Age (1650), every citizen of Amsterdam occupied an average of 15 m² of city space. In the seventeenth century, urban expansion plans were developed to counter densification and to accommodate economic and population growth. A distinctive feature of two such plans in Amsterdam, the Grachtengordel and the Jordaan, was the increase in the scale of urban planning. This was the first time in the Netherlands that public authorities introduced building regulations and zoning to guide private developments. Through these expansions, the density in Amsterdam fell to around 400 inhabitants per hectare in 1795. By 1815 a further fall in population density to 320 inhabitants per hectare had occurred, following economic stagnation and periods of war in the eighteenth century.

LIBERAL-COMPETITIVE CAPITALISM (1815–1900)

Following a period of relative stagnation, the Dutch population began to grow once more during the nineteenth century. The population increased from 2.3 million in 1815 to 3.1 million in 1850, and reached 5.1 million by 1900. Industrialization and the agrarian crisis precipitated an even more rapid population growth in the cities with a huge migration to them, especially after 1870. In the late nineteenth century this rapid population growth led to problems with overcrowding, ill health and human misery. The population density in Amsterdam reached almost 600 inhabitants per hectare in 1880, comparable to the peak density of 1650. Scientists, urban experts and the state began to recognize the relationship between city form, density and health problems. Influential books about 'better cities' began to focus on both hygiene and aesthetics. Still, plans of the time tended to be little but compromises between ideals and stark economic pragmatism.

STATE-MANAGED CAPITALISM (1900–1979)
The main developments of this period have their origins in the late nineteenth century as capitalism slowly evolved from a liberal-competitive status to a more state-managed and centrally controlled mode. Criticism of the overcrowded and unhealthy industrial city of the nineteenth century led in the Netherlands to the introduction of the *Housing Act* (*Woningwet*) in 1901, which had a profound impact on urban planning and design. Central government and municipalities assumed a greater role in city development. During the first half of the twentieth century, Berlage drew up expansion plans for Amsterdam and The Hague, inspired by the work of Sitte. *The General Extension Plan* of Amsterdam (AUP, 1934), planned by Van Eesteren and Van Lohuizen, represented a unique example of Dutch modern urbanism, while the utopian ideas of Le Corbusier and Gropius contributed to the design of the vertical garden city, a concept that reached its peak in the Netherlands with the realization of the Bijlmermeer in 1973.

Before the Second World War, the new ideals were mostly realized at the city level, leading to a rapid growth of areas of relatively low density. The average population density of Amsterdam decreased from almost 600 inhabitants per hectare at the end of the nineteenth century (1880) to 195 inhabitants per hectare by 1939. After the Second World War, this process of urbanization in ever-lower densities changed into one of suburbanization. The advent of the car in less crowded cities and a rapid colonization of the countryside became synonymous with progress. Population density in Amsterdam continued to decrease to 70 inhabitants per hectare by 1984.

NEOLIBERAL CAPITALISM (1979–the present)

The oil crisis of 1973 and a global recession ended an unusually long period of economic growth. This had a great effect on all levels of society. The centralized state-managed planning approach, dominant since the Second World War, gave way to a market-oriented, project- and negotiation-based approach. The basic assumption was that market competition would increase efficiency. Private parties would be forced to be sensitive to the wishes of investors and housing consumers. By being closer to the action, it was assumed that they would be able to respond more quickly to social and economic changes. This was in stark contrast to the image sketched of a preceding period of a bureaucratic, expensive, and inefficient state apparatus that had relied on its planning and housing monopoly to realize top-down developments. Such a collectivist construction was deemed unsuitable for individualized and emancipated postmodern consumers whose postindustrial wealth seemed to be ever increasing. This very affirmative approach to capitalist dynamics paralleled other social and economic reforms of the welfare state that were taking place in the 1980s. The neoliberal TINA stance of the late 1980s expressed this fundamental view on the power of the market: There Is No Alternative (to the market).

During the last decades of the twentieth century, population density in Amsterdam continued to decline and fell to a little more than 60 inhabitants per hectare in 2000. However, the trend of decreasing densities seemed to be slowing down somewhat, probably influenced by the new spatial policy in which the concept of concentrated dispersal was replaced by the concept of the compact city, and the fact that Amsterdam had reached the physical limits of its administrative boundaries.

The patron saint of San Gimignano (Italy) holds an image of the city crowned by feudal towers in a fourteenth-century altarpiece by Taddeo di Bartolo (Kostof 1991: 297).

2
CITY DEVELOPMENT AND SPACE CONSUMPTION

This chapter looks at the history of city development[1] and discusses the role of the differing views on density in this process. The concept of density has acquired both descriptive and prescriptive connotations. On the one hand it is used to analyse problems, and on the other to offer solutions. This chapter sketches the development of density from a mere outcome of complex circumstances (roughly until 1850); through the birth of density as a tool for analysis and diagnosis (1850–1900); via a concept used to propagate alternatives and prescribe maximum densities in order to guarantee certain qualities (1900–1960); to, more lately, an instrument that is used to argue for minimum densities to support amenities and public transport, and produce less unsustainable environments with potential for vital urban interaction.

In addition, this chapter highlights two forces in city development – described briefly in the previous chapter – using a historical perspective. The first relates to the dialectic between an unregulated market and collective intervention[2] and the transition from government to governance; the second focuses on the tension between programme- and image-based planning. These developments are described with the use of examples from Dutch cities, supplemented from time to time by background information on the international context.

We further look at how land use and human space consumption has changed and how this has affected the practice of city development. The city of Amsterdam is used to illustrate these historical shifts.[3] ♟ Certainly, Amsterdam is just one example. Other cities are of different sizes, have different historical backgrounds, and developed in their own unique ways. Nevertheless, Amsterdam can serve as a suitable point of reference for other larger Dutch cities and for many of the general trends that took place in Europe.

The chapter ends with some critical questions on the effects of these developments and its impact on city development. We highlight the need for a better understanding of the relationship between quantity and quality, or between programme and the performance of the urban landscape.[4]

DUTCH DENSITY DEVELOPMENTS

The subsequent analysis delineates four distinct periods. The shift from one period to the next is sometimes rather imperceptible as ideas of previous periods extend into, and continue to influence subsequent periods. The role density has played is central to this historical examination, whether it has been used as a tool or merely manifests itself as an outcome. The periods described are:

— *Mercantile Capitalism* (1400–1815). This period stretches from the end of the Middle Ages to the beginnings of the nineteenth century. It sees the birth of Dutch cities and sets the scene for later industrial expansions. Two distinct practices of city development coexist. One concerns public streets laid out by the feudal ruler or municipality, the other individual lots developed by users. Density is a mere outcome.

1
The notion of city development is used to include both intentionally planned developments and more organically generated settlements.

2
Collective intervention through state institutions (municipalities, provinces, ministries), and/or corporativist organizations.

3
The calculations are all made by the authors based on historical maps of Amsterdam and different sources for the statistics concerning the amount of inhabitants. Berghauser Pont, M. and P. Haupt, *Space Density and Urban Form* (Delft: 2009), 235–271
4
Concerning the use of the term 'urban landscape' we follow the argument put forward in Moudon, A.V., 'Getting to Know the Built Landscape: Typomorphology', in: K. Franck and L. Schneekloth (eds.), *Ordering Space: Types in Architecture and Design* (New York: Van Nostrand Reinhold, 1994), 289–311.

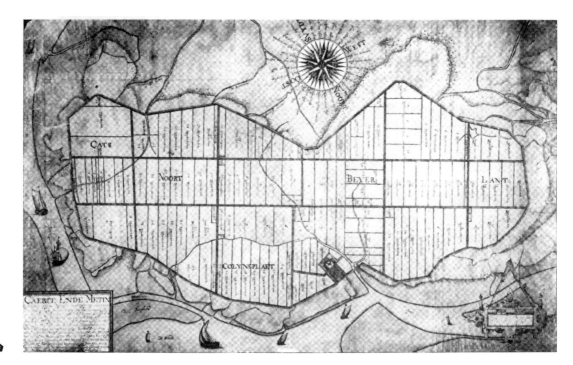

Map of Oud-Noord-Beverlandpolder with Colijnsplaat, drawn by Lucas Sinck, 1598.

Amsterdam in 1665; the realization of Grachtengordel and Jordaan (dienst der Publieke Werken, based on the map of Daniel Stalpaert).

— *Liberal-Competitive Capitalism* (1815–1900). During this period the dynamics of the market, industrialization and city growth are only marginally influenced by political and public sector interference. Towards the end of the century, the density concept is introduced. It is used to diagnose and compare cities that quickly have to absorb growing populations, but plays a limited role in the creation of new expansion plans.

— *State-Managed Capitalism* (1900–1979). This period, starting from around 1900 and extending to the end of the 1970s, is often dubbed as a state-driven planning tradition. The *managerial state* and public institutions dominate, from start to finish, throughout the entire urban development planning process. The term *embedded liberalism* is sometimes used to describe this period and to distinguish it from the previous one. During this period, density is used to prescribe preferred densities. The Garden City Movement in England and the early functionalists in Germany are the first to systematically engage with the concept. The use of density resonates well with the scientific, positivist ideal of the time.

— *Neoliberal Capitalism* (1979–the present). Referred to as the period after the late 1970s when planning practice is to a large extent privatized. The state becomes more of an *entrepreneurial state,* facilitating the demands of private investors and consumers in the marketplace. An urban crisis (unemployment, declining population and budget deficits) defines the first part of this period. The postmodern critique of centralized, modernist planning also tarnishes the reputation of density as a 'technocratic' instrument that had played an important role in the 'crimes' of the earlier period. However, problems of sprawl, mobility and unsustainability, and economic demands for profitable developments turn the attention to the need for minimum densities.

MERCANTILE CAPITALISM (1400–1815)

One can distinguish two types of Dutch towns prior to the nineteenth century.[5] A regular pattern of streets developed in a rather short period of time characterized the first type. These towns were established by powerful rulers (such as counts, bishops, dukes) or through large-scale land reclamation projects. ❂

The second type of late medieval towns are characterized by a gradual urbanization. Growth was driven by a flourishing economy, rising population and increases in commercial activity. Amsterdam is a good example of this type. The initial inhabitants of Amsterdam were farmers who settle on both sides of the Amstel River on terps.[6] In 1300 Amsterdam acquired city rights, but not until after 1450 did large numbers of people settle in the city (more than 10,000 inhabitants).[7] During an economic boom in the first half of the seventeenth century – the Golden Age – the population density grew substantially until it peaked in 1650 at 650 inhabitants per hectare. By the seventeenth century, Amsterdam had grown from being a small town into being one of the largest cities in Europe.[8]

Large-Scale Expansion

At the beginning of the seventeenth century, Amsterdam undertook new expansion plans to combat increasing densification and to facilitate economic growth. The plans cover the Grachtengordel and the Jordaan. ❂

5
Rutte, R., *A Landscape of Towns: Urbanization in the Netherlands from the 11th to the nineteenth Centuries* (Delft: Delft University of Technology, Faculty of Architecture, 2004).
6
A *terp*, an artificial dwelling hill, is a mound created to provide safe ground during high tide and river floods. The first terp-building period in the Dutch province of Friesland dates from 500 BC.
7
Dijkstra, C., M. Reitsma and A. Rommerts, *Atlas Amsterdam* (Bussum: Uitgeverij THOTH, 1999).
8
Abrahamse, J.A., 'De ruimtelijke ontwikkeling van Amsterdam in de zeventiende eeuw en de opkomst van de stedebouw als wetenschap', in: B. Bakker and E. Schmitz (eds.), *Het aanzien van Amsterdam: Panorama's, plattegronden en profielen uit de Gouden Eeuw* (Bussum: Uitgeverij THOTH, 2007), 24–41.

Living conditions at the beginning of the twentieth century in the Joden Houttuinen, Amsterdam (Gemeentearchief Amsterdam).

These expansions contain something different in comparison to previous expansions. The Grachtengordel plan incorporated the aesthetic, classicist preferences of that time. This plan results in a regular and symmetrical layout with rectangular blocks and lots, whereby appearance, functionality and profit go hand in hand. The municipality not only designated the building lots, streets and canals, but a new type of land management emerged that influenced the way in which private lots were developed and utilized. The city expropriated the land needed for new expansions and sold the lots. In specific contracts, the city authorities stipulated the requirements concerning the use and types of the development permitted within the plan.[9] The plan was in effect instrumental in sealing agreements between the various parties involved.[10]

The two expansion plans for the Grachtengordel and the Jordaan culminated in zoning plans (functional and socioeconomic) that had never existed before on such a scale in the Netherlands.[11] The first two canals of the Grachtengordel (Herengracht and Keizersgracht) were in effect housing developments, especially for the ruling class. Specific conditions were linked to the lots sold along these canals, so called standards (*keuren*). These standards laid down strict conditions for the building of the houses, including construction time (usually one year) and how the resulting structures should be aligned in the street to ensure a neat row of façades. Height and depth of the houses were also limited to allow for large gardens in the courtyards behind the buildings.[12] These stipulations directly or indirectly had a bearing on the final built form and on density.

9
Heeling, J., H. Meyer and J. Westrik, *Het ontwerp van de stadsplattegrond* (Amsterdam: SUN, 2002);
10
Terlouw, E., 'A House of One's Own', *OASE* 52 (1999), 32–77.
11
Abrahamse, 'De ruimtelijke ontwikkeling', op. cit. (note 8).

12
Ibid., 29.

The Jordaan area originally arose in a part of the city outside the walls that had sprung up illegally (*de voorstad*, or *faubourgs*). The redevelopment plan, consisting of industry and housing, included the widening of streets and the demolition of some existing structures to align the streets. In this plan no additional standards (*keuren*) were enforced. In 1859 the density of the Jordaan was 830 inhabitants per hectare while the Grachtengordel housed only 270 inhabitants per hectare.[13] When the last bubonic plague struck Amsterdam in 1664, 25,000 people, almost 10 per cent of the population, perished.[14] The poorest and most densely populated areas, such as the Jordaan, were most severely affected.

After 1672, the year of catastrophe (*het Rampjaar*), the Dutch economy stagnated and the market for land and property in the southern part of the Grachtengordel collapsed. No Dutch town or city grew until well into the nineteenth century. Amsterdam even lost a quarter of its population between 1735 and 1815. The area covered by the city remained very much the same, but the diminished population spread out. This translated into a fall in population density in Amsterdam from 650 inhabitants per hectare during the Golden Age of the seventeenth century to 320 inhabitants per hectare by 1815. ∎

LIBERAL-COMPETITIVE CAPITALISM (1815–1900)

Following a period of relative stagnation, the Dutch population began to grow once more during the nineteenth century. Amsterdam had developed into a strong, innovative financial centre and the period saw the completion of a series of major national and international infrastructure projects, such as the opening of the Suez Canal (1869), and the Noordzeekanaal (1876). The middle part of the period has been referred to as the Mini Golden Age and the glorious Age of Capital.[15] In 1815 Amsterdam had 180,000 inhabitants, in 1850 224,000 and by the end of the nineteenth century 510,000. Rotterdam actually tripled its population between 1850 and 1900.[16]

The increases in population prior to 1875 were absorbed into a city that had not grown in size since the seventeenth century.[17] Between 1750 and 1850, the amount of families living in Amsterdam increased by 20,000 to 40,500, while the amount of houses only increased by 900, to 27,600. A doubling of the population thus had to be accommodated in an (almost) unchanged housing stock. Only after the introduction of the *Fortification Law* (*Vestingwet*) in 1875 could the population growth once more be accommodated in (legal) urban expansions outside the fortifications.[18]

Population density in the Jordaan increased between 1859 and 1889 by more than 50 per cent, from 830 to 1,265 inhabitants per hectare.[19] Cheap dwellings were constructed in the courtyards of existing city blocks. This meant that 40 to 60 per cent of the dwellings lacked the required amount of sunlight.[20] In Rotterdam the percentage of the dwellings with more than ten inhabitants increased from 43 per cent in 1840, to 70 per cent by 1849.[21] Despite this process of intensification, street plans were relatively unchanged due to their 'inertia': a high level of resistance from an established form. Structures were often rebuilt to accommodate a higher density within the same street layout, illustrating the robustness of the urban ground plan (*stadsplattegrond*).[22]

13
Based on an 1859 census. Sources: Laloli, H.M., 'Beter wonen? Woningmarkt en residentiële segregatie in Amsterdam 1850–1940', in: O.W.A. Boonstra et al. (eds.), *Twee eeuwen Nederland geteld: Onderzoek met de digitale volks-, beroeps- en woningtellingen 1795–2001* (The Hague: DANS and CBS, 2007); and www.amsterdamhistorie.nl, accessed August 2008.
14
Moll, H., 'Vuile teringstad: Vijf eeuwen besmettelijke ziekten in Amsterdam', *NRC Handelsblad* 31 January 2001.
15
Wintershoven, L., *Demografisch eeuwboek Amsterdam: Ontwikkelingen tussen 1900 en 2000* (Amsterdam: dRO, 2000); Hobsbawm, E., *The Age of Capital: 1848–1875* (London: Weidenfeld and Nicholson, 1975).
16
Cammen, H. van der, and L. de Klerk, *Ruimtelijke Ordening: Van grachtengordel tot Vinex-wijk* (Utrecht: Het Spectrum, 2003), 45.
17
Martin, M. and C. Wagenaar, 'Stadsverfraaing en stadsuitbreiding', in: E. Taverne and I. Visser (eds.), *Stedebouw: De geschiedenis van de stad in de Nederlanden van 1500 tot heden* (Nijmegen: SUN, 1993), 124–129, 124.
18
Klerk, L. de, *De modernisering van de stad 1850–1914: De opkomst van de planmatige stadsontwikkeling in Nederland* (Rotterdam: NAi Publishers, 2008), 15. Exception in Amsterdam is the Singelgracht area, added between 1820 and 1860; see Plas, G. van der, 'Amsterdam 1750–1850: van stadsstaat naar hoofdstad', in: Taverne and Visser, *Stedebouw*, op. cit. (note17), 148–159, 159.
19
Based on the censuses of 1859 and 1889. Sources: Laloli, 'Beter wonen?', op. cit. (note 13); and www.amsterdamhistorie.nl, accessed August 2008.
20
Plas, 'Amsterdam 1750–1850', op. cit. (note 18), 150.

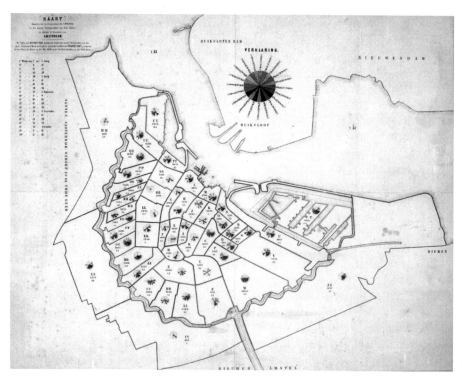

1866 cholera map of Amsterdam on which the number of deaths per neighbourhood is registered (Hameleers 2002: 24).

Growth Pains

This tendency for higher densities represented one of the factors that led to serious health problems in industrializing cities. The first cholera pandemic in Europe reached London and Paris in 1832. In London, the disease claimed 6,500 victims, in Paris 20,000 of a population of 650,000. Throughout France 100,000 people died of cholera during the pandemic. In 1866, a fourth cholera pandemic led to 21,000 victims in Amsterdam. ⬟ Just as in 1664 when the bubonic plague struck Amsterdam, the majority of the victims were in the most densely populated areas.[23]

In the second half of the nineteenth century people started to reconsider and criticize the poor living conditions of overcrowded cities. People living in disadvantaged areas with high population densities suffered from the combined effects of a lack of access to daylight, fresh air, clean water and adequate sewerage.[24] Established in 1844 in London, the *Society for improving the condition of the labouring classes*, an organization dealing with public health issues, exerted considerable influence throughout Europe. This was followed by the British *Public Health Act* in 1848. This regulation, and the investments in public works in England (water, sewer, parks, pavement), served as an example for many cities.[25] In Amsterdam, the architect J.H. Leliman designed several dwellings for the working class inspired by the activities of this society.[26] Still, such charitable initiatives were exceptions, as financial returns remained the driving force in town planning. By the onset of the second half of the nineteenth century, a mere 1 per cent of new buildings consisted of such social housing. They remained 'islands in the sea of slums'.[27]

21
Cammen and De Klerk, *Ruimtelijke Ordening*, op. cit. (note 16), 45.
22
Rutte, *A Landscape*, op. cit. (note 5), 48; Heeling, Meyer and Westrik, *Het ontwerp*, op. cit. (note 9); Plas, 'Amsterdam 1750–1850', op. cit. (note 18), 149.
23
Moll, 'Vuile teringstad', op. cit. (note 14).

24
Ruijter, P. de, *Voor volkshuisvesting en stedebouw* (Utrecht: Matrijs, 1987), 34–45.

25
Ibid., 40; Rådberg, J., *Doktrin och täthet i svenskt stadsbyggande 1875–1975* (Stockholm: Statens råd för byggnadsforskning, 1988), 106.
26
De Ruijter, *Voor volkshuisvesting*, op. cit. (note 24), 41.
27
Ibid., 42.

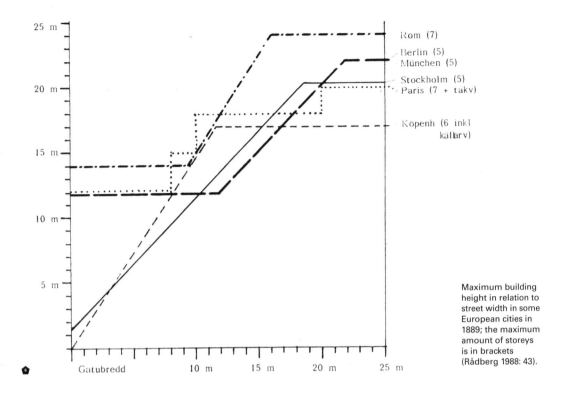

Rom (7)
Berlin (5)
München (5)
Stockholm (5)
Paris (7 + takv)
Köpenh (6 inkl källarv)

Maximum building height in relation to street width in some European cities in 1889; the maximum amount of storeys is in brackets (Rådberg 1988: 43).

At the same time, more centrally ruled countries implemented grand classicist schemes such as the boulevards in Paris (1851) and the Ringstrasse in Vienna (1857).[28] The oldest parts of Paris were occupied at a density of almost 1,000 inhabitants per hectare.[29] The poor living conditions in the overcrowded city were not only a problem for the poor, as diseases and criminality originating in poor areas quickly spread to the rest of the city:

> According to [a] report from 1855, published by the Royal Institute of Engineers on the request of king Willem III, diseases originating from workers districts have a wide influence on the surroundings, and affect all classes, spreading a scourge of disaster to the houses of the more civilized.[30]

Squalid living conditions affected large segments of society and led to riots and social unrest.[31] Later, after the First World War, this fear was evident in England from the deliberations leading to the Housing and Town Planning Act: 'The money we are going to spend on housing is an insurance against Bolshevism and Revolution.'[32] In 1870, jhr. mr. D.O. Engelen in his dissertation *Over arbeiderswoningen* clearly underlined the interdependence of productivity and good housing in the Netherlands: 'One is starting to recognize that the worker, like the machine, needs a good dwelling to be able to produce well.'[33]

28
Taverne, E., *De wortels van de contemporaine stad*, Reader Architectuur- en Stedenbouw- geschiedenis (Groningen: Rijksuniversiteit Groningen, 2000); Castex, J., J-C. Depaule and P. Panerai, *De rationele stad: Van bouwblok tot wooneenheid* (Amsterdam: SUN, 2003), originally published in 1977 as *Formes urbaines: de l'ilot a la barre*.
29
Rådberg, *Doktrin*, op. cit. (note 25), 40.
30
Ottens, E., 'De aanloop naar de Woningwet: "de holen der mensen…"', in: J. Keesom (ed.), *Wonen. Woning. Wet. Wij wonen – 100 jaar Woningwet* (Amsterdam: Stedelijke Woningdienst Amsterdam, 2000), 9–40, 24.
31
Hall, P., *Cities of Tomorrow* (Oxford: Blackwell Publishers, 1996), 14–46.
32
Ibid., 71.
33
Cammen and De Klerk, *Ruimtelijke Ordening*, op. cit. (note 16), 74.

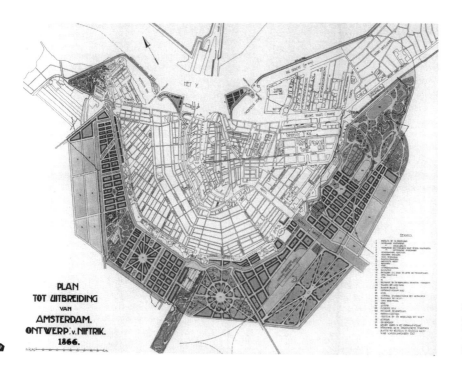

Expansion plan for Amsterdam drawn by Van Niftrik in 1866 (De Klerk, 2008: 258).

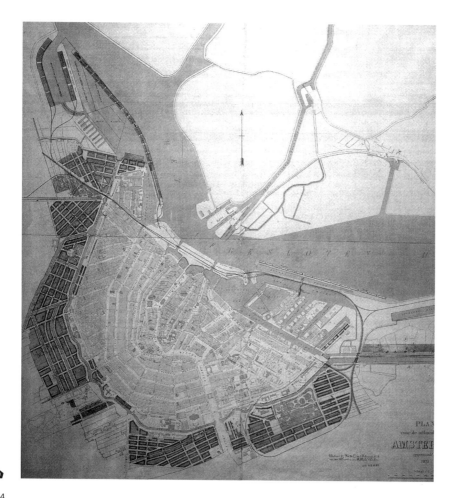

Expansion plan for Amsterdam drawn by Kalff in 1877 (De Klerk, 2008: 259).

Regularism versus Laissez-Faire

In Germany, by the end of the nineteenth century, a scientific approach was increasingly the norm when dealing with the problems of hygiene and social misery in overcrowded cities. Reinhard Baumeister advocated such an approach. With a modern perspective on urbanism he aimed to link the artistic, technical, and economic aspects of city development.[34] He argued in his book *Stadterweiterungen in technischer, baupolizeilicher und wirtschaftlicher Beziehung* (Urban expansions from a technical, regulatory and economic perspective, 1876) that municipalities should take an active role in coordinating development. He argued that decisions should be supported by statistical research, comparative density figures, and systematic survey methods covering population, real estate, and traffic conditions.[35]

Baumeister, and his colleague Joseph Stübben, adhered to a rather pragmatic approach to city development. This combined the need for access to daylight and fresh air with practical economic considerations. Although they believed that low-rise solutions resulted in improved living conditions, they accepted the need to increase density in cities. Single-family dwellings were not an option for many people. Standards dealing with the maximum building height, lot size and the distance between buildings came into force to counter some of the negative effects of the increase in density. ◉ Baumeister introduced a normative building ordinance (*Normalbauverordenung*) in 1880 that stipulated a maximum of four storeys and prescribed that the building height should never exceed the street width. Although such rules had earlier been applied during the rebuilding of London (1667), in Paris (eighteenth century) and Barcelona (1859), Baumeister and Stübben can be regarded as the first to systematically engage with urban density (directly and indirectly) in their analyses of the problems of existing cities and prescriptions for new expansion plans. Density does not yet play a role as a norm in specific plans, but is more a tool used in the process. Later, in plans such as the AUP in Amsterdam, density becomes a guiding framework for the plans themselves.

Baumeister and Stübben's convictions that healthy cities should be realized by public authorities required public intervention and land ownership that did not correspond to the views of the conservative-liberal elite in Dutch cities. They perceived entrepreneurs as being the leading force of city development and private property a sacred institution. The state should confine itself to sorting out street width, building alignment and some minimal guidelines covering housing hygiene standards.[36] Two different expansion plans for Amsterdam can illustrate the tension between state-managed and market-oriented development plans. ◉ ◉ One was drafted by Jacobus van Niftrik (1867) and the other by Jan Kalff (1877). Van Niftrik's plan included plenty of public space, a strict division between social classes, and a functional zoning that did not consider the existing distribution of land ownership.[37] In addition, the plan stipulated that the street width should be at least 1 to 1.5 times the height of the highest building to guarantee enough daylight inside the buildings and in the streets.[38] However, these aspects made the plan too expensive and an alternative was drawn up by Kalff, the director of public works in Amsterdam.

34
Rådberg, *Doktrin*, op. cit. (note 25), 47.

35
De Ruijter, *Voor volkshuisvesting*, op. cit. (note 24); Rådberg, *Doktrin*, op. cit. (note 25), 47.

36
Ibid., 78; Wagenaar, M., 'Amsterdam 1860–1940: Een bedrijvige stad', in: Taverne and Visser, *Stedebouw*, op. cit. (note 17), 218–234, 220.

37
Dijkstra et al., *Atlas Amsterdam*, op. cit. (note 7).

38
De Ruijter, *Voor volkshuisvesting*, op. cit. (note 24), 51.

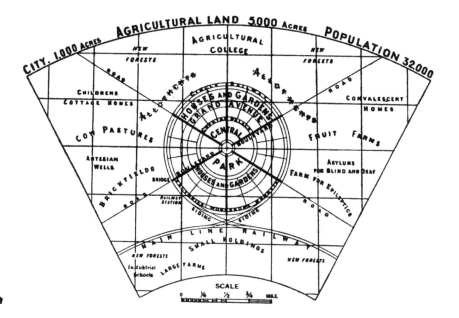

Diagram of the
Garden City by
Ebenezer Howard,
1898 (Kostof, 1991:
203).

Kalff's plan retained the existing pattern of streets and, in contrast to the plan made by Van Niftrik, it respected the distribution of land ownership. The word *expropriation* was not mentioned once during the process, and private developers were frequently able to adapt the street layout to accommodate their own preferences.[39] According to the architect Willem Kromhout, it rendered 'narrow, long and depressing streets', known today as De Pijp (the pipe).[40] The population density in De Pijp was approximately 700 inhabitants per hectare; less than the Jordaan, but still three times more than in the Grachtengordel.[41] The more aesthetic elements of town planning were largely ignored by Kalff's plan. Almost 60 years later, Cornelis Van Eesteren described it as:

> [A] plan, that by its lack of character is typical of the period of cultural collapse in which it was developed . . . The tradition of city development from the seventeenth and eighteenth centuries has been lost; any form of spatial guidance from the state is absent; urbanism is left up to developers and other private enterprises, speculation entered the urban planning process. Neighbourhoods such as 'De Pijp' and the not so very poetic 'Dichterbuurt' are witnesses in stone of the societal and artistic incapability of its time.[42]

In the light of the economic developments of the second half of the nineteenth century, one could interpret the Van Niftrik Plan as expressing the self-secured bourgeoisie ambitions of an ever-expanding economy (The Age of Capital), while Kalff's plan, in contrast, illustrates the choice for a less costly and more pragmatic plan at the beginning of what was to become the Great Depression of 1875–1895.[43]

The Vondelparkbuurt in Amsterdam is a good example of a development where enough means were present to let aesthetic considerations

39
Wagenaar, 'Amsterdam 1860–1940', op. cit. (note 36), 228.
40
De Ruijter, *Voor volkshuisvesting*, op. cit. (note 24), 51. The word *pijpenla* in Dutch is used to describe a long narrow room. In this case De Pijp is used to describe an area with long narrow streets.
41
Based on the dwelling density as mentioned on the 1956 map *Woningdichtheden* ('dwelling densities') from the Dienst der Publieke Werken, Department Stadsontwikkelin in Hameleers, M. (ed.), *Kaarten van Amsterdam 1866–2000* (Bussum: Uitgeverij THOTH, 2002), 270. The dwelling density of the oldest parts of De Pijp was between 190 and 220 dwellings per hectare, and the occupancy rate of Amsterdam in 1958 was 3.5.
42
Municipality of Amsterdam, *Algemeen Uitbreidingsplan van Amsterdam (AUP): Nota van toelichting* (Amsterdam: Stadsdrukkerij Amsterdam, 1934), 7.
43
Hobsbawm, E., *The Age of Empire: 1875–1914* (London: Weidenfeld and Nicholson, 1987).

play a central role. This new part of Amsterdam was targeting a different segment of the urban population. In 1864, eight wealthy inhabitants of Amsterdam took the initiative to create a park on the south-western edge of the city. The only urban green area present in the older parts of the city, the Plantage, was to a large extent built upon in 1857.[44] The sale of the lots adjacent to the Vondelpark yielded sufficient profit to commission garden architect Jan David Zocher to design the park. Only the wealthy segment of the city could afford to undertake this kind of privatized urban development. The expansion also had a very explicit programme. Houses were permitted, while workshops or factories were forbidden. The initial development, to only build large villas that would compete with the attractive rural settlements of the immediate surroundings (Gooi, Kennemerland), was never realized because of the higher development costs.[45] Even so, population density in the Vondelparkbuurt was only between 190 and 225 inhabitants per hectare, which was less than a third of the density in De Pijp.[46] It is important, however, not to forget that the Vondelparkbuurt represented an exception. The norm for Amsterdam was the continuing speculation that dominated the housing market in the city, leading to the related problems of overcrowding and poor hygiene.

By the end of the nineteenth century, aesthetic ideas on town planning began to gain influence, especially in Austria and Germany. In 1889 Camillo Sitte published a small polemic entitled *Der Städtebau nach seinen künstlerischen Grundsätzen* (*City Planning According to Artistic Principles*). This book made him the leading proponent of a new school in town planning.[47] Sitte argued that town planning should be more than only land-use planning whereby streets and lots are determined. In this polemic he expressed his concern about city development leading too often to the creation of wide and straight streets accompanied by monotonous buildings of uniform height. Sitte instead believed in compact urban patterns with narrow winding streets. The ideas of Sitte immediately had an impact in the Netherlands, leading to a discussion about the role of the engineer and the artist in city development.

At about the same time, in 1899 in England, Ebenezer Howard founded the Garden City Association to promote the 'Social City'.[48] This new, decentralized city offered an alternative to the overcrowded and unhealthy cities with their lack of natural environments. In the book *Garden Cities of Tomorrow: A Peaceful Path to Real Reform*, published in 1898, Howard explained his ideas about the ideal town. ◓ Garden cities should have a maximum of 30,000 inhabitants and should be built on an area of 1,000 acres (approximately 400 ha). This translates to a population density of 75 inhabitants per hectare. The most important amenities are in clusters at the centre of each town. Housing is located in spacious settings surrounding the centre and industry on the outer ring.

STATE-MANAGED CAPITALISM (1900–1979)

Around the turn of the century city development became increasingly influenced by the ideas of the 'Healthy City' (Baumeister), the 'Beautiful City' (Sitte), and the 'Social City' (Howard). In response to rampant speculation and poor public health in the city, and the fears of the powerful working-class movement that since 1890 was becoming a factor that

44
Dijkstra et al., *Atlas Amsterdam*, op. cit. (note 7).

45
Wagenaar, 'Amsterdam 1860–1940', op. cit. (note 36), 228–230.
46
Based on the dwelling density as mentioned on the 1956 map *Woningdichtheden* ('dwelling densities') from the Dienst der Publieke Werken, Department Stadsontwikkeling in Hameleers, *Kaarten*, op.cit. (note 41), 270. The dwelling density in the Vondelparkbuurt was between 55 and 65 dwellings per hectare. The occupancy rate of Amsterdam in 1958 was 3.5.
47
De Ruijter, *Voor volkshuisvesting*, op. cit. (note 24), 53, 162–164.

48
Rådberg, *Doktrin*, op. cit. (note 25), 54–57.

could not be ignored, the *Housing Act* (*Woningwet*, 1901) and the *Long Land Lease Regulation* (*Erfpachtregeling*, 1896) came into force.[49] Through the Housing Act it became not only possible to plan land use on a large scale, but, at the same time, it offered public institutions the means to plan space in a manner that was both socially and aesthetically responsible. Public or semi-public services (local Government Departments and Housing Associations) became not only responsible for the layout of streets and the required infrastructure, but also for large social housing developments. This constituted a qualitative break with the past. At the beginning of the twentieth century, population density fell throughout Amsterdam. This was caused by a combination of a massive home building programme, the demolition of small slum dwellings during the first decades of the century, and a decrease in the occupancy rate from an average of 4.4 persons per dwelling in 1900 to 3.6 by 1938.[50]

Amsterdam's Plan Zuid 🖉, designed during the first decade of the twentieth century by Hendrik Petrus Berlage,[51] was one of the first examples whereby a public street plan and the architecture of the lots and the buildings represented a synthesis of public planning policy and art, a *Gesamtskunstwerk*.[52] Unlike any previous city expansion plan, it was not a pragmatic exercise using entrepreneurial principles. Plan Zuid embraced both the aesthetic and the social dimensions of Sitte and Howard. The quality of the public space, improved housing for the working class, more schools, and better recreational opportunities; all were central to the plan: 'Plan Zuid was to be the first large-scale demonstration of a modern twentieth-century city, based on social-democratic ideals of social justice and cultural elevation.'[53] Dwellings were larger and occupied by fewer people. More public space had been added (wide streets), and the open spaces within the building lots were more spacious through private and communal gardens. However, although the density of Plan Zuid with 315 inhabitants per hectare was less than half the density of De Pijp (700 inhabitants per hectare), it was still four times higher than the ideal of 75 inhabitants per hectare proposed by Howard 20 years earlier.[54]

The Garden City Movement

The ideas of Howard and the Garden City Movement were also very influential in alternative housing developments built in other countries during this period. In Germany and France this led to the founding of the *Gartenstadtgesellschaft* and the *Association des Cité Jardins*.[55] Despite the call by some for similar changes in the Netherlands, such as by Bruinwold Riedel in his book *Tuinsteden* (Garden cities) of 1906, no such association was established here. The architect Jan Leliman explained in 1908 at the opening of an exhibition of the German *Gartenstadtgesellschaft* in Amsterdam the numerous reasons for this. According to him, the problems in Dutch cities were not quite as bad or as widespread as in many other European cities. In addition, the decentralized tradition and legal autonomy of municipalities had made it rather difficult to establish new towns. Last but not least, Dutch planners were not convinced that the ideas of Howard fulfilled a real need.[56] Ideas like those expressed in the regional plan developed by the *Tuinstadcommissie* (the garden city commission) in Amsterdam, which included garden cities located 10 to 20

49
De Ruijter, *Voor volkshuisvesting*, op. cit. (note 24); Hall, *Cities*, op. cit. (note 31); Heeling et al., *Het ontwerp*, op. cit. (note 9); De Klerk, *De modernisering*, op. cit. (note 18).

50
Wintershoven, *Demografisch eeuwboek Amsterdam*, op. cit. (note 15).
51
1st plan 1905, 2nd plan 1917.
52
Wagenaar, 'Amsterdam 1860–1940', op. cit. (note 36), 232.

53
Heeling et al., *Het ontwerp*, op. cit. (note 9), 44.

54
Based on the dwelling density as mentioned on the 1956 map *Woningdichtheden* ('dwelling densities') from the Dienst der Publieke Werken, Department Stadsontwikkeling in Hameleers, *Kaarten* op.cit. (note 41), 270, and the average occupancy in 1958 of 3.5 in Amsterdam from Wintershoven, *Demografisch eeuwboek Amsterdam*, op. cit. (note 15).
55
De Ruijter, *Voor volkshuisvesting*, op. cit. (note 24), 184–185.

56
Ibid; 187.

Second version of
Plan Zuid (1917),
Amsterdam, by
H.P. Berlage
(Taverne 1993: 233).

km from the existing city, were not taken seriously until the 1960s when
the policy of new towns was introduced in the so-called Second National
Policy Document on Spatial Planning.[57]

Some of the ideas of the Garden City Movement did, however, influence Dutch practice. Especially the work of Raymond Unwin, a socialist
and self-educated planner, was influential. The Arts and Crafts ideals of
William Morris and the historical references of Middle Age communities were combined by Unwin with analytical studies of urban form and
land use. The garden suburbs in Letchworth and Hampstead, designed
together with Barry Parker, are the most well known. Unwin, best known
for *Town Planning in Practice* (1909) and his pamphlet *Nothing Gained by
Overcrowding!* (1912), set a norm of 12 dwellings to the net acre (30
dwellings per hectare) and argued that it was cheaper to build in such
low densities. He demonstrated this by comparing two schemes with
single-family housing with densities of respectively 30 and 60 homes per
hectare.[58] The most important difference, besides the number of
dwellings, was the price for infrastructure (streets) needed to access the
dwellings. In the first scheme (30 dwellings per hectare) almost £5,000
was needed to construct the street plan, and in the second scheme (60
dwellings per hectare) £10,000. As the total land price (for 5 ha) in both
schemes was similar (£5,000), the costs per dwelling would have been
£67 and £50 respectively. In other words, the denser scheme was cheaper
when measured per dwelling, but the price of the lots (per m²) were in
the less-dense scheme only 20 pence while in the second scheme this
was 30 pence. Unwin argued, therefore, that the economic results of
overcrowding are less favourable when the price per square meter of
land is considered.[59] Another argument often used against low densities,

57
VROM, *Tweede nota over de
ruimtelijke ordening* (The
Hague: Ministry of Public
Housing and Spatial
Planning, 1966).

58
Unwin, R., *Nothing Gained
by Overcrowding! How the
Garden City Type of
Development May Benefit
Both Owner and Occupier*
(Westminster: P.S. King &
Son, 1912), 6–8.

59
Ibid., 3–10.
60

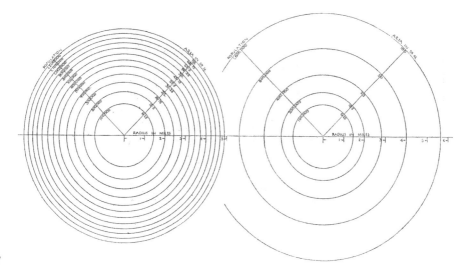

refuted by Unwin in his pamphlet, was that it took up more land and, therefore, caused an increase in commuter traffic. Unwin used the radius and the surface of a circle to argue that when the radius of a circle was doubled, and thus the distance from the circumference to the centre of that circle, the surface of 'land' added is quadrupled. ♙

Scientific Design

Mathematical reasoning of this kind was used by more urban planners in this period. In the 1920s in Germany, Anton Hoenig is an exponent of this approach. Others included L.H.J. Angenot, Aad Heimans, and the people associated with SAR (*Stichting Architectuur Research*) in the Netherlands (1950s–1960s); and Leslie Martin and Lionel March in England (1960s–1970s). The work of Hoenig is particularly interesting as he introduced the concept of spaciousness (*Weitraumigkeit*) in an attempt to measure 'urban quality'.[60] This concept stemmed from the Berlin Building Ordinance, passed in 1925. ♙ This ordinance defined five different building categories based on building height (*Stockwerksanzahl*; from two to five storeys), and lot coverage (*Ausnutzung der Grundstücks*; from 10 to 60 per cent). For each category the built density (*Ausnutzungsziffer*) could be calculated as the product of building height and lot coverage.

Hoenig used the same definitions given in the building ordinance, but added spaciousness, defined as the ratio between the non-built land and the total amount of building stock. Put another way, spaciousness expresses the amount of non-built land that each dwelling has at its disposal. In the article 'Baudichte und Weitraumigkeit' (Building density and spaciousness), Hoenig discusses the relation between urban density, spaciousness and building height.[61] He showed that the lowest and highest building densities in Berlin's building ordinance differ by a factor 15, but when spaciousness is added to the equation, the densities differ by a factor 35. Each square metre of floor area in the highest category

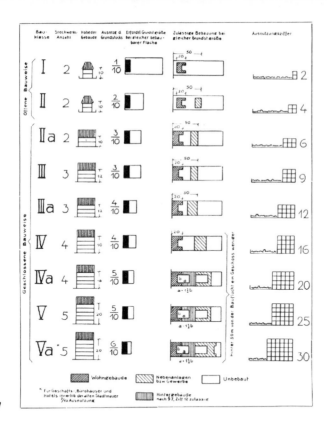

Building categories within the construction ordinance of Berlin effectuated in 1925 (Rådberg 1988: 69).

(*Bauklasse Va*) has 0.13 m² of non-built space available, while in the lowest category (*Bauklasse I*), the figure is 4.5 m². Hoenig argued further that quality can only be guaranteed when each square metre of floor area is at least compensated for by one square metre of non-built land. This applied only to the first three categories of Berlin's building ordinance, all of which concerned single-family housing.

In 1933 Le Corbusier presented an alternative to the compact nineteenth-century city and the spacious garden city: *La Ville Radieuse.* This was a model for a 'Green City' with plenty of open space, light, sun and fresh air. Densities were high – up to 1,000 inhabitants per hectare, comparable to the density of the Jordaan 50 years earlier, which had often been characterized as being heavily overcrowded. The rationale for such a high density was to minimize land use and distances travelled. High-rise buildings were used to realize such high densities. Hoenig used the work of Le Corbusier to illustrate the relationship between density and spaciousness. Le Corbusier's plan for Paris (Plan Voisin) consisted of buildings of 60 storeys and 95 per cent of the lots left open. The built density (*Ausnutzungsziffer*) achieved in this way was comparable to the highest building category in Berlin's building ordinance. The spaciousness, however, of *Plan Voisin* was three times higher than in Berlin (0.32 compared to 0.13) and, Hoenig concluded, when high densities had to be achieved, better qualities could be realized with high-rise buildings.

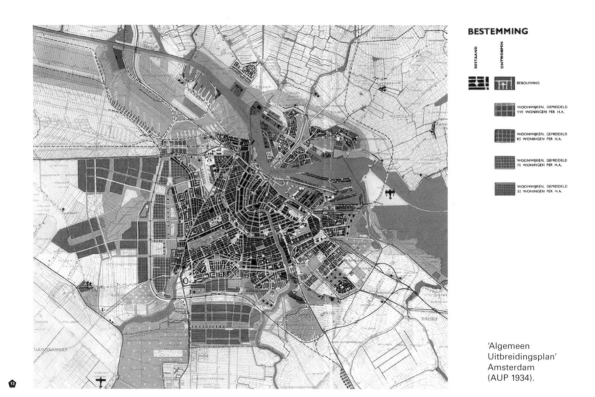

'Algemeen
Uitbreidingsplan'
Amsterdam
(AUP 1934).

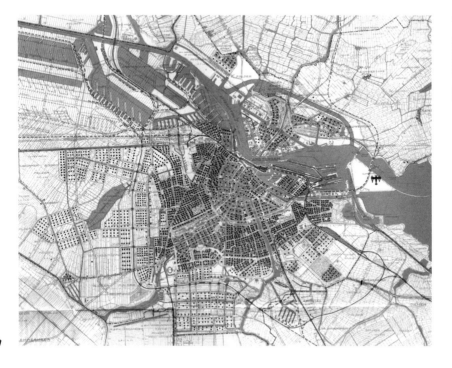

'Algemeen
Uitbreidingsplan'
Amsterdam.
Dwelling densities
in 2000 (AUP 1934).

This scientific ideal of analysis in planning was important to the international movement CIAM (*Congrès Internationaux d'Architecture Moderne*), founded in 1928 at the initiative of Le Corbusier and Siegfried Gideon in La Sarraz, Switzerland. The CIAM perceived the urban landscape as the sum of collective functions of a city. *Die Funktionelle Stadt* was not determined aesthetically, but functionally.[62] Cornelis van Eesteren, chairman of CIAM from 1930 until 1947, developed a model for the modern functional city in Amsterdam: the General Extension Plan (*Algemeen Uitbreidingsplan Amsterdam* or *AUP*).[63] ♟ ♟ Van Eesteren, with Th.K. van Lohuizen, did not seek to realize an ornamental plan with a formal layout based on intuition or artistic inspiration, but aimed instead to create the appropriate conditions for the modern city based on scientific methods. The AUP was to become a model for the modern functional city. This model included such elements as housing, amenities, industry, roads and parks, all developed based on their own intrinsic rules and ideals. Most of the housing types reflect functionalist views on living; they are oriented towards the sun, have access to fresh air and good housing schemes, and are characterized by the well-known open block structures.[64] Prior to the urban plan, Van Lohuizen undertook a thorough survey that was used to predict the population growth of Amsterdam. A survey of this nature was comparable to the statistical research and demographic prognoses mentioned by Baumeister at the end of the nineteenth century, the scientific method advocated by Hoenig, and, even earlier, to the work on the 1860 expansion of Barcelona by Cerda. Patrick Geddes's call for 'survey before plan' had also influenced Dutch planning through Unwin's 1909 book *Town Planning in Practice*.[65]

Van Lohuizen estimated that the population of Amsterdam would not exceed one million inhabitants by 2000, and satellite cities, as advocated by the Garden City Movement, would not be necessary. This methodology adhered to prevailing optimistic ideas about science and its ability to predict social developments using extensive, often quantitative analysis of human behaviour and socioeconomic phenomena. The exact area required for the extension could be calculated with precision based on the number of houses required (111,200) and the preferred urban densities, defined as the number of dwellings per hectare.[66] Adhering to the ideas of the Garden City Movement, the initial idea was to provide single-family homes on a large scale, including homes for the working class. However, to prevent excessive sprawl and to keep the price of land acceptable, a mix of housing types was suggested. Research into different lot patterns had shown that within a density of 70 dwellings per hectare, 50 to 60 per cent of the dwellings could still be realized as single family homes. With high land prices adjacent to the existing city, densities were higher on central locations (85–110 dwellings per hectare), and lower in the more peripheral areas (55–70 dwellings per hectare).[67] This is probably the first time in Dutch planning practice that density was used in such a prescriptive, normative fashion.

Despite the studies carried out in advance of the realization of the AUP, the actual densities turned out to be lower than were envisaged. The peripheral areas had between 45 and 60 homes per hectare instead of 55 to 70, and there were fewer single-family units than originally planned (32 per cent instead of 50 to 60 per cent).[68] As a result, the envi-

62
Rådberg, *Doktrin*, op. cit. (note 25), 115–124; Taverne, *De wortels*, op. cit. (note 28), 64; Cammen and De Klerk, *Ruimtelijke Ordening*, op. cit. (note 16), 137.
63
Municipality of Amsterdam, *Algemeen Uitbreidingsplan*, op. cit. (note 42).

64
Engel, H. and E. van Velzen, 'De vorm van de stad: Nederland na 1945', in: Taverne and Visser, *Stedebouw*, op. cit. (note17), 276–282; Hereijgers, A. and E. van Velzen, *De naoorlogse stad, een hedendaagse ontwerpopgave* (Rotterdam: NAi Publishers, 2001); Venema, H., 'Bos en Lommer', in: S. Komossa et al. (eds.), *Atlas van het Hollandse bouwblok* (Bussum: Uitgeverij THOTH, 2002), 112–123.
65
Cammen and De Klerk, *Ruimtelijke Ordening*, op. cit. (note 16); De Ruijter, *Voor volkshuisvesting*, op. cit. (note 24), 200.
66
Municipality of Amsterdam, *Algemeen Uitbreidingsplan*, op. cit. (note 42), 83.
67
Based on the assumed occupancy rate of 3.37 from Ibid., 82.
68
Based on the dwelling density as mentioned on the 1956 map *Woningdichtheden* ('dwelling densities') from the Dienst der Publieke Werken, Department Stadsontwikkeling in Hameleers, *Kaarten*, op.cit. (note 41), 270. The dwelling density in Geuzenveld-Slotermeer was between 45 and 60 dwellings per hectare and the occupancy rate in Amsterdam in 1958 was 3.5. In Slotermeer, 32 per cent of the dwellings were single-family houses, 11 per cent consisted of two-storey houses (so called duplexes) and 57 per cent were multi-family apartments. From Cammen and De Klerk, *Ruimtelijke Ordening*, op. cit. (note 16), 144.

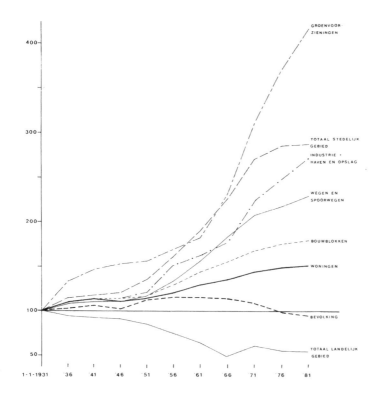

Relative growth of land use in Amsterdam from 1931 to 1981 (1931 = 100) (Hellinga & de Ruijter 1985: 128).

sioned mix of dwellings and commercial activities (shops and small-scale industry) was never actualized for the simple reason that there were not enough people living in the area. The housing shortage just after the Second World War further decreased the amount of commercial activities in favour of dwellings. The idea of concentrated shopping areas, dominant since the 1950s, caused a further specialization in separate living and shopping areas.

There were two important reasons for the fall in densities in the AUP.[69] First, the rate of occupancy had fallen much faster than expected. The expected number of 3.37 in 2000 had already been reached by 1960. In 2000, the rate of occupancy was 1.98.[70] Based only on this decline, space consumption for housing rose by 70 per cent from 1960 to 2000. Secondly, economic growth caused a general increase in space consumption. Houses became larger, with wider lots (*beukmaat*), leading to an increase in land use. For instance, single-family housing units in Slotermeer (part of the AUP) had lots of 5.4 m wide, instead of the originally calculated 4.5 m in the AUP. Also, more cars, public buildings (schools), cultural and health facilities, office and industrial areas, and public green space (sport facilities and parks) were needed than had been projected in the plan.

The lower densities in the AUP, in combination with enormous transformations of the housing stock in the centre of Amsterdam and the

69
Hellinga, H. and P. de Ruijter, *Algemeen Uitbreidingsplan Amsterdam 50 jaar* (Amsterdam: Amsterdamse Raad voor de Stedebouw, 1985), 128.
70
Wintershoven, *Demografisch eeuwboek Amsterdam*, op. cit. (note 15).

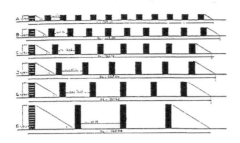

Scheme by Gropius
(1930), illustrating
the relation between
building height, sun
angle, land use and
built density
(Rådberg 1988: 83).

process of 'city forming' (decrease of housing and increase of shops and work places), made new large-scale expansion areas necessary. Parts of North Amsterdam (Buikslotermeer) and, later, the south-east of the city (Bijlmermeer) were developed in the 1960s with a large proportion of the dwellings in high-rise buildings. The realization of the Bijlmermeer, a vertical garden city planned by Siegfried Nassuth and the municipality of Amsterdam, was the last modernist project in the Netherlands and represented one of the best examples of a plan in which the CIAM ideals and the Green City of Le Corbusier and Walter Gropius were realized.[71] Both had earlier researched the advantages of high-rise buildings. Between 1928 and 1931 Gropius developed his ideas about high-rise developments consisting of 8 to 12 storeys.[72] By using simple schemes he argued that high-rise buildings had many advantages:

— Given the same sun angle and plan area, higher built densities were possible;
— Less land was needed to realize the same number of dwellings;
— Using the same density and available land, improvements in quality (in terms of daylight access, sun, view, and privacy) could be achieved.

In the Bijlmermeer, these arguments were put into practice: the housing density matched that of the AUP (about 45 dwellings per hectare), but as the buildings were higher, more land was available on which to construct large green parks between the buildings.[73] The spaciousness in the Bijlmermeer matched the minimal standard introduced by Hoenig: one square metre of open space for each square metre of floor area. We can thus conclude that the same methodology (mathematical analysis) led Unwin to advocate the advantages of low-rise developments with a maximum density of 30 dwellings per hectare; led Hoenig to argue for a

71
Cammen and De Klerk, *Ruimtelijke Ordening*, op. cit. (note 16), 200–202.
72
Rådberg, *Doktrin*, op. cit. (note 25), 79–84, 118.

73
Based on the numbers of dwellings in 2007 of the Bijlmermuseum in which all high rise slabs are still present (area T94c and n, O&S, Amsterdam). The dwelling density was 44 dwellings per hectare in 2007.

spaciousness of at least 1.0; and was used by Le Corbusier and Gropius to promote high-rise developments in their critique of both the traditional city and the Garden City Movement:

> Le Corbusier ... argued that the evil of the modern city was its density of developments and that the remedy, perversely, was to increase that density. Le Corbusier's solution, whereby an all-powerful master planner would demolish the entire existing city and replace it by a city of high-rise towers in a park [illustrates this].[74]

In the 1960s and 1970s, at the Centre for Land Use and Built Form Studies in Cambridge, Martin and March developed a comparable approach to investigate the relationship between density and urban form. In the first volume of a series of monographs emanating from this institute, Martin and March explained that their approach moved beyond the usual boundaries of architecture to include the measurement of the urban landscape.[75] Similar research existed in the Netherlands. Angenot published the book *Verhandelingen over het vraagstuk van de dichtheid van de bebouwing* (Discussions on the subject of built density),[76] Heimans the book *Bebouwingsdichtheid en grondgebruik voor de woningbouw in de stadsuitbreiding* (Building density and land use in urban housing expansions),[77] and the SAR (Stichting Architecten Research) developed the tissue method (*weefselmethode*).[78]

Heimans distinguished different types of allotments (from closed to open building blocks) and related these to their dimensions. He stated that one cannot speak of the density of a building type as it was also dependent on the dimensions of the ground plan. Within the SAR method, the type of lot division (tissue models) was central. Two basic models are mentioned: closed blocks and strip developments. The distribution and function of public space (streets, parking and green space) and building height were important elements that needed to be added to characterize tissue models. In the book *Urban Space and Structure*, Martin and March argued that more floor space could be realized in semi-detached housing types in the countryside than with high-rise buildings in inner-city centres.[79] As the city expands with equal-width bands, the outer bands would be able to accommodate more built space than the inner bands. To compensate for this, the same area of floor space in the inner bands had to be achieved in the sky. ✪ This choice between central and peripheral dispositions of space was also central in the models of Unwin, as discussed earlier, and the Dutch architect Hans van der Laan.[80] The latter concluded that when cities were built following the concept of peripheral disposition, a large open square could be positioned in the centre, but when the periphery had to remain open, the city would be crowded at its centre.

The three plans discussed in this section, Plan Zuid, AUP and Bijlmermeer, all illustrate clear breaks with nineteenth-century urban planning. These twentieth-century plans relied on the idea that it was possible, and preferable, to create a new (part of a) city by design. These ideas of deliberate city design were supported by the legal instruments embodied in the Housing Act and the Long Land Lease Regulation. Berlage, inspired by the work of Sitte and Howard, viewed the city as a harmo-

74
Hall, *Cities*, op. cit. (note 31), 9.

75
Martin, L. and L. March (eds.), *Urban Space and Structures* (Cambridge: Cambridge University Press, 1972).
76
Angenot, L.H.J., *Verhandelingen over het vraagstuk van de dichtheid van bebouwing* (Alphen aan den Rijn: N. Samsom NV, 1954).
77
Heimans, A., *Bebouwingsdichtheid en grondgebruik voor de woningbouw in stadsuitbreidingen* (The Hague: Ten Hagen, 1965).
78
Stichting Architectuur Research, *Deciding on Density: An Investigation into High Density Allotments with a View to the Waldeck Area, The Hague* (Eindhoven, 1977).
79
Martin and March, *Urban Space*, op. cit. (note 75), 51–53.

80
Tummers, L.J.M. and J.M. Tummers-Zuurmond, *Het land in de stad: De stedebouw van de grote agglomeratie* (Bussum: Uitgeverij THOTH, 1997).

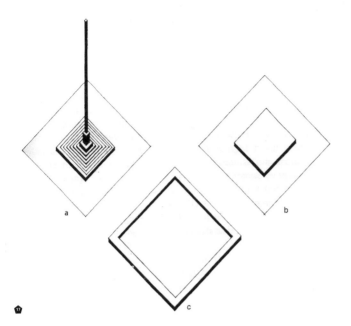

Housing density in relation to its distribution (Martin and March 1972: 52). [a] Each band (with equal width) accommodates an equal amount of built space: in the outermost ring, a building is only one storey high and in the centre 72 storeys are required. [b and c] Two examples showing the same built space and plot ratio, whether distributed in a concentrated or a linear form.

nious, three-dimensional artefact. The city could be designed like a building, uniting all levels of scale in a *Gesamtkunstwerk*.[81] In a baroque fashion Berlage strived for visual unity. The Sittean picturesque, combined with a baroque composition, puts the plans of Berlage in stark opposition to nineteenth-century pragmatic engineering plans.[82]

The approach of Van Eesteren, in contrast, did not aspire to a final image. Instead, city expansions were designed relying on the ideals of CIAM, with 'a collection of land uses that through their functional relations would become a productive whole'.[83] This also applied to the 1947 Plan for the Reconstruction of Rotterdam by Cornelis van Traa.[84] As with the AUP, but in contrast to Berlage's Plan Zuid, the new plan for Rotterdam did not prescribe any specific architectural form or final image, but offered an open plan of structures. Van Traa's plan was even more radical in its functionalism and flexibility than the AUP.[85] This shift from three-dimensional city development by urban design (for example Sitte, Berlage, 'City Beautiful'), to a two-dimensional functional organization of the city, represented a triumph for the ideas of CIAM. Scientific and technology-based ideals became the main driving force for urban planning:

> The Plan [for Rotterdam by van Traa] does not only propagate the structuring of space, but also the structuring of time by deliberately leaving options open. That which was smouldering before 1940 had inflamed: on an urban scale, spatial planning as organization of land uses has taken over from urban design [*vormgevende stedebouw*].[86]

Based on scientific urban surveys, the modern city could be planned with great precision. This belief in the possibility to predict population growth, housing needs, traffic patterns, and so forth made spatial plan-

81
Castex, *De rationele stad*, op. cit. (note 28); Wagenaar, 'Amsterdam 1860–1940', op. cit. (note 36).
82
Cammen and De Klerk, *Ruimtelijke Ordening*, op. cit. (note 16), 93.

83
Engel and van Velzen, 'De vorm van de stad', op. cit. (note 64), 277.
84
Klerk, L. de, *Particuliere plannen: Denkbeelden en initiatieven van de stedelijke elite inzake volkswoningbouw en de stedebouw in Rotterdam, 1860–1950* (Rotterdam: NAi Publishers, 1998), 244–247.
85
Cammen and De Klerk, *Ruimtelijke Ordening*, op. cit. (note 16), 182.

86
De Klerk, *Particuliere plannen*, op. cit. (note 94), 247.

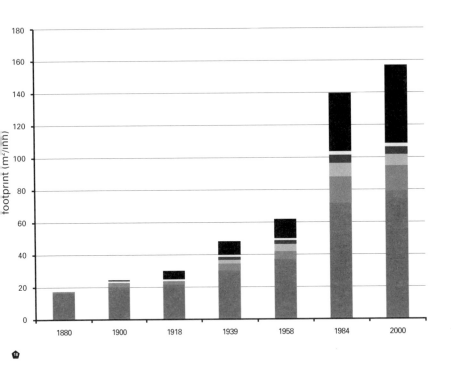

Legend:
- Industry and offices
- Cemeteries
- Garden allotments
- Sports facilities
- Parks
- Housing

footprint (m²/inh)

1880 1900 1918 1939 1958 1984 2000

Different land uses per inhabitant in Amsterdam at different moments between 1880 and 2000.

ning one of the most important political tools after the Second World War. Peter Hall describes this as 'the golden age of planning'.[87] The Fordist-Keynesian welfare state under construction after the Second World War had planning and state management of the economy at its core: 'Everything was subordinated to growth.'[88] This model, however, must not so much be seen as the opposite of capitalism as such, but as a stabilizing and facilitating apparatus necessary to guarantee future accumulation, although with a different agency compared to the character of the state half a century earlier.

Spatial Policies
Between 1958 and 1984, the population of Amsterdam shrank from 871,580 inhabitants to 676,520.[89] Rotterdam experienced a similar development during this period; falling from 731,000 in 1965 to 555,000 inhabitants in 1984.[90] Still, although the population of Amsterdam decreased by 22 per cent between 1958 and 1984, the urbanized area of Amsterdam grew by 75 per cent, from 5,400 to 9,460 hectares! A large part of this growth came from the harbour, which attracted workers from Amsterdam and the surrounding area. However, even if one only examines the relationship between population decline and growth in the area of housing, the figures show the same trend.[91] The total size of the area occupied by housing grew by 50 per cent during this period, from 3,240 to 4,865 hectares. Statistically speaking, an inhabitant in Amsterdam had 37 m² of residential area at his or her disposal in 1958, and by 1984 this had almost doubled to 72 m² per person.[92] Some of the relatively well-off middle classes escaped from the city to low-density environments and thereby drained cities like Amsterdam and Rotter-

87
Hall, *Cities*, op. cit. (note 31), 324.
88
Henri Lefebvre, quoted in Brenner, N., *New State Spaces: Urban Governance and the Rescaling of Statehood* (Oxford: Oxford University Press, 2004), 131.

89
Wintershoven, *Demografisch eeuwboek Amsterdam*, op. cit. (note 15).
90
Bik, M. and D. Linders, *Factsheet – prognose: Bevolkingsontwikkeling Rotterdam 2003–2017* (Rotterdam: Centrum voor Onderzoek en Statistiek, 2003).
91
This excludes large scale green areas and larger working areas such as the harbour.
92
See Berghauser Pont and Haupt, *Space, Density*, Op.cit. (note 3).

dam of much tax income and vitality. With fewer taxpayers and citizens in the city centre, the advantages of scale that higher densities offered in terms of amenities, community interaction and transport efficiency were threatened. In turn this led to a further depopulation of the city centre. All over Europe, and even more so in the USA, the trend of suburbanization led to an exodus of the middle class from the cities, especially from the big cities.

Various subsidies in the Netherlands were created to control the rapid (sub)urbanization of the Randstad (conurbation in West Netherlands). One measure was to stimulate the regions furthest away from the Randstad to again make them economically viable. The scale of urban planning was upgraded, with national planning becoming an accepted tool to organize land uses and restore the economic viability of peripheral regions. The first National Policy Document on Spatial Planning of 1960 was about such an equal distribution of population and economic activities.[93] The juridical and organizational framework for the planning on all different levels of scale was laid down in *The Spatial Planning Act* (*Wet op de ruimtelijke ordening*) of 1965.[94]

The policy was successful, partly due to positive economic developments. Industries in need of cheap labour relocated from the Randstad to the peripheries of the country. The economic boom continued during the 1960s and the Dutch Statistical Institute (*Centraal Bureau voor Statistiek*) predicted in the mid 1960s that the Dutch population would reach 20 million people by the year 2000. This was 7 million more than had been predicted in the National Policy Document on Spatial Planning five years earlier.[95] In 1963 the international planner and advisor for the State Service for the National Plan (*Rijksdienst voor het Nationaal Plan*), J.P. Thijsse Jr, presented a plan for the Netherlands in the year 2000. The plan was to accommodate 20 million inhabitants in two huge agglomerations.[96]

An alternative to combat the growth of such huge agglomerations and to react to the laissez-faire character of suburbanization was presented in The Second National Policy Document on Spatial Planning: concentrated dispersal (*gebundelde deconcentratie*).[97] New and existing towns and cities (satellite cities, or *groeikernen*) were to be (further) developed at a distance of 10 to 20 km from the existing larger cities of the Randstad. ✪ By assigning areas where urbanization could take place, the demands for suburban living environments could be accommodated, green open spaces would be saved and the size of the Randstad agglomerations would be controlled. Fifty years after its birth, one could conclude that Howard's regional planning model had finally been adopted in the Netherlands. The Dutch approach to new towns, however, had not been implemented to counter the negative effects of overcrowding. Instead it focused, above all, on channelling residential investments into less developed or marginalized areas, on preserving open space within the Randstad's Green Heart, on expanding regional transportation infrastructures, and on managing demographic expansions throughout the whole country.[98] The satellite cities consisted of the expansion of existing towns such as Alkmaar, Hoorn and Zoetermeer and the newly created new towns of Lelystad (1967) and Almere (1975). Although the prognosis for Dutch population growth turned out to be inaccurate – in 2000 the Netherlands had less than 16 million inhabitants and not the

93
VROM, *Nota inzake de ruimtelijke ordening* (The Hague: Ministry of Public Housing and Construction Industry, 1960); Brenner, *New State Spaces*, op. cit. (note 88), 142–143.
94
VROM, *Wet op de ruimtelijke ordening* (The Hague: Ministry of Public Housing and Spatial Planning, 1965); Cammen and de Klerk, *Ruimtelijke Ordening* op.cit.(note 16), 174.
95
Cammen and De Klerk, *Ruimtelijke Ordening*, op. cit. (note 16), 211–212.
96
Ibid., 212.

97
VROM, *Tweede nota over de ruimtelijke ordening* (The Hague: Ministry of Public Housing and Spatial Planning, 1966); Cammen and De Klerk, *Ruimtelijke Ordening*, op. cit. (note 16), 213–217.

98
Brenner, *New State Spaces*, op. cit. (note 88), 156.

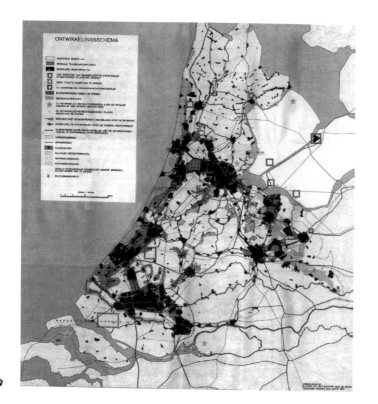

'Ontwikkelings-
schema Westen des
Lands 1980',
proposing regional
urbanization with
satellite towns such
as Almere, Hoorn
and Zoetermer (van
der Cammen & de
Klerk 2003: 221).

predicted 20 million – all the space that had been set aside was used up by a rapid increase of space consumption per capita. In an analysis by L. Wijers it is shown that human space consumption over a ten-year period (1945–1955) more than doubled in the new expansion plans, from 80 m² to 180 m² per person.[99]

Reactions to Modernism

During the last part of the period of state-managed capitalism, some people came to criticize what they saw as the failure of modern planning and architecture. People such as José Luis Sert and Jane Jacobs contributed through their books to a change in the theory and practice of city development. The titles of their publications expressed the urgency of their ideas: *Can Our Cities Survive?* and *The Death and Life of Great American Cities*.[100] Sert reached the conclusion that high density was often mistaken for overcrowding and that the solutions of the Garden City Movement and the high-rise solutions promoted by Le Corbusier and Gropius were to blame for much of the decline of city life. Jacobs argued that modern planning had ignored the complexity of the city and had forgotten that social and economic vitality were essential ingredients for achieving a city that functions well. To arrive here Jacobs propagated a minimum density of 100 dwellings per acre (175 dwellings per hectare).

Jacobs's conclusions on the effects of modern planning and architecture on existing habitats and cities marked the beginning of a move towards typomorphological research in architecture and urbanism.

99
Cammen and De Klerk,
Ruimtelijke Ordening, op.
cit. (note 16), 225.

100
Sert, J.L., *Can Our Cities
Survive? An ABC of Urban
Problems, Their Analysis,
Their Solutions Based on
Proposals Formulated by
the CIAM* (Boston: Harvard
University Press, 1942);
Jacobs, J., *The Death and
Life* (New York: Random
House, 1992), originally
published in 1961.

Anne Vernez Moudon describes the origins and different schools of morphological research in her text *Getting to Know the Built Landscape: Typomorphology*.[101] In Italy, typomorphological studies have their origins in the 1940s with the work of Saverio Muratori, an architect who argued that the roots of architecture were to be found not in the fantastic projections of the modernists, but from within the more continuous tradition of city development emanating from antiquity until the 1930s. The French, and especially the Versailles school, followed the Muratorian philosophy, believing that modernism had created a complete break with the past that could not be repaired. They believed that the roots of architecture had to be rediscovered in past traditions. The shift to the morphological perspective in architecture and urbanism led to an emphasis on the formal and historical characteristics of urban patterns. Demographic surveys, social statistics and abstract zoning diagrams by planners gave way to matters more intrinsic to the design profession such as typologies, historical map analyses and detailed drawings of settlement patterns. And besides, as a reaction to the dominance of the regional scale and the autonomous architectonic structure in modernist planning, the attention also shifted towards the 'intermediate scale'. Especially Manuel de Solà-Morales called attention to the lack of interest in this intermediate scale, or the urban project, in modern planning.[102]

The counterculture of the 1960s and 1970s was, among many things, a reaction against industrialized mass production, large-scale projects and the wholesale post-war demolition of existing city-centre environments. Plan areas became smaller in the 1970s and the long-term perspectives were replaced by solutions addressing the local problems of the day. This can be described as a transition 'from a technocratic to a sociocratic process'.[103] Concepts such as advocacy planning and urban renewal came to dominate professional discussions. Architects and urban planners affiliated with the Dutch magazine *Forum* heavily criticized functionalist planning as inhumane and argued for a (re)turn to human scale in planning and design. Hall caricatured these rapid shifts of professional attitude from the 1950s to the 1970s in his *Cities of Tomorrow* as follows:

> In 1955, the typical newly graduated planner was at the drawing board, producing a diagram of desired land uses; in 1965, s/he was analyzing computer output of traffic patterns; in 1975, the same person was talking late into the night with community groups, in the attempt to organize against hostile forces in the world outside.[104]

NEOLIBERAL CAPITALISM (1979–THE PRESENT)

In the early 1970s, the economic boom of the Fordist-Keynesian period that had followed the Second World War turned into a worldwide recession.[105] This economic stagnation forced countries and municipalities to cut spending. Furthermore, much industrial production was unable to compete with the emerging Asian economies and sectors such as shipyards and textiles, but also consumer goods, shrank while the service sector grew. The programme of economic reform in China of 1978 instigated after the death of Mao by Deng Xiaoping, and the opening up of new populations for production and consumption with the fall of the

101
Moudon, A.V., 'Getting to Know the Built Landscape: Typomorphology', in: K. Franck and L. Schneekloth (eds.), *Ordering Space: Types in Architecture and Design* (New York: Van Nostrand Reinhold, 1994), 289–311.

102
Meyer, H., *City and Port: Transformation of Port Cities London, Barcelona, New York, Rotterdam* (Utrecht: Internationaal Books, 1999).

103
Cammen and De Klerk, *Ruimtelijke Ordening*, op. cit. (note 16), 242.

104
Hall, *Cities*, op. cit. (note 31), 334.

105
Brenner, R., *The Economics of Global Turbulence: The Advanced Capitalist Economies from Long Boom to Long Downturn, 1945–2005* (London: Verso, 2006); Harvey, D., *A Brief History of Neoliberalism* (Oxford: Oxford University Press, 2005); Brenner, *New State Spaces*, op. cit. (note 88).

Iron Curtain during the 1990s, further increased the global competitive character of life at the end of the twentieth century. The global recession of the 1970s, the transition from regional, via national, to global competition between corporations, and the rise of unemployment in the 1980s had a significant impact on the development of Dutch cities. In Amsterdam unemployment more than doubled from a relatively high level of 8 per cent to 17 per cent between 1980 and 1984.[106] Housing associations were privatized and while in 1980 the national housing production in the Netherlands consisted for 90 per cent of social housing, by 2000 this had shrunk to 20 per cent.[107]

After an almost standstill in the housing construction in Amsterdam between 1977 and 1980, the production of social housing quickly increased between 1981 and 1984. These counter-cyclical investments during the severe recession marked the end of a long period of collective investments in housing that started after the Second World War and the beginning of a market-oriented urban governance. Neil Brenner in his book *New State Spaces* summarizes this general shift as a reorientation 'from the managerial, welfarist mode of the Fordist-Keynesian period to an entrepreneurial, growth-oriented, and competitiveness-driven framework during the post-1970s period'.[108]

After the criticism of a centralized and technocratic state paradigm on many levels of society, a reorientation on the social and human scale of the city took place. This period was characterized by urban renewal and regeneration. Political protests and social unrest at the end of the 1960s and beginning of the 1970s led to an increased democratization of the urban process, and advocacy planning paved the way for locally focused 'building for the neighbourhood' (*bouwen voor de buurt*). The need to revitalize the cities after a long period of depopulation and 'urban crisis' was expressed in the *Structuurschets stedelijke gebieden* (Structure scheme urban areas).[109] Here the focus was less on collective investments in social housing. These had become too expensive to the bleeding treasuries, and seemed to only reproduce an expensive social structure of low-income groups with little purchasing power to support amenities and with the wrong qualifications to suit the new service economy. The educated middle class that had migrated to the suburbs and smaller towns was what the large cities were in need of. 'People with an above average income [were needed] back in the city.'[110] Gentrification had thus become not only a neighbourhood phenomenon, but was rescaled to play out over whole regions. Such an uneven geographical development became accepted as a fact, and policies that were set up in the 1960s to geographically redistribute wealth were abandoned.

Spatial Privatization

The socially engaged criticism of the 1960s and 1970s of technocratic planning paved the way for an interactive consensus planning approach. The assumption of the latter was that market forces would increase efficiency, making all those involved sensitive to the wishes of housing consumers and investors. Proximity to 'real life' would enable them to respond more adeptly to social and economic changes. This market orientation was initiated not only because of a general revaluation of private initiative's competence and ability, but also because municipalities

106
Brenner, *New State Spaces*, op. cit. (note 88), 179.

107
Cammen and De Klerk, *Ruimtelijke Ordening*, op. cit. (note 16), 405.

108
Brenner, *New State Spaces*, op. cit. (note 88), 177.

109
VROM, *Structuurschets stedelijke gebieden* (The Hague: Ministry of Housing, Spatial Planning and the Environment, 1983).

110
Cammen and De Klerk, *Ruimtelijke Ordening*, op. cit. (note 16), 279.

and the state simply lacked the resources.[111] It became a pragmatic necessity in the 1980s to invite market parties to participate in the (re)building of the cities to cover (local) government budget deficits. The private sector now operated on an equal footing with the state. This was in stark contrast to the past when developers and private building firms used to be mere minions who executed the grand designs of government and municipal planning agencies.

In recent decades private developers and investors have gained a central position in city development through strategic investments in land: 'Attention of all private parties has shifted from buying land that has been prepared for housing development to the purchase of undeveloped land.'[112] In the quarterly bulletin of the Dutch National Bank (*De Nederlandse Bank*) of March 2008, it was stated that 85 per cent of released land for new housing projects came from private developers and not from municipalities.[113] Private developers have hereby become more powerful in project negotiations with local authorities. They have a greater say on the quantitative goals (number of dwellings to be developed) and qualitative ambitions (type of dwellings, amount of green space, parking options) of such projects. This gradual shift from government to governance has created a receptive environment for a project-based approach, an approach in which public and private partners sign agreements (under private law) *before* the spatial aspects of these agreements become legally binding through zoning plans (under public law). This phenomenon of 'after-zoning' has been criticized for its democratic deficit as most of the project formulation takes place outside democratic institutions.[114]

A more adaptive planning approach was propagated for the first time in the Netherlands in the 1988 national planning policy of The Fourth National Policy Document on Spatial Planning, and *Vinex;* The Fourth National Policy Document on Spatial Planning Extra of 1994.[115] With hindsight, these policy documents officially mark the end of a long tradition of government-controlled housing construction that began with the introduction of the *Housing Act* in 1901.

Policy Reactions

Despite this shift, the Dutch government has continued to produce spatial policy documents. In 1983 The Third National Policy Document on Spatial Planning introduced the concept of the 'Compact City', aiming to temper the depopulation of the larger cities that was signalled in the 1976 Policy Document on Urbanization.[116] In the *Vinex* report (1994), the policy was formulated as follows: to build preferably within existing cities through intensification, or, if not possible, adjacent to existing cities to accommodate suburban living environments. Between 1995 and 2005, 455,000 houses were needed according to the survey underpinning the *Vinex* report. In Amsterdam (including Almere) more than 100,000 houses were foreseen of which 35 per cent were projected as 'infill' projects and 65 per cent in areas adjacent to the city. ● An example of the first strategy of this policy was the development of the South Bank of the IJ in Amsterdam (IJ-oevers). Cities, together with private developers, tried to create top locations to attract both real estate investments and economically viable activities in high-density mixed developments. The

111
Brenner, *New State Spaces,* op. cit. (note 88); Harvey, *A Brief History,* op. cit. (note 105).

112
Segeren, A., *De grondmarkt voor woningbouwlocaties* (Rotterdam: NAi Publishers, 2007), 10.
113
Leeuwen, H. van, 'Geef bouwgrond niet aan speculanten', NRC *Handelsblad* 18 August 2008.

114
Meyer, H., 'In dienst van de stad onder postmoderne condities/Working for the City under Post-modern Conditions', in: H. Meyer and L. van den Burg (eds.), *In dienst van de stad/Working for the City* (Amsterdam: SUN, 2005), 64–68.
115
VROM, *Vierde nota over de ruimtelijke ordening* (The Hague: Ministry of Housing, Spatial Planning and the Environment, 1988); VROM, *Vierde nota over de ruimtelijke ordening extra* (The Hague: Ministry of Spatial Planning and the Environment, 1994).
116
VROM, *Derde nota over de ruimtelijke ordening* (The Hague: Ministry of Housing, Spatial Planning and the Environment, 1973–1983);

density of the IJ-oevers in Amsterdam was 90 dwellings per hectare (200 inhabitants per hectare) and although these numbers were higher than those realized earlier in the AUP and Bijlmermeer, they were still far lower than the minimum density for vital cities of 175 dwellings per hectare proposed by Jacobs in the 1960s.[117]

The suburban expansion De Aker in the western part of Amsterdam is a good example of the second Vinex strategy of developments adjacent to existing cities. As is the case in most of the other extension areas of that period in the Netherlands, De Aker consists of mostly single-family housing (more than 70 per cent) and has a density of approximately 35 dwellings per hectare.[118] This is similar to the density proposed by Unwin. Such densities could, according to Jacobs, be viable and safe and even ecologically sustainable (although heavily car dependent), but it would not generate city liveliness or public life for the simple reason that there would not be a sufficient concentration of inhabitants.

Preparations for a Fifth National Policy Document on Spatial Planning at the end of the 1990s included a national inventory of spatial claims for all functions that needed to be accommodated until 2030.[119] For infrastructure, housing and businesses alone, an extra 200,000 hectares of land would be required, an increase of 45 percent.[120] Following market research, housing needs were noted for green suburban areas with low densities and urban areas with higher densities. As was the case already in the *Vinex* report, The Fifth National Policy Document on Spatial Planning inclined towards a compromise to accommodate both claims. Alongside the continuation of a liberalized housing policy, it argued for the liberalization and decentralization of spatial planning. Although The Fifth National Policy Document on Spatial Planning was never approved, the following report, The Spatial Planning Policy Document of 2004, formalized these ambitions with an even clearer choice for decentralization.[121] Spatial planning and design became key instruments for contributing to a better economic performance in the current globalized and competitive environment.

The Image of the City

Parallel to changes in spatial planning, the architecture policy of the government was summed up in the Belvedere Memorandum.[122] Here, in line with the transition from a predominately industrial production society to a de-industrialized consumer society, with its postmodern 'aesthetification of life', the image of the city in terms of cultural heritage, identity and spatial quality dominated. This shift from planning to design matched the increased emphasis on competition between cities:

> It was an approach that saw the city largely in design terms and it accorded well with another theme from the 1980s and 1990s: marketing them like cars or kitchens, which was part and parcel of globalization in an era where the old locational advantages had blown away.[123]

This development corresponded to a more general reorientation from planning to design. Technical content gave way to form, instrumental engineering was replaced by image design, or 'seduction engineering'. Of course, the rationality of engineering, technology and economics

117
Java island, KNSM island, Borneo and Sporenburg (O+S Amsterdam). AUP had 50 dwellings per hectare in 2007 and the Bijlmer 45 dwellings per hectare (O+S, 2007).
118
Based on the amount of dwellings and inhabitants in 2007 (O+S Amsterdam), the population density is 103 inhabitants per hectare in 2007.

119
VROM, *Vijfde nota over de ruimtelijke ordening* (The Hague: Ministry of Housing, Spatial Planning and the Environment, 2001).
120
Cammen and De Klerk, *Ruimtelijke Ordening*, op. cit. (note 16), 423.

121
VROM, *Nota ruimte – ruimte voor ontwikkeling* (The Hague: Ministry of Housing, Spatial Planning and the Environment, 2004).

122
RACM, *Nota Belvedere* (The Hague: The National Service for Archaeology, Cultural Landscape and Built Heritage, 1999).

123
Hall, *Cities*, op. cit. (note 31), 416.

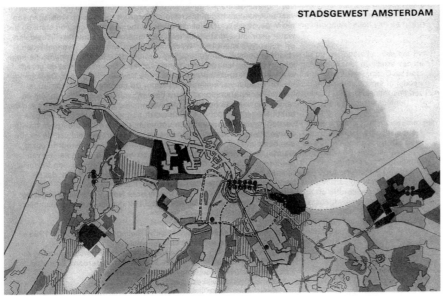

STADSGEWEST AMSTERDAM

ONTWIKKELINGEN TOT 2005:

   woningbouwlocaties –
stedelijk capaciteit

uitbreidingsmogelijkheden
voor woningbouw

uitbreidingen stadsgewestelijk
openbaar railvervoer

kantoorfuncties binnen
stedelijk gebied

industrie en handel

OPTIES NA 2005:

zoekruimte voor woning
bouwlocaties

zoekruimte voor industrie
en distributie

zoekruimte voor
glastuinbouw

Vinex policy in the
Amsterdam city
region:
intensification with
20,000 to 25,000
dwellings and city
expansions with
65,000 dwellings
(VROM 1994: 46).

remained keys to success, but the carefully produced imagery became
more central to the sales effort of plans and projects.

The interest in morphology and premodernist city development mentioned earlier are good examples of this shift. The use of morphology in
analysis and design corresponded with the scaling down of urban planning. This was in contrast to the earlier all-encompassing blueprint
expansions and the mechanist functionalism that expressed the view
that form was merely a result of technique, economy, programme and
organization. The 'postmodern turn' in urbanism was illustrated by the
renaissance of more romantic humanist architects such as Sitte, the
'City Beautiful' movement, and the birth of the New Urbanism movement, the latter labelled by Michael Sorkin 'the Opus Dei of urban
design'.[124] With New Urbanism, traditional urban form and the cultural
significance of the city development received a greater emphasis.[125]

In the Dutch practice 'culture – in the sense of image and image production – again received a position in spatial planning when the mainly
on programming and containment fixated planning was substituted by
one concerned with seduction and inspiration'.[126] In the policy report
Nota wonen: Mensen, wensen, wonen citizens were defined as consumers
with different lifestyles that needed to be matched with a suitable object
in an appropriate setting.[127] These could then be translated into a series
of urban environment types (*stedelijke milieutypen*). Urban and architectural 'qualities' were looked after by detailed image and quality plans
(*beeld- en kwaliteitsplan*) and supervisors (quality coordinators) to ade-

124
Sorkin, M., 'The End(s) of
Urban Design', *Harvard
Design Magazine* fall
2006/winter 2007, 5–18, 12.
125
Harvey, D., 'New
Urbanism and the
Communitarian Trap', in:
W.S. Saunders (ed.),
Sprawl and Suburbia, A
Harvard Design Magazine
Reader (Minneapolis:
University of Minnesota
Press, 2005).
126
Taverne, E., 'Kan de
erfgoed de ruimtelijke
ordening redden?', in: F.
Claessens and H. Engel
(eds.), *OverHolland 2*
(Amsterdam: SUN, 2005),
107–110, 107–108.
127
VROM, *Nota wonen:
Mensen, wensen, wonen*
(The Hague: Ministry of
Housing, Spatial Planning
and the Environment, 2000).

quately enhance the image. In a way, this marked a return of blueprint planning, this time not as a programme, but as the image quality of a plan.[128] One of the best known examples of such an image-based plan was Kattenbroek in Amersfoort (1990) where the architect Ashok Bhalotra used metaphors and themes to diversify the image of a neighbourhood with some 4,500 homes. ⚲ Despite the diverse image, the programming of the area is rather uniform: almost 80 per cent of the housing stock consisted of single-family homes in a homogenous density of 30 dwellings per hectare.[129]

Urbanity and Sceptics
'Urbanity' (*stedelijkheid*) is another concept that, next to 'spatial quality', achieved an important status in defining the ambitions for city extensions and transformations during the 1990s. In the Netherlands different books and reports were published trying to define urbanity, for instance *Strategie voor stedelijkheid (Strategy for urbanity)*; *Structuurplan Amsterdam: Kiezen voor stedelijkheid (Structural Plan Amsterdam: The choice for urbanity)*; and *Stedelijkheid als rendement: Privaat initiatief voor publieke ruimte (Urbanity as result: Private initiatives for public space)*.[130] The concept tends to be very elastic and there is little consensus on how it should be defined. François Barré described two related meanings of urbanity in the article 'The Desire for Urbanity'. The first was morphological and described the physical space of the city and its conditioning aspects for urbanity. The second was socioeconomic and concerned the actual use of the city.[131]

Gert Urhahn and Milos Bobic emphasized 'complexity' as the main attribute in their 1996 book *Strategie voor stedelijkheid*. Their emphasis was on the spatial, physical and strategic conditions that stimulate the socioeconomic complexity of life. This adherence to complexity was also expressed by Heeling, et al. in *Het ontwerp van de stadsplattegrond (The design of the urban plan)*:

> The urbanity of a city is primarily determined by the degree to which the spatial configuration is able to contain a large pluriformity of land use, economic activity, institutions, life forms, cultural life styles and social relations. The more complex and pluriform the city is, the more it will be experienced as urban.[132]

Jane Jacobs, Richard Sennet and Marshall Berman discussed the civic dimension of urbanity in terms of public interaction and accessibility. Both Sennet and Berman emphasized the need for spaces in which public urban life can flourish.[133] Jacobs saw vitality, diversity and concentration as being central to urbanity: 'Dense concentrations of people are one of the necessary conditions for flourishing city diversity.'[134] She added the need for high lot coverage (60 to 80 per cent) as a condition for urban vitality to indirectly force people into the public streets and parks and so increase social interaction. Jacobs suggested, as mentioned earlier, a minimum density of 175 dwellings per hectare to arrive at a vital and diverse urban landscape.[135]

The emphasis on urbanity as an attractive part of city life fit in well with two problems that cities were confronted with in the 1980s: competition

128
Cammen and De Klerk, *Ruimtelijke Ordening*, op. cit. (note 16), 309–310, 360–361.

129
Municipality of Amersfoort, *Amersfoort in cijfers* (Amersfoort: Onderzoek en statistiek, 2006).

130
Urhahn, G.B. and M. Bobic, *Strategie voor stedelijkheid* (Bussum: Uitgeverij THOTH, 1996); Municipality of Amsterdam, *Structuurplan Amsterdam: Kiezen voor stedelijkheid* (Amsterdam: dRO, 2003); Lengkeek, A., *Stedelijkheid als rendement: Privaat initiatief voor publieke ruimte* (Haarlem: Trancity, 2007).
131
Barré, F., 'The Desire for Urbanity', *Architectural Design* 11/12 (1980), 4–7.

132
Heeling et al., *Het ontwerp*, op. cit. (note 9), 101.
133
Meyer, H., F. de Josselin de Jong and M.J. Hoekstra (eds.), *Het ontwerp van de openbare ruimte* (Amsterdam: SUN, 2006); 10–13.
134
Jacobs, *The Death and Life*, op. cit. (note 100), 205.
135
Density as dwelling units per net acre of residential land, excluding public streets. If public streets are included, this corresponds to approximately 175 dwellings per hectare (with 30 per cent of the land used for streets).

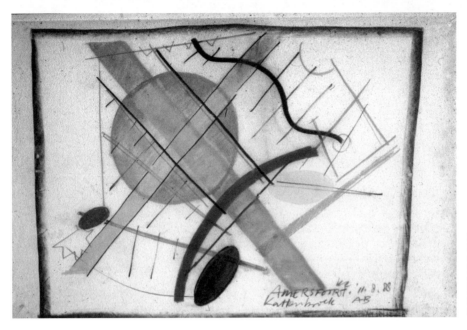

Design sketch for Kattenbroek in Amersfoort. Example of the conceptual, image-based urbanism of the 1980s (Ashok Bhalotra).

with suburbia, and a general degeneration of city economies as a result of recession and de-industrialization. Cities reinvented their identities in what, somewhat tautologically, was seen as the essence of the city: *urbanity*. Cultural sociologist Anton Zijderveld claimed in the Van Eesteren lecture in 1992 that:

> Urbanity has the same function as a management culture to a corporation or an administration. Cities without urbanity have no face and lack propulsion. There is then a lack of administrative legitimacy and conviction and the economy is adrift, not capable to attract the necessary investments.[136]

Following the politically tumultuous 1970s, this re-branding of the city and its way of life partially helped to stem the exodus from the physically and economically decaying cities to the suburbs. Furthermore, the postindustrial boom of services led to a focus on innovation, financial services, entertainment, leisure and tourism. These were all activities that for many were inherently connected to urbanity.[137] For Dutch cities, these urban ambitions contributed to the realization of compact inner city (re)developments, such as Zuidas and the IJ-oever projects in Amsterdam, The Resident in The Hague, and Kop van Zuid in Rotterdam. The enthusiasm for the concept probably also contributed to some increase of densities in more suburban developments such as Noorderhof in Amsterdam and Brandevoort in Helmond. However, with around 50 dwellings per hectare these areas were still far from vital if we are to believe Jacobs.

Despite a consensus in recent decades on the positive effects of the concepts of urbanity and spatial quality on city development, some people were critical of these concepts.[138] What kind of vitality and intensity was actually being striven for when all parties unite around the flag of

136
Quoted in Cammen and De Klerk, *Ruimtelijke Ordening*, op. cit. (note 16), 361.
137
Florida, R., *Cities and the Creative Class* (New York: Routledge, 2005); Hall, P., *Cities in Civilization* (London: Phoenix, 1999); Municipality of Amsterdam, *Structuurplan Amsterdam*, op. cit. (note 130); Urhahn and Bobic, *Strategie*, op. cit. (note 130).
138
E.g. Brenner, N. and N. Theodore, *Spaces of Neoliberalism: Urban Restructuring in North America and Western Europe* (Oxford: Blackwell Publishing, 2002); Davis, M. and D.B. Monk (eds.), *Evil Paradises: Dreamworlds of Neoliberalism* (New York: The New Press, 2007); Sorkin, M. (ed.), *A Theme Park: The New American City and the End of Public Space* (New York: Hill and Wang, 1992); Sorkin, 'The End(s)', op. cit. (note 124).

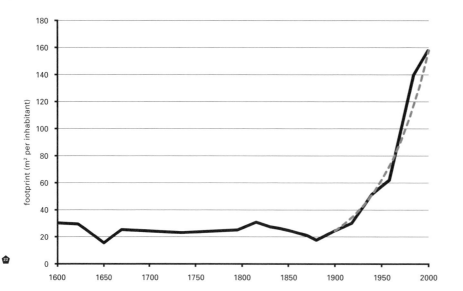

Urban footprint
for the city of
Amsterdam from
1400 to 2000.

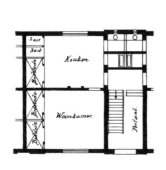

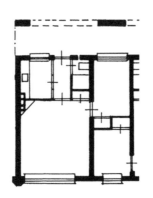

1   2

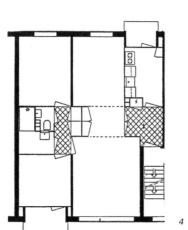

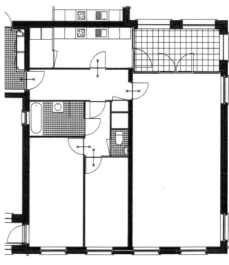

3   4

Floor plans of four
dwellings, scale
1:200 (Kloos 2000:
15; Floet 2001: 247,
399, 440).

1
One-room
apartment 1876,
Amsterdam: 30 m²
2
Two-room
apartment 1926,
Mathenesserhof
Rotterdam: 50 m²
3
Four-room
apartment 1958,
Sloterhof
Amsterdam: 80 m²
4
Three-room
apartment 1998,
Wolveschans Leek:
120 m²

'urbanity'? Was it the friction and 'accident and mess' that seemed to be an important part of Jacobs's urban vitality? Or was it the concentration of retail outlets and gentrification, the nice front of diversity and 'cappuccino urbanism'[139] that led to a less diverse social reality? The main points of Jacobs's criticism on the monofunctional sleep city and her plea for street vitality and people power seemed to have been lost along the way.

The Battle for Growth

Throughout much of the twentieth century private financers, developers and construction companies had been viewed with some suspicion. They were central actors during the housing boom at the end of the nineteenth century and were seen by many as profiteers, contributing little to the common good. A rather statist top-down approach had in the 1960s and 1970s forced most of the private initiatives to the periphery of spatial and urban development. In the 1990s the economy was no longer seen as the enemy but rather as the motor for social and spatial transformations. The economic reality had to be accepted and growth stimulated with the help of the creativity of, among others, architects and urban designers. Ranking Randstad, a research project initiated at the Faculty of Architecture of Delft University of Technology, illustrated this by recognizing the struggle of cities in a competitive global economy. The programme examined how 'spatial quality and spatial characteristics account for the competitive/comparative advantages/ disadvantages in various city-regions'.[140] The right spatial interventions in combination with appropriate fiscal and social policies could attract improvements in corporate investments, tourism, expatriates and well-educated immigrants. This would result in a higher ranking and, one supposes, sustained economic growth.

If we are to believe Rem Koolhaas, the affirmative stance of the neoliberal epoch had made urban planning and design meaningless and even undesirable as it intervened in the self-organizing power of cities.[141] Apart from producing marketing imagery the most the urban designer could achieve was to engage with the physical components that made the flows of people, money and goods possible. In this way urban designers became spatial engineers, optimizing the techniques of physical organization. The machinery that needed greasing was different from the rationally organized city of Le Corbusier, though. If *La Ville Radieuse* attempted to fetter the beast of corporate profit and individual desire through embedded capitalism, Koolhaas's *Generic City* was created by the beast and was proud of it. The title of a book by Crimson reflected the *zeitgeist* of such an extremely ironic and hedonistic pragmatism: *Too Blessed to be Depressed*.[142]

RUNAWAY SPACE CONSUMPTION?

Predictions in the past about future land use in the Netherlands have often been inaccurate. This was also the case with the prediction of a dramatic increase of the Dutch population from 12 million in 1966 to 20 million inhabitants by 2000 that The Second National Policy Document on Spatial Planning used as its point of departure.[143] However, it transpired that the space that had been reserved was still needed to accommodate the Dutch population. Part of the explanation for this can be found in

139
Saunders, W.S., 'Cappuccino Urbanism, and Beyond', *Harvard Design Magazine* fall 2006/winter 2007, 3.

140
www.ranking-randstad.net, accessed October 2008.

141
Koolhaas, R., *S,M,L,XL* (Rotterdam: 010 Publishers, 1995), 1248–1264; Haupt, P., 'Adriaan Geuze, Rem Koolhaas och staden som inte längre finns', *Arkitektur*, 1 1996, 68–73.

142
Crimson, *Too Blessed to Be Depressed: Crimson Architectural Historians 1994–2002* (Rotterdam: 010 Publishers, 2002).

143
VROM, *Tweede nota*, op. cit. (note 57). The Netherlands had 15,864,000 inhabitants in 2000, and 16,500,000 in March 2009 (CBS).

the fact that anticipated occupancy rates were too high. For example, the calculations in the surveys undertaken in the 1930s for the AUP were based on an estimated 3.37 inhabitants per dwelling by 2000. The real level in Amsterdam in 2000 was 1.98 inhabitants per dwelling.[144]

Predictions of demographic developments and their influence on city growth and contraction remain dubious. A lesson that a city like Amsterdam could draw from past experience, however, is that its urban footprint[145] has been exponentially increasing since the end of the nineteenth century. Amsterdam's urban footprint increased with a factor 6.4 during the twentieth century.[146] This is comparable to an annual growth of 1.9 per cent, and equivalent to a doubling of the urban footprint every 37 years. ☻ Expressed another way, one could say that every new generation in Amsterdam since 1900 has had the double amount of urban space at its disposal – or lives half as densely – as their parents.[147]

People during the twentieth century tended to live in ever-smaller households,[148] in larger houses,[149] at greater distance from each other and from their places of work. ☻ The increase in individual housing allocations, the functional zoning of cities into separate areas for housing, green space (for example parks, graveyards and sport fields), offices and industries, and the increased use of the car (wider streets with more parking facilities) have since 1900 all contributed to an increased urban footprint.

SCENARIOS FOR SPACE CONSUMPTION

Based on the changes in land use in the past, and considering the twentieth-century developments in Amsterdam as a point of reference for the Netherlands as a whole, the continuation of the micro-scale trends described above – people living in larger houses, with less people in lower densities – could theoretically result in a situation in 2050 whereby more than 30 per cent of the country would be covered by urbanized areas. This should be compared to 12 percent in 2000.[150] In the Randstad almost 50 per cent of the area would be urbanized, compared to 19 per cent in 2000. (Scenario 1 ☻) Even when a less polemic, and perhaps more realistic scenario is set out, one based on the growth of the land use in the Netherlands between 1993 and 2000, we still arrive at a substantially larger amount of urbanized areas by 2050: 22 per cent for the country as a whole and 33 per cent of the Randstad. (Scenario 2 ☻) This last scenario corresponds almost exactly to the trend described in The Fifth National Policy Document on Spatial Planning.[151] (Scenario 3 ☻) The Netherlands Institute for Spatial Research predicted in a recent report, *Demographic Decline and Spatial Development*, that a number of Dutch municipalities would soon experience a decrease in population.[152] However, in a situation where this coincides with economic growth and a continuation of current behaviour patterns, the increase in spatial footprint may well outpace any population decrease. People will continue to prefer bigger houses in the countryside and many of them will be able and willing to pay for them.

The issue of rapid urbanization, conflicting spatial claims, and 'spatial chaos' has recently been placed at the top of the political agenda in the Netherlands by the media.[153] A Christian Democratic Party (CDA) report argued for the creation of an additional 5 million parking spaces in the Netherlands between now and 2020, and the policy report *Structu-*

144
Wintershoven, *Demografisch eeuwboek Amsterdam*, op. cit. (note 15).
145
The urban footprint is defined as the total amount of land needed for housing fabrics (areas dominated by dwellings), urban green (parks, sports fields, garden allotments and graveyards) and working areas divided by the total amount of inhabitants.
146
In 1900, each person in Amsterdam had 25 m² of city at his or her disposal; in 2000 this was 157 m² per person. See Berghauser Pont and Haupt, *Space, Density,* op.cit. (note 3), 235–271.
147
Ignoring a temporary interruption in population increases during the 1970s and 1980s.
148
The occupancy rate in Amsterdam in 1900 was 4.37 persons per dwelling; in 2000 this was 1.98. From Wintershoven, *Demografisch eeuwboek Amsterdam*, op. cit. (note 15).
149
The amount of rooms per dwelling can serve as an indicator for size. In 1899, 75 per cent of the dwellings in the Netherlands had less than three rooms. In 1989, only 12 per cent had less than three rooms. From CBS, *Historie bouwnijverheid vanaf 1899* (The Hague: Statistics Netherlands, 2008).
150
Housing, working areas, and infrastructure. Based on Schuit, J. van der, et al., *Ruimte in cijfers 2006* (The Hague: Netherlands Institute for Spatial Research, 2006). This calculation assumes zero population growth. See Berghauser Pont and Haupt *Space, Density,* op.cit. (note 3), 247, for further details.
151
VROM, *Vijfde nota*, op. cit. (note 119).
152
Netherlands Institute for Spatial Research, *Demographic Decline and Spatial Development: Planning for the Consequences of Population Changes, Summary* (The Hague, 2006).
153
The Netherlands Environmental Assessment Agency (MNP), NOVA (TV news maga-

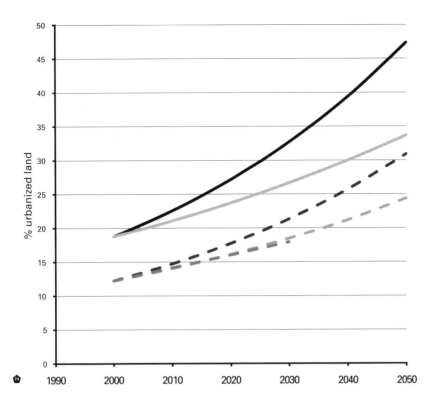

Different scenarios for the percentage of urbanized area in 2050, (Berghauser Pont and Haupt 2009: 64).

urvisie Randstad 2040 predicted the addition of 500,000 dwellings within the Randstad.[154] The number of parking spaces suggested in the first report would correspond roughly to the whole area of Amsterdam.[155] The half million new homes that have been proposed for the Randstad would cover an area almost three times the size of Amsterdam, if constructed at an average density of 30 dwellings per hectare.[156] When lower densities are chosen, such as proposed in the study *Waterland 2020* for the provincial executive of North Holland, the increase in urbanized land would reach even higher values. This study suggested that the countryside may be saved from the periods of overproduction crisis of agriculture in the Netherlands by people looking for big houses at very low densities.[157] The introduction of a variety of traditional housing types at low densities in rural areas, it is claimed, would not substantially influence the quality of the landscape in any negative way. Critics of these ideas suggest that sprawl and suburbanization go hand in hand with car mobility, social segregation and a decline in public services.[158] The increased mobility that accompanies sprawl undermines the overriding aim of curbing energy consumption and the emission of greenhouse gases. After all, it is no secret that both the SUV (Sports Utility Vehicle) and sprawl are the last in line for a green energy label. Furthermore, the insecurity of food prices and the increasing demand for meat in the world has already begun to ameliorate the agricultural crisis in the Netherlands. Food production may not be characterized by surpluses and subsidies in the near future, but by increases in demand and necessity.[159] Any general agricultural crisis

zine produced by NPS and Vara), and the Netherlands Architecture Institute (NAi).
154
ANP, 'CDA wil 5 miljoen extra parkeerplaatsen', *de Volkskrant* 1 July 2008; VROM, *Structuurvisie Randstad 2040: Naar een duurzame en concurrerende Europese topregio* (The Hague: Ministry of Housing, Spatial Planning and the Environment, 2008), presented by the Dutch cabinet on 5 September 2008.
155
The amount of space needed per car is estimated to be 25 m², resulting in a need for 12,500 ha of parking space (5 million cars x 25 m²). The urbanized territory of Amsterdam was 11,475 ha in 2000.
156
With a housing density of 30 dwellings per hectare on the scale of the fabric (the average density of most suburban areas in the Netherlands), the amount of land needed to accommodate 500,000 dwellings is 16,667 ha

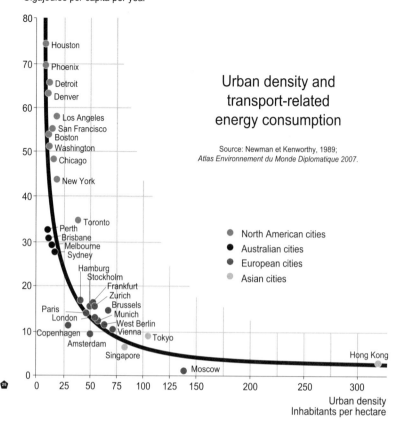

Transport-related energy consumption
Gigajoules per capita per year

Urban density and
transport-related
energy consumption

Source: Newman et Kenworthy, 1989;
Atlas Environnement du Monde Diplomatique 2007.

- North American cities
- Australian cities
- European cities
- Asian cities

Houston
Phoenix
Detroit
Denver
Los Angeles
San Francisco
Boston
Washington
Chicago
New York
Toronto
Perth
Brisbane
Melbourne
Sydney
Hamburg
Stockholm
Frankfurt
Zurich
Brussels
Paris
London
Munich
West Berlin
Copenhagen
Vienna
Amsterdam
Tokyo
Singapore
Moscow
Hong Kong

Urban density
Inhabitants per hectare

Urban density and
transport-related
energy
consumption.
(UNEP 2008).

is then difficult to apply as an argument in favour of transforming arable land into housing estates.

Economic bubbles expand and burst. The spatial bubble, fed by financial abundance and the transformation of finance capital into fixed capital in the form of built landscapes, risks bursting.[160] Many parts of the world may run into huge difficulties when/if real estate values deflate and transportation costs become prohibitive. Sprawl might have a short-term attraction and deliver much consumer satisfaction, but in the long run one could certainly argue that it is unviable. In his polemic on Robert Bruegmanns pro-sprawl book *Sprawl: A Compact History*, James Howard Kunstler undermines this blind idolization of the consumer:

His book fails entirely to acknowledge the fact that we are entering a permanent global energy crisis that will put an end to the drive-in utopia whether people like it or not ... The stark truth of the situation is that we are simply going to have to make other arrangements – and I'm sorry to have to repeat that this will be the case whether we like it or not. Suburbia will be coming off the menu. We will no longer be able to resort to the stupid argument that it is okay because we chose it.[161]

fabrics. Considering all other land uses (parks, infrastructure, working areas, etcetera), the land needed on city scale is then approximately 33,000 ha (based on the same ratio between fabric area and total area as in the case of Amsterdam).
157
Province of North-Holland, *Bouwen voor Waterland 2020* (Haarlem, 2004).
158
Carbonell, A. and R. Yaro, 'American Spatial Development and the New Megalopolis', *Land Lines*, 17 (2) 2005; Couch, C., L. Leontidou and G. Petschel-Held, *Urban Sprawl in Europe: Landscapes, Land-Use Change & Policy* (Oxford: Blackwell Publishing, 2007).
159
See for instance FAO's initiative on Soaring Food Prices, 30 May 2008.

CLIMATE CHANGE AND SPACE CONSUMPTION

Given the urgency of climate change, emission reductions and depleted world carbon fuel supplies, we have to reconsider current trends in urban land use. In low-density cities in North America energy consumption per inhabitant for transport is far higher than the same energy used by Europeans, and even more so when compared to very high-density cities in Japan. ● North Americans are almost totally dependent on the private car, while the Japanese in general cluster in higher densities and are able to sustain a more efficient public transport network.[162] Denser urban environments certainly do not automatically mean less transport and energy consumption. Distances between homes and places of work, regulations and fiscal policies probably have far greater impacts on car use than the mere physical layout of cities and regions.[163] However, if the argument is turned around, one has to admit that dense settlements are a necessary prerequisite if we are to aspire to a radical cut in car and lorry transportation. Only dense settlements offer feasible circumstances for the large investments needed for a more energy-efficient and environmentally responsible movement of goods and people. Such settlements are also the only environments that can be successful when it comes to healthy and sustainable modes of transportation, such as walking and cycling. Also, proximity and mixing of functions seem to be a prerequisite for lower mobility and energy consumption. The urban patterns that are appropriate for such goals are those with a qualified urban density and a balanced mix of functions.[164]

The trigger for the critical density analyses of planners and architects of the Garden City Movement and the early modernists a century ago was rapid industrialization. Such problems of too much in too little space seem a long way off today (except for road congestion), as they have largely been displaced from the command centres of our global economy to booming production zones elsewhere in the world. There, as Mike Davis describes in his book *Planet of Slums,* urbanization is taking place that dwarfs the growth pains of Western Europe a century ago, the period when the concept of density was introduced.[165] In the Netherlands the challenges facing spatial planning and design are quite the opposite of those that confronted planners and architects a century ago. Our affluence has brought with it suburbanization and sprawl that seem to threaten the very vitality of cities, aggravate social segregation and feed burgeoning car mobility. As mentioned earlier in this chapter, trends towards intensification have been evident in many urban developments during the last couple of decades (for example the waterfront developments in Amsterdam and Rotterdam, and the Zuidas in Amsterdam). The average space consumption per capita hereby seemed to increase less rapidly than it did a couple of decades ago. Nevertheless, these developments were mostly targeting high-end consumers and businesses. They were not addressing the vast stretches of less appealing industrial areas and suburban expansions that were added to the Netherlands each year. Sorkin, in his article *The End of Urban Design,* pointed to an important polarization 'between inevitabilism and nostalgia' in American cities over the last decade.[166] On the one hand the sprawl of traditionalist suburbia (in the New Urbanism social and aesthetic fashion) with low, but not very low densities, and, on the other

160
Harvey, D., *The Urbanization of Capital* (Baltimore: John Hopkins University Press, 1985), 1–31. As of September 2008, the real estate markets in many countries are contracting. Prime examples are Spain, Ireland, UK, Denmark, the USA and Dubai. See articles on the subject in *The Guardian, The Financial Times, The Economist,* etcetera from winter 2008/2009.
161
Kunstler, J., 'Review of Sprawl: A Compact History', *Salmagundi* 152 (Fall 2006), 175–183; Bruegmann, R., *Sprawl: A Compact History* (Chicago: University of Chicago Press, 2005).
162
Newman, P. and J. Kenworthy, *Sustainability and Cities: Overcoming Automobile Dependence* (Chicago: University of Chicago Press, 1999); Nozzi, D., *Road to Ruin: An Introduction to Sprawl and How to Cure It* (Westport: Praeger Publishers, 2003).
163
Neuman, M., 'The Compact City Fallacy', *Journal of Planning Education and Research* 25 (2005), 11–26.
164
Kann, F. van and W. Leduc, 'Synergy between regional planning and energy as a contribution to a carbon neutral society – energy cascading as a new principle for mixed land-use'. Paper presented at the SCUPAD conference (Salzburg, Austria, 2008).
165
Davis, M., *Planet of Slums* (London/New York: Verso, 2006).

166
Sorkin, 'The End(s)', op. cit. (note 124).

gentrified inner-city developments with many of the characteristics of 'urbanity' and with high, but not very high, densities.

On the issue of energy consumption, a strong consensus has emerged among experts and policymakers concerning efficiency and energy saving. Urban planning and design lack a similar drive to innovate and experiment in making land use more efficient and less unsustainable. If reining in the energy and space consumption of individuals is preferable to runaway climate change and depleted resources, we might need to rethink some elements of past liberal spatial policies. At the beginning of the twentieth century the threat of social upheaval and revolution made housing and urban reform a necessity. During a period of political turmoil Le Corbusier in 1923 spelled out the options at the beginning of that century: 'It is a question of building which is at the root of the social unrest of today: Architecture or Revolution.' At the beginning of the twenty-first century, as we face real estate overproduction, financial turmoil, energy and food shortages, climate change and serious doubts about continuous economic growth, this might be restated as a choice between Urbanism or Meltdown.

REINVENTED DENSITY, DIFFERENT DOCTRINES

In this chapter we have discussed changes in the process of city development, focusing on changes in the role state institutions played and the role of density in planning. During the first part of the twentieth century an active role of the state was accepted in response to dealing with public health issues. Density was used to diagnose this situation and propagate alternatives. Interventions and legislation countered the negative effects of overcrowding and laissez faire capitalism. Still, this interventionism was fairly modest compared to the state-managed economies that took form after the Second World War. Coordinated planning and state investments played an important role in the Keynesian growth strategy, peaking in the 1960s and coming to an end in the crises of the 1970s. With the neoliberal shift in the 1980s and 1990s, liberals of a less fundamentalist character – those ascribing to the Third Way social-democracy of the 1990s – argued that many of the direct impacts of inevitable reforms (read deconstruction of the welfare system) would be softened by economic trickledown effects and win-win situations. Instead of striving for more healthy and social cities, urban designers produced marketing imagery to attract investments.

In 2008, it surely seemed difficult to plea for direct public intervention in spatial and urban planning, since the current managerial state is just one of many forces that determine the direction of future space consumption. Furthermore, decentralization, competition between cities and the fragmentation of urban developments into separate competing urban projects described by Brenner, Harvey, and so forth, run against such public activism on all levels, be it national, regional or global. At the end of the nineteenth century private developers were the drivers of city development when the practice of speculation was flourishing. They had at the end of the twentieth century, again, assumed centre stage, following an interval of 75 years of more or less continuous state management. Today private and public actors work together in project based agencies. Such projects are, to use the words of Harvey, 'concerned with the construction of place (the image of a specific place) and the enhancement of property values rather than the amelioration of conditions (housing, health, poverty, etc.)'.

However, the quick turns of the most recent crisis of capitalism – acknowledged not only by its sternest critics, but by just about everyone – makes fundamental reconsideration of the neoliberal spatial strategies of the last decades necessary. A post-neoliberal path will certainly, at least temporarily, include more state intervention (so far mostly in the form of the socialization of private losses) and collectively formulated guidelines and regulations to once again save capitalism from itself. That the de-financialization of large swaths of society will bring about fundamental changes in the realm of fixed capital, that is, the physical development of cities and countryside, seems quite self-evident.[167] Whether it will lead to a more democratic society or further strengthen the corporative character of the state is an open question. In both cases, a larger involvement of state institutions will mean that new instruments are (again) needed to reconnect national, regional and urban planning with urban and architectural design.

Whatever the political and economic constellation will be in the near future – a return to neoliberalism, a solidification of state interventions, or other not yet imaginable arrangements – some urgent issues will need to be responded to. As we discussed before, an infinite urban growth cannot be sustained in a finite world. Even if many parts of the world spatially seem able to absorb almost endless urban expansions, the associated consequences for transportation, energy consumption, climate change and loss of arable land will be immense. The need for density discussions today can be likened to the one a century ago, but with some fundamental differences. Then, attempts were made to describe and understand the problems of the industrializing cities (for example diseases) and their causes (such as overcrowding), alternatives were suggested (for example the Garden City), and instruments created and implemented, often in the form of maximum densities. Today, overcrowding, extreme poverty and human misery have moved from Manchester to Manila (where legally binding maximum densities would be part of radical emancipation!). The proximity of production and consumption, wealth and poverty, that earlier was present in one and the same city in Western Europe (for instance the Jordaan next to the Grachtengordel in Amsterdam), structure many developing metropolises today. At the same time, large swaths of affluence here and predominant production there have created new problems (such as exploitation of humans, climate change, pollution, resource scarcity), driven by overconsumption of resources (transport, goods, energy, humans) and space (sprawl). If industrialization took off with urbanization and overcrowding, the fossil-fuel-driven economic growth and developments in transport techniques of the last century have dispersed and thinned out our cities. The consequences of the present overconsumption and overshoot of the earth's resources, as well as possible responses (such as (re)intensified cities, compact villages, rural self-sufficiency), should be investigated through, among other things, the concept of density. A future step would be to further integrate density into the legal process of contracting, plan making and zoning documents. Instead of

167
Sassen, S., 'Too Big to Save: The End of Financial Capitalism'. Available online at www.opendemocracy.net, accessed 24 November 2009; Harvey, D., *The Urbanization*, op. cit. (note 160).

the maximum densities that are often (indirectly) prescribed, a shift to minimum densities should in many cases be made. The ambitions for intensifying Dutch cities are present, mainly as part of the limitation of development costs and creation of 'urbanity'. However, other, more urgent, reasons (such as survival) to consciously and more firmly guide, plan and regulate the exploitation of space should give the question a very high priority. Carbon taxing and rationing are being discussed in some countries, and cars and buildings have to confirm to tightening CO_2 and energy performance requirements respectively. Why should one of the most fundamental conditions, the spatial stage set, or the urban plan, be exempt of such regulations? This rather naive question surely shortcuts many reality constraints and vested interests, but still, it should be of great importance to speculate about and develop appropriate instruments that can be part of such a shift.

In this chapter we have shown how the dominating emphasis in urban planning during the twentieth century in the Netherlands shifted from quantifying urban developments through scientific surveys and mathematic reasoning (Unwin, Hoenig, Van Eesteren and Lohuizen, Martin and March) to grasping the qualitative aspects of city development in terms of urban form, identity and urbanity (Sitte, Berlage, Jacobs, Urhahn, Bhalotra). Morphological research at one stage became part of the answer, but as this approach focused mainly on the traditional city (read the one before the modernist takeover), this often resulted in preservationism, selectively extracting elements and symbols of the city to create a culture of 'niceness'.

When considering quantity and quality too much in isolation, the primacy of one may be to the detriment of the other. To arrive at more sustainable urban developments we need to reconcile spatial quality at the micro level (variation in built environments, housing typologies, public spaces, and so forth) to the structural effects on society as a whole (programme, mobility, socioeconomic effects, integration/segregation, energy consumption). Gains can be made if quantity and quality can be engaged simultaneously.

Associated architects and developers playing with miniature Rockefeller Centers: '... combine the maximum of congestion with the maximum of light and space' (Koolhaas 1994: 178).

3
MULTIVARIABLE DENSITY: SPACEMATRIX

As Arza Churchman describes in *Disentangling the Concept of Density*, there is not one accepted measure of density in, or shared by, different countries.[1] In general, density measures vary according to the manner in which numerators and denominators are defined.[2] Some countries define density using the number of people per given area (population density), while others define it using the number of dwelling units or the building mass per given area (Floor Space Index, or land use intensity). It is important to realize that one can translate one density measure into another by making assumptions or applying known statistics, such as dwelling size and occupancy rate. A purely physical density, such as FSI, can be translated into a more socially relevant form of density, such as dwelling and population density. A variety of land units, including acre, hectare, square mile and square kilometre can be used for denominators. These measures are not difficult to convert.

More important – and problematic – is the definition of the boundary of an area, as this, to a large extent, determines the outcome of density calculations. Although it is common to distinguish between net and gross density, the definition of net and gross varies from place to place, and has been a source of great ambiguity. This book aspires to formulate a clear set of definitions for these boundaries. Most important, however, is to be consistent when comparing different areas.

Related to the discussion of boundaries is the issue of scale and averages. An average density does not necessarily mean that the whole area has a uniform density. The larger the area over which the density is measured, the more heterogeneous it is likely to be. Moreover, as the scale increases, the amount of non-built land (roads, railways, green areas and water) also increases in relative terms, and density, be it population density or another measure, decreases. Thus, the definition of the denominator – the total area of the land – in the quotient is crucial when determining density.

The first part of this chapter critically assesses the density measures introduced in Chapter 2 and their potential to describe built form. We demonstrate that existing density indicators have a programmatic and statistical character and are indeed, as is discussed in Chapter 1, inadequate in describing central spatial properties of urban landscapes. The second part of this chapter presents a method designed to simultaneously assess different density variables and describe spatial properties with more precision. The use of this method is demonstrated with the help of the examples from Amsterdam used in the previous chapter. Chapters 4 and 5 then further discuss in greater detail the relationship between urban density, urban types and performance.

PERCEIVED DENSITY
Before discussing different measuring methods, it is important to realize that density can be approached in different ways. One important distinction is between physical density and perceived density.[3] Depending on a range of individual and sociocultural factors, a person (inhabitant,

1
Churchman, A., 'Disentangling the Concept of Density', *Journal of Planning Literature*, 13 (4) 1999, 389–411.

2
The numerator (A) is the number above and the denominator (B) is the number below the line in a vulgar fraction A/B.

3
Rapaport, A., 'Toward a Redefinition of Density', *Environment and Behaviour* 7 (2) 1975, 7–32.

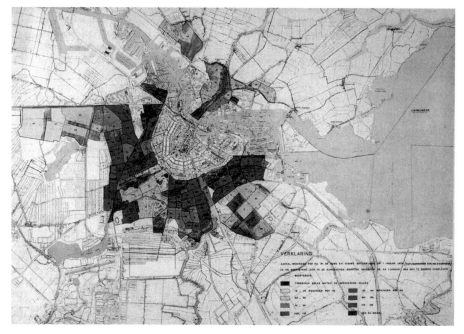

Dwelling density in the old expansion areas on 1 January 1956 (1956, k226–9 and 226–10 in Hameleers 2002: 270).

visitor) will evaluate and react differently to perceived density. The concept of 'crowding' highlights, in this case, a negative evaluation of perceived density.[4] An example: a shy person from a rural area will react in a specific manner to a busy inner-city street; this reaction might be described as a feeling of 'crowdedness'. On the other hand, the reaction of a streetwise metropolitan dweller to the same physical and social situation might be described as the joy of 'urbanity'.[5] He or she might appreciate the pace of the city and enjoy the random, social forms of intercourse.

Although these more multifaceted aspects of density are of great importance to the evaluation of design and understanding people's reactions to different urban environments, in our research we limit ourselves primarily to physical density as defined by Ernest Alexander.[6] We return to the distinction between perceived and physical density in Chapter 5 in a discussion of the issue of performance as it relates to density.

PHYSICAL DENSITY

Different physical density measures have been used to describe and prescribe human space consumption. In this section we describe the most conventional methods used to measure density and draw conclusions about their effectiveness in describing urban form. The measurement methods discussed are:
— Population and dwelling density;
— Land use intensity;
— Coverage;
— Building height;
— Spaciousness.

4
Churchman, 'Disentangling', op. cit. (note 1).

5
This concept will be further discussed in Chapter 5.

6
Alexander, E.R., 'Density Measures: A Review and Analysis', *Journal of Architectural and Planning Research* 10 (3) 1993, 181–202.

POPULATION AND DWELLING DENSITY

Population density can be expressed in terms of the number of people or households in an area, while dwelling density measures the number of dwellings in an area. Families vary in size (social and historical spread) and a household can range from a single person to multiple family units. Population density calculations are used to plan for new schools, retail, utilities and the transit expansion needed for an area. As social transformations generally are quicker than physical transformations, the population density of an area can have changed through history even if the number of dwellings has remained the same. Dwelling density is thus the more robust of the two and is often used in descriptions of urban developments.

Raymond Unwin stated in his 1912 pamphlet *Nothing Gained by Overcrowding* that density should be limited to 12 dwellings per acre (30 dwellings per hectare).[7] Frank Lloyd Wright, on the other hand, proposed in Broad Acre City an ideal density of one dwelling per acre (2.5 dwellings per hectare).[8] In the Netherlands, Cornelis van Eesteren and Th.K. van Lohuizen were the first to use dwelling density in a planning document. They studied the relationship between dwelling type and density and arrived at a density that would allow for feasible land use in combination with the construction of as many single-family houses as possible.[9] Research into different allotment patterns had shown that with a density of 70 dwellings per hectare, 50 to 60 per cent of the dwellings could be constructed as single-family houses.[10] In the Netherlands, this ratio between the number of dwellings and a hectare of land was recommended as a standard for measuring density in 1942.[11]

In most cases a differentiation is made between net and gross density, or between net residential density, neighbourhood density (*wijkdichtheid*) and city density (*generale dichtheid*).[12] Net density mostly excludes all public streets and residential density usually describes the portion of the neighbourhood used solely for housing. Gross, or neighbourhood density, also covers neighbourhood facilities such as primary schools and grocery shops, and city density adds the more general amenities, such as a city library, hospitals, etcetera.

A residential area is in the Netherlands often defined as a unique combination of street systems, lot patterns and building configurations (size and shape) and is delineated by boundaries drawn in the middle of the streets surrounding the lots and buildings.[13] The gross density, or neighbourhood density, is calculated by adding the amount of land needed for amenities to serve the population in a residential area.[14] The 1956 density map of Amsterdam, ⬡ which applied Van Lohuizen's method for calculating density, included the residential area, the neighbourhood facilities and the main roads, and thus corresponds to the gross density, or neighbourhood density.[15] The definition of the neighbourhoods (*buurten*) used today by the Dutch municipalities and Statistics Netherlands (CBS) are similar to the boundaries set in 1956, although the exact borders are often revised to match municipal borders. The effects of these different definitions for measured density are enormous and make comparisons between areas difficult. ⬡

The previous chapter referred to a series of areas in Amsterdam as representatives of different periods in the history of city development in

7
Unwin, R., *Nothing Gained by Overcrowding! How the Garden City Type of Development May Benefit Both Owner and Occupier* (Westminster: P.S. King & Son, 1912).
8
Wright, F.L., *The Disappearing City* (New York: W.F. Payson, 1932).
9
Municipality of Amsterdam, *Algemeen Uitbreidingsplan van Amsterdam (AUP): Nota van toelichting* (Amsterdam: Stadsdrukkerij Amsterdam, 1934).
10
Hellinga, H. and P. de Ruijter, *Algemeen Uitbreidingsplan Amsterdam 50 jaar* (Amsterdam: Amsterdamse Raad voor de Stedebouw, 1985).
11
Angenot, L.H.J., *Verhandelingen over het vraagstuk van de dichtheid van bebouwing* (Alphen aan den Rijn: N. Samsom NV, 1954).
12
Alexander, 'Density Measures', op. cit. (note 6); Angenot, *Verhandelingen*, op. cit. (note 11); Churchman, 'Disentangling', op. cit. (note 1); Forsyth, A., 'Measuring Density: Working Definitions for Residential Density and Building Density', *Design Brief*, 8 2003, Design Center for American Urban Landscape, University of Minesota; Rådberg, J., *Doktrin och täthet i svenskt stadsbyggande 1875–1975* (Stockholm: Statens råd för byggnadsforskning, 1988).
13
Angenot, *Verhandelingen*, op. cit. (note 11).
14
Ibid.

15
Ibid.

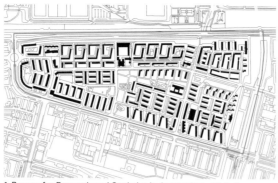

1 Bureau for Research and Statistics in Amsterdam: 40 dw/ha

2 Van Lohuizen: 50 dw/ha

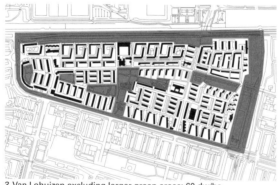

3 Van Lohuizen excluding larger green areas: 60 dw/ha

Dwelling density in Slotermeer Noord, Amsterdam, calculated based on three different boundary definitions (in red the subtracted area).

16
Based on the dwelling density as mentioned on the 1956 map *Woningdichtheden* ('dwelling densities') from the Dienst der Publieke Werken, Department Stadsontwikkeling in Hameleers, M.(ed.), *Kaarten van Amsterdam 1866–2000* (Bussum: Uitgeverij THOTH, 2002), 270; and Laloli, H.M., 'Beter wonen? Woningmarkt en residentiële segregatie in Amsterdam 1850–1940', in: O.W.A. Boonstra et al. (eds.), *Twee eeuwen Nederland geteld: Onderzoek met de digitale volks-, beroepsen woningtellingen 1795–2001* (The Hague: DANS and CBS, 2007).

the Netherlands. We will use these again here to demonstrate the different density measures. The Jordaan (seventeenth century) and De Pijp (nineteenth century) had among the highest population densities in Amsterdam. The former had 1,265 inhabitants per hectare in 1889, the latter 700 inhabitants per hectare in 1956.[16] During the same periods, two other areas were built for the well-to-do inhabitants of Amsterdam: Grachtengordel (seventeenth century) and Vondelparkbuurt (nineteenth century). These had, respectively, densities of 270 (Grachtengordel in 1889) and 200 (Vondelpark in 1956) inhabitants per hectare. One reason for the difference in density between Jordaan and De Pijp, on the one

Grachtengordel
Jordaan

h/ha

1200

1000

800

600

400

200

0

1850   1900   1950   2000 YEAR

Development of the
population density
based on censuses
held in 1859, 1899
and 1930 (Laloli,
2007), and statistics
(O+S 2007).

Grachtengordel

Jordaan

Aerial and street
view of Grachten-
gordel and Jordaan.

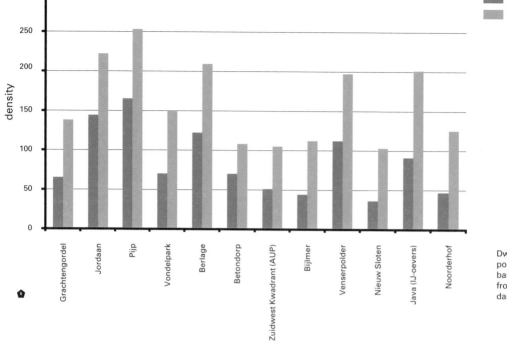

density

Grachtengordel
Jordaan
Pijp
Vondelpark
Berlage
Betondorp
Zuidwest Kwadrant (AUP)
Bijlmer
Venserpolder
Nieuw Sloten
Java (IJ-oevers)
Noorderhof

Dwelling and population density based on statistics from O+S Amsterdam (2007).

Bijlmer: 112 inh/ha and 44 dw/ha

Betondorp: 108 inh/ha and 70 dw/ha

Aerial and street view of Bijlmer and Betondorp.

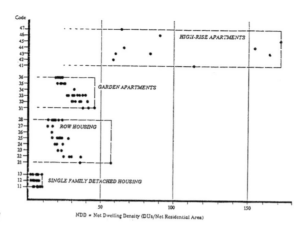

Code

HIGH-RISE APARTMENTS

GARDEN APARTMENTS

ROW HOUSING

SINGLE FAMILY DETACHED HOUSING

50   100   150

NDD = Net Dwelling Density (DUs/Net Residential Area)

Distribution of Net Dwelling Density (dwelling units per net residential area) by dwelling type (Alexander 1993: 193).

hand, and Grachtengordel and Vondelparkbuurt, on the other, is that the first two areas, built for immigrants and the working class, contained large numbers of small dwellings, inhabited by large families. The dwellings in Grachtengordel and Vondelparkbuurt were much larger. A family was allowed to construct only one house per lot. Later, when the economic situation changed, dwellings were subdivided or transformed into offices, thus changing the population density. Today, especially in the Grachtengordel, more people work in the area, resulting in a decrease in population density.[17] A different type of transformation has taken place in the Jordaan and De Pijp. Small dwellings have been united into larger ones and industries have been moved to the periphery of the city. Relatively few people now work in these areas.[18] Also, the average number of people per dwelling (occupancy rate) in Amsterdam decreased from 4.36 towards the end of the nineteenth century to 1.97 in 2000.[19] ⬟ demonstrates how the transformations in Grachtengordel and Jordaan brought about less extreme differences in population density. ⬟

The changes in population density in these four examples occurred without much change in the layout of the urban fabric. We can therefore conclude that there is little relation between population density and urban form. ⬟ demonstrates that the high-rise development in Bijlmermeer has a lower dwelling density than the garden city of Betondorp, which comprises low-rise housing. ⬟ The same dwelling density can thus be achieved through very different urban forms, and we can therefore question Alexander's conclusions, presented in ⬟, which show a relationship between dwelling types and net dwelling density.[20] The reasons that dwelling and population density demonstrate a weak relation to built form are threefold: the occupancy rate of dwellings differs, the size of the dwellings differs and the amount of non-residential space is not taken into account when expressing dwelling density.

Of course, the differences in the numbers of inhabitants influence such characteristics of an area as the user and traffic intensity, or the potential for different programmes, etcetera. In short, the quality of life in

17
The ratio between people living and working in the Grachtengordel is 1:1.5 and in Vondelparkbuurt 1:0.6. Source: O+S, Statistics for the areas A02c and V47d available online at www.os.amsterdam.nl (2007).
18
The ratio between people living and working in the Jordaan is 1:0.3 and in De Pijp 1:0.2. Source: O+S, Statistics for the areas A06c and V24d available online at www.os.amsterdam.nl (2007).
19
These numbers are averages for the whole city, based on Wintershoven, L., Demografisch eeuwboek Amsterdam: Ontwikkelingen tussen 1900 en 2000 (Amsterdam: dRO, 2000).
20
Alexander, 'Density Measures', op. cit. (note 6), 193.

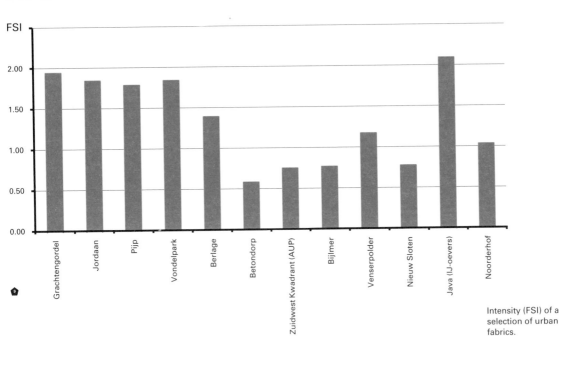

FSI

2.00

1.50

1.00

0.50

0.00

Grachtengordel
Jordaan
Pijp
Vondelpark
Berlage
Betondorp
Zuidwest Kwadrant (AUP)
Bijlmer
Venserpolder
Nieuw Sloten
Java (IJ-oevers)
Noorderhof

Intensity (FSI) of a selection of urban fabrics.

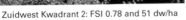

Zuidwest Kwadrant 2: FSI 0.78 and 51 dw/ha

Nieuw Sloten: FSI 0.77 and 36 dw/ha

Aerial and street view of Zuidwest Kwadrant and Nieuw Sloten.

an area is dependent on the dialectic relation between the physical environment and the social activities taking place. However, these variations take place in a physical context that is largely characterized by stability and robustness.[21] A monofunctional working area does not physically transform during the night although it is crowded during the day and empty at night. Its physical form can certainly change, but occurs in time spans measured in decades and centuries, rather than days and years.

LAND USE INTENSITY

Today, population and dwelling densities are still widely used in the urban profession. The Dutch Ministry of Spatial Planning and the Environment (VROM) for instance, uses households per hectare as a classification of urban environments.[22] Another, purely physical, density measure only recently became more popular in the Netherlands for expressing land use intensity: the Floor Space Index (FSI).[23]

The 1925 Building Ordinance of Berlin made use of the so called *Ausnutzungsziffer* (exploitation number).[24] This variable expresses the relation of the amount of built floor area to the area of a plan. This is one of the first examples in Europe of the use of a more neutral indicator that combined *all* floor space to describe and prescribe density, independent of its use. In 1944, the British Ministry of Health suggested using the building bulk (floor area) as the numerator, expressed as floor-space-index, or FSI.[25] It was particularly to be used in areas dominated by commercial buildings. An international conference in Zurich in 1948 established this index as the common standard in Europe. A comparable term used in New York City's Zoning Resolution is the floor to area ratio (FAR), which expressed the building bulk in relation to lot size.[26]

Under the guidance of the *Centrale Directie van de Wederopbouw en de Volkshuisvesting* Central Service for Reconstruction and Public Housing, the Land Index was developed in the Netherlands in 1949 to measure built density.[27] This quotient uses the ratio of the land area (in the numerator) to the floor area (in the denominator), and is inversely equivalent to the *Ausnutzungsziffer*, FSI or FAR. This measure has, however, never been widely accepted in the Dutch urban profession. The number of dwellings per hectare has remained popular. The first time FSI was used in an official Dutch planning document was, as far as we have been able to trace, in the 2003 *Structuurplan Amsterdam*.[28] In this document, built environments are defined by, among other things, density measures, expressed as FSI.[29] This plan was preceded by two studies by Bureau Parkstad in Amsterdam,[30] and the report *Meten met twee maten* in which a distinction was made between lot FSI, net FSI and gross FSI.[31] The boundary of the net plan area was defined by the urban project and therefore sometimes took into account streets, water and green areas, but on other occasions consisted of only a single lot. This makes comparisons risky. The gross plan area was calculated by drawing a boundary line 30 m from the borders of the lot or, when adjacent lots were in close proximity, by drawing the boundary exactly in the middle of the lot lines. To a large extent, both definitions are arbitrary and were criticized in an expert meeting organized by the municipality of Amsterdam in 2001.[32]

21
Heeling, J., H. Meyer and J. Westrik, *Het ontwerp van de stadsplattegrond* (Amsterdam: SUN, 2002); Rutte, R., *A Landscape of Towns: Urbanization in the Netherlands from the 11th to the 19th Centuries* (Delft: Delft University of Technology, Faculty of Architecture, 2004).
22
In the most recent National Policy Document on Spatial Planning, VROM, Nota ruimte–ruimte voor ontwikkeling (The Hague: Ministry of Housing, Spatial Planning and the Environment, 2004), and in the report VROM, Nota wonen: Mensen, wensen, wonen (The Hague: Ministry of Housing, Spatial Planning and the Environment, 2000), five urban environments are defined with a density for working and living, expressed in households and work places per hectare.
23
Municipality of Amsterdam, *Structuurplan Amsterdam: Kiezen voor stedelijkheid* (Amsterdam: dRO, 2003); Municipality of Rotterdam, *De Rotterdamse woonmilieu-profielen-atlas* (Rotterdam: dS+V, afdeling Wonen, 2003); Municipality of Amsterdam, *Meten met twee maten: Referentieplannen bebouwingsintensiteit* (Amsterdam: dRO, coördinatieteam Optimalisering Grondgebruik, 2001); Urhahn, G.B. and M. Bobic, *A Pattern Image* (Bussum: Uitgeverij THOTH, 1994).
24
Rådberg, *Doktrin*, op. cit. (note 12), 68.
25
Angenot, *Verhandelingen*, op. cit. (note 11).
26
City of New York, *Zoning Handbook: A guide to New York City's Zoning Resolution* (New York, 1990). Probably this term was not established in the first resolution of 1916. The introduction of the *Zoning Handbook* states that the current resolution, in which FAR is mentioned, came into effect in 1961.
27
Angenot, *Verhandelingen*, op. cit. (note 11).
28
Municipality of Amsterdam, *Structuurplan*, op. cit. (note 23).

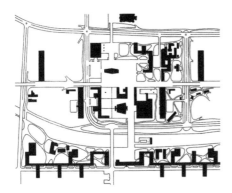

Figure-ground analysis from 'Collage City' by Rowe and Koetter (1978).

When assessing the samples from Amsterdam,[33] we see that the four oldest areas (Grachtengordel, Jordaan, De Pijp and Vondelparkbuurt) have a similar FSI although the population and dwelling density, as we have seen in the former paragraph, differs significantly. ◑ When comparing the FSI with the spatial characteristics of these areas, it appears thus that FSI expresses form in a better way than population and dwelling density.

However, other samples show that although FSI takes all functions into account, it is not nuanced enough to convey urban form. The typical post-war open block structures of Zuidwest Kwadrant (part of the AUP), the high-rise developments of the Bijlmermeer and the single-family houses of Nieuw Sloten have identical built intensities (FSI), but they differ greatly in terms of urban form. ◑ ◑ ◑

COVERAGE

The concept of coverage was frequently used throughout the twentieth century to express the relationship between built and non-built land. Colin Rowe used the figure-ground analysis to visually represent coverage as the distribution of (built) mass and open space.[34] He used this representation to decode two opposite doctrines at the core of modern and traditional planning: the first an accumulation of solids in an endless floating void, the other dominated by mass and cut through by voids. ◑

In Germany, the coverage measure was applied to limit the negative effects of solid urban patterns. Reinhard Baumeister, Joseph Stübben, Karl Hoepfner and Anton Hoenig all worked with the concept of coverage and in 1925 it became part of the official planning policy in the Building Ordinance of Berlin.[35] Coverage was actively used even earlier in planning. The expansion plan of Barcelona by Ildefonso Cerdà is a good example. Here the coverage was restricted to a maximum of 50 per cent of the lots to guarantee good hygienic conditions.[36] This was, however, to a large extent ignored during implementation and, over time, coverage reached almost 90 per cent in many areas. Interestingly, Jane Jacobs argued in 1961 for high lot coverage (between 60 and 80 per cent for the building blocks). This was to bring people out into the public streets and parks, and to create a lively city.[37] Jan Gehl recently used the same argument for a high degree of coverage in his study for Ørestad Syd in Copenhagen.[38]

29
Ibid. Another physical measure mentioned in *Structuurplan* is Ground Space Index, or coverage. This measure is discussed in the following paragraph.
30
Permeta architecten, *FSI-GSI-OSR: Atlas Westelijke Tuinsteden, instrumentarium voor verdichting en verdunning*, commissioned by Bureau Parkstad (Amsterdam, 2001); Permeta architecten, *FSI-GSI-OSR als instrumentarium voor verdichting en verdunning: Case study Nieuw West*, commissioned by Bureau Parkstad (Amsterdam, 2000).
31
Municipality of Amsterdam, *Meten*, op. cit. (note 23).
32
Persons present at the meeting: I. Kleijnjan (coordinatieteam Optimalisering Grondgebruik, dRO), K. van Zanen & L. de Laat (authors *Meten met Twee Maten*, dRO), M. Berghauser Pont (Permeta architecten), E. van der Kooij & G. de Boo (dRO), R. Meertens & J. Westrik (Delft University of Technology), L. Vrolijks (Urhahn Urban Design), J. Harts (URU, University Utrecht), C. Maat (OTB, Delft University of Technology), M. de Koning Gans (RPD), A. Oude Ophuis (Tauw), F. de Jong (SEV), C. de Boer (Slotervaart/Overtoomse Veld), D. Dicke (EGM), M. Simons, C. de Koning, R. Mertens, N. van Eeghem, and M. van Kessel (dRO).
33
Based on calculations and field work by the authors. Areas are defined as urban fabrics consisting of a reasonably homogenous urban

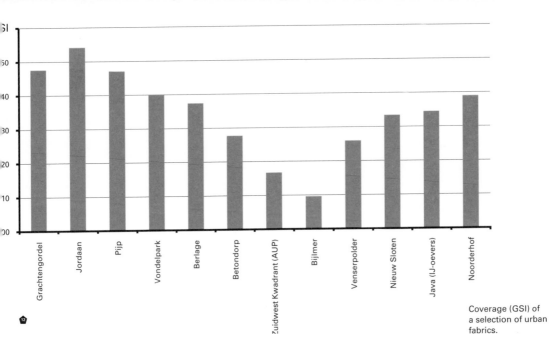

Coverage (GSI) of
a selection of urban
fabrics.

Aerial and street
view of Berlage,
Plan Zuid, and
Noorderhof.

Berlage, Plan Zuid: GSI 0.37

Noorderhof: GSI 0.39

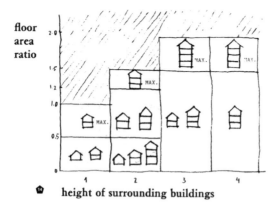

floor area ratio

height of surrounding buildings

Relationship between the maximum heights of the buildings, based on the height of the adjacent buildings and the floor area ratio (FAR), according to Alexander (1977: 476).

The 1916 New York City's Zoning Resolution restricted the amount of ground that could be covered by buildings.[39] In the Netherlands, coverage is used in zoning plans (*bestemmingsplannen*) to regulate maximum utilization of an area.

When we look at the areas with identical FSI values discussed in the former section – namely Zuidwest Kwadrant, Bijlmermeer and Nieuw Sloten – we observe that the coverage (or Ground Space Index, GSI) differs. In fact, GSI can be said to be a better standard with which to distinguish the spatial differences of these samples. ♟ However, a part of Plan Zuid by Hendrik Petrus Berlage and Noorderhof, an area in Amsterdam designed by Rob Krier and Christoph Kohl in 1999, have similar GSI values although the spatial characteristics are remarkably different. ♟ The land use plan of Noorderhof is composed of small blocks with low-rise housing and little public space. Plan Zuid is composed of rather big blocks with apartment buildings of four to five storeys and wide streets. We conclude from this that coverage alone also has a rather weak relation to urban form.

BUILDING HEIGHT

In most European countries at the end of the nineteenth and the beginning of the twentieth century, building height and street width were regulated through ordinances.[40] In Paris, the Ordinance of 1902 regulated that buildings of seven storeys, plus attics, were allowed on streets of at least 20 m width. In Berlin, the maximum height was five storeys. In the Netherlands in 1878, Jacobus van Niftrik argued that streets should be 1 to 1.5 times wider than the highest building on a street.[41] His plan for the expansion of Amsterdam, in which he put this approach into practice, was never executed. It was perceived as too expensive, partly due to its wide streets. Baumeister and Stübben went even further and proposed to also relate building height to the size of the courtyards.[42] The relation between street width (or court size) and building height was also a factor in the studies of Walter Gropius. He argued that by planning for higher buildings, one could provide more open space without losing out on the number of dwellings (and population density). Later, Christopher Alexander, arguing against the modernist high-rise developments,

pattern of streets and islands (building or urban blocks) and thus rather similar to the definition of net residential density. However, all functions are expressed in the total amount of floor area. Floor area is defined as gross floor area of buildings as described in the Dutch standard NEN 2580.

34
Rowe, C. and F. Koetter, *Collage City* (Cambridge, MA: MIT Press, 1978).

35
Rådberg, *Doktrin*, op. cit. (note 12).

36
Busquets, J., *Barcelona, the Urban Evolution of a Compact City* (Rovereto: Nicolodi, 2005), 130.

37
Jacobs, J., *The Death and Life of Great American Cities* (New York: Random House, 1992), 214.

38
Presentation of Jan Gehl's studies by Jan Christiansen, city architect of Copenhagen, at the conference *Scale, Form and Process. Scales in Urban Landscapes*, Aarhus School of Architecture, Department of Landscape and Urbanism, Aarhus, Denmark, 23-24 February 2006.

39
City of New York, *Zoning Handbook*, op. cit. (note 26).

40
Rådberg, *Doktrin*, op. cit. (note 12), 43, 106.

41
Ruijter, P. de, *Voor volkshuisvesting en stedebouw* (Utrecht: Matrijs, 1987).

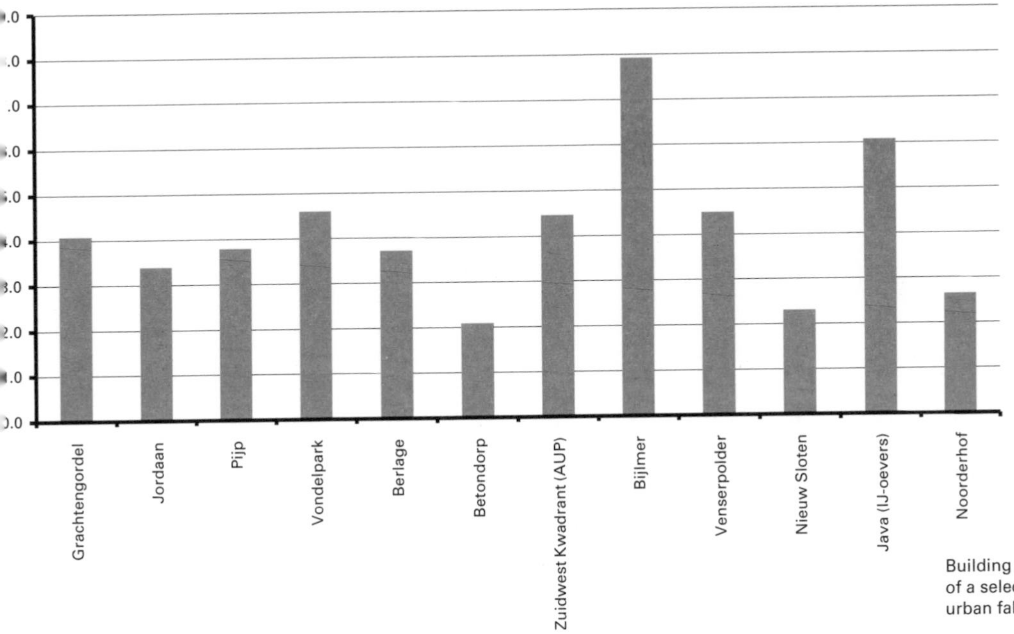

Grachtengordel
Jordaan
Pijp
Vondelpark
Berlage
Betondorp
Zuidwest Kwadrant (AUP)
Bijlmer
Venserpolder
Nieuw Sloten
Java (IJ-oevers)
Noorderhof

Building height (L) of a selection of urban fabrics.

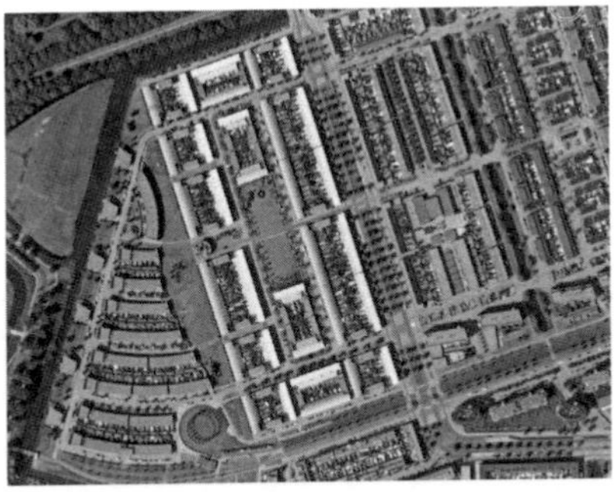

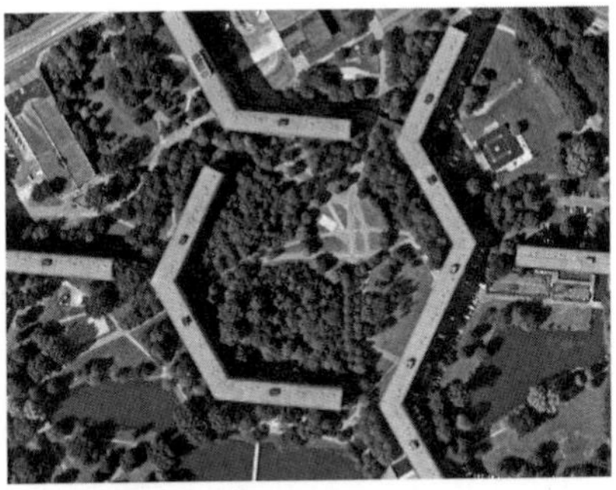

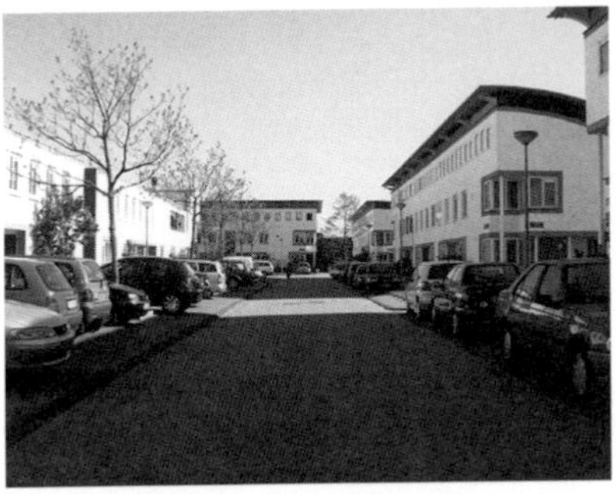

Nieuw Sloten: L 2.31 and FSI 0.77

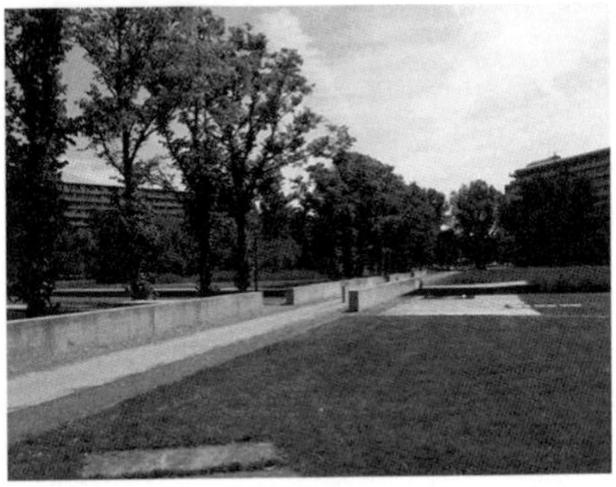

Bijlmer: L 7.92 and FSI 0.76

Aerial and street view of Nieuw Sloten and Bijlmer.

introduced psychological arguments to subject all buildings to height restrictions.[43] ♠ Based on evidence from the *British Medical Journal* and Newman's experience since the early 1970s of carrying out and analysing 'Defensible Space' projects, Alexander claimed that 'there is abundant evidence to show that high buildings make people crazy'.[44] To protect people from becoming crazy, Alexander advocated limiting the height of the majority of buildings in any urban area to four storeys or less, no matter how dense the area.

When looking at samples from Amsterdam with the same average building height, say two storeys, we find examples ranging from villas in a spacious layout to compact old villages. We can thus conclude that building height alone does not contribute much to an understanding of density and urban form or to the relation between the two. Of the Amsterdam samples, the Bijlmermeer has the highest buildings. ♠ Despite the height of the buildings, the FSI is similar to Nieuw Sloten. Here the floor space is evenly distributed over the area, while in the Bijlmermeer it is concentrated to leave large amounts of open green space. ♠

SPACIOUSNESS

Hoenig was the first to systematically study the density and spaciousness of the urban environment.[45] In his article *Baudichte und Weiträumigkeit,* he introduced the concept of *Weiträumigkeit,* or spaciousness, defined as the relationship between open space and total floor area, as a measurement of the quality of an urban plan.[46] Spaciousness is equivalent to the Open Space Ratio (OSR) mentioned in the New York City's Zoning Resolution.[47] OSR was used as an instrument to stipulate that a development must provide a certain amount of open space on a zoning lot in specified districts. It can be viewed as an expression of the trade-offs between the desire to maximize the building bulk (programme or FSI) and the public and private demand for adequate open space.

At the level of a lot (or building block), Hoenig proposed a minimum of one square metre of open space for every square metre of built floor area. He believed that when this standard was met, the area could be described as spacious (*weiträumig*). Built areas with less open space were not acceptable and were described as cramped or crowded (*engräumig*).

In Amsterdam, the only example that, on the scale of the building block, meets the spaciousness standard proposed by Hoenig is the Bijlmermeer. The other Dutch areas analysed have lower figures. In Berlin, however, most low-rise samples built from the 1920s to the 1960s fulfil Hoenig's requirements. Other locations do not, but are structurally more spacious than their counterparts in the Netherlands.[48]

Two samples, Venserpolder and Noorderhof, with similar OSR values, consist of respectively large building blocks of 4.5 storeys high and small blocks of 2.5 storeys. ♠ We can thus conclude that OSR alone does not contribute much to the understanding of urban form. However, it does reveal the character of the areas in terms of pressure on the non-built space. If all of the inhabitants of the dwellings in these houses would go out onto the streets and into the courtyards at the same time, each person would have the same amount of open space at his/her disposal in both samples.

42 Rådberg, *Doktrin*, op. cit. (note 12), 48, 51.
43 Alexander, C., et al., *A Pattern Language: Towns, Buildings, Construction* (New York: Oxford University Press, 1977), 114–119.
44 Ibid., 115.

45 Rådberg, *Doktrin*, op. cit. (note 12), 68–70.
46 Hoenig, A., 'Baudichte und Weitraumigkeit', *Baugilde* 10 1928, 713–715.
47 City of New York, *Zoning Handbook*, op. cit. (note 26).

48 Based on all empirical data used in the research for this book (Berghauser Pont, M. and P. Haupt, *Space, Density and Urban Form* (Delft: 2009), 273–295.

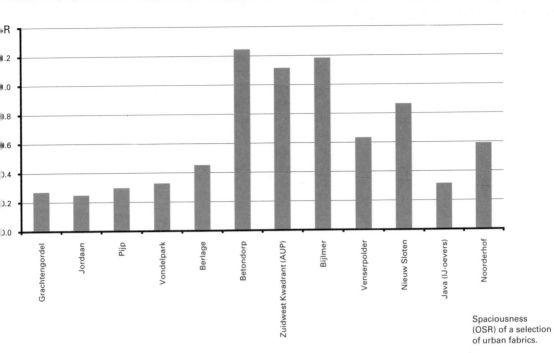

Spaciousness (OSR) of a selection of urban fabrics.

Aerial and street view of Venserpolder and Noorderhof.

Venserpolder: OSR 0.63 and L 4.5

Noorderhof: OSR 0.60 and L 2.5

EVALUATION OF DENSITY MEASURES

As we have discussed, population and dwelling density have some serious shortcomings when it comes to establishing a relation with urban form. When working with dwelling density, the floor space allocated to employment is not taken into account. It is further impossible to determine whether people reside in large or small dwellings. In addition, issues of health and hygiene, which led to the introduction of the concept of density in urbanism, are not only influenced by the number of people residing in an area. Also relevant are dwelling size, building height and the distance between buildings. In 1880, the Jordaan had a dwelling density of 1,265 inhabitants per hectare. The area more than once faced high death rates due to diseases; in 1664 from the bubonic plague and in 1866 as a result of a cholera outbreak.[49] The bad living conditions (read: high population density) were perceived as part of the reason that the area was so badly affected by these pandemics. But were the pandemics caused by high population density or by the fact that a large number of people were living in small and cramped dwellings? Is it possible to imagine such a circumstance, a ratio of 1,265 people per hectare, without the problems that European cities encountered at the end of the nineteenth century? In the Jordaan, in 1880, the space allocation was 15 m² of floor area per inhabitant. In 2007, this had increased to 85 m².[50] Accommodating a density of 1,265 persons per hectare with the same amount of floor area per person, as is thought to be appropriate today, would result in a FSI increasing from 1.9 to 10.8![51]

We observe that land use intensity (FSI or FAR) is more effective but still does not allow us to differentiate between different spatial layouts. The same can be said about the other density indicators discussed here. All are, to a certain degree, informative, but none can be used on their own to adequately describe spatial properties as a step towards defining urban types with the use of density. This conclusion corresponds with the opinion commonly held by professionals, as well as researchers, as mentioned earlier.

An alternative approach is to use more variables to describe an urban area. The New York City's Zoning Regulation contained three indicators of density: FAR (or FSI), coverage (GSI) and population density. In Barcelona, both building height and coverage were considered and the building ordinance in Berlin of 1925 mentioned *Ausnutzungsziffer* (FSI), *Ausnutzung der Grundstücks* (GSI) and *Stockwerksanzahl* (building height). More recently, a combination of different indicators have been used to differentiate between various development patterns.[52] These approaches highlight the advantage of using a multivariable approach to density.

An example of a multivariable approach to density can be illustrated by looking at a children's game in which a circle is divided in two, three or four pieces. This game is portrayed in 🔵. In the first instance, the pieces are positioned in such a way that four full circles are constructed. In terms of intensity (FSI), coverage (GSI), height (L) and spaciousness (OSR) these solutions are identical (1, 1, 1, and 0 respectively). In the second case, the same pieces are stacked on top of each other. The first solution, consisting only of one piece, is identical to the one in the first picture. The second solution consists of two pieces stacked on top of each other, resulting in a halving of the GSI (0.5) and a doubling of the

49
Moll, H., 'Vuile teringstad: Vijf eeuwen besmettelijke ziekten in Amsterdam', *NRC Handelsblad* 31 January 2001.

50
The FSI in the Jordaan is assumed for this calculation to be unchanged (FSI=1.89). The population density in 1889 was 1,265, in 2007 it was 222 inhabitants per hectare. Other functions within the area were not taken into account.

51
Derived from the situation in the Jordaan in 2007: FSI=1.89 and population density of 222 inhabitants/ha.

52
CETAT, *Indicateurs morphologiques pour l'amenagement: Analyse de 50 périmetres batis situes sur le canton de Geneve* (Geneva: Departement des traveaux publics, 1986); Rådberg, *Doktrin*, op. cit. (note 12); Yoshida, H. and M. Omae, 'An approach for analysis of urban morphology: methods to derive morphological properties of city blocks by using an urban model and their interpretations', *Computers, Environments and Urban Systems*, 29 (2005), 223–247.

DENSITY MEASURE	YEAR	USE	NORM
Population density			
Inhabitants per hectare	1899	Howard	< 75 inh/ha (district)
	1933	Le Corbusier	1,000 dw/ha
Dwelling density			
Dwellings per hectare	1909	Unwin	< 30 dw/ha (island)
	1934	Van Eesteren	55-110 dw/ha (fabric)
	1961	Jacobs	> 250 dw/ha (island)
Land use intensity			
Ausnutzungsziffer = FSI*100	1925	Building Ordinance Berlin	20-300 (lot)
Land Index = 1/FSI	1949	Central Service for Reconstruction and Public Housing	
Floor to Area Ratio (FAR) = FSI	1961	New York Zoning Resolution	maximum FAR (lot)
Floor Space Index (FSI)	2003	Structuurplan Amsterdam	minimal FSI (fabric)
Coverage			
Coverage = GSI*100	1961	New York Zoning Resolution	maximum coverage (lot)
	1860	Cerdà	< 50% (lot)
	1925	Building Ordinance Berlin	0.10-0.60 (lot)
	1961	Jacobs	0.60-0.80 (island)
Ground Space Index (GSI)	2003	Structuurplan Amsterdam	minimal GSI (fabric)
Building height			
Building height	1961	New York Zoning Resolution	maximum height
Amount of stories	1667	Rebuilding Law London	
	1880	Baumeister	< 4
	1902	Ordinance Paris	< 7 + attic
Spaciousness			
Weitraumigkeit = OSR	1928	Hoenig	> 1.0 (lot)
Open Space (Ratio) = OSR*100	1961	New York Zoning Resolution	minimal OSR (lot)

Examples of density measures used through history.

height. Also, the OSR has changed from zero to 0.5. The FSI, though, remains the same (1.0). The other two solutions in the second picture, still with the same FSI, have both different GSI, L and OSR values (third solution: 0.33, 3, and 0.67; fourth solution: 0.25, 4, and 0.75). We suggest that such a combination of indicators is needed to better relate density to potential urban form.

A shortcoming of this combination of density indicators, however, is their focus on the built mass and the absence of a reference to size. In the example of the children's game nothing indicates the size of the wooden pieces. For all we know, they could represent a villa or an industrial shed with identical density measures. By introducing network density, we can add the non-built space more profoundly and arrive at an abstract indication of measure.

Children's game, illustrating the relation between FSI, GSI, OSR and L.

1
The four solutions are identical in terms of FSI, GSI, OSR and L

2
The four solutions are identical in terms of FSI, but differ in terms of GSI, OSR and L

NETWORK DENSITY

Network density is defined by us as the amount of network per area unit, and is expressed as metres of network (length) per square metres of ground area (surface). The type of network included should be made explicit (motorized, bike, pedestrian, or a combination). To justify the choice of network as a fundamental characteristic of urban areas, the following section looks at the basic elements of the urban ground plan as defined in morphological and quantitative research.

We use the arguments of Conzen, the founder of the British school of morphology, in defining the main research entities of the urban landscape. The spatial entities identified by Conzen as essential to the town plan (or ground plan) are the street system, the lot pattern and the building configuration. These three entities are similar to the distinction made by Jan Heeling, et al., between the public streets (street system) and private islands (consisting of lots and buildings).[53] ◉ The combination of streets and a series of islands surrounded by these streets constitute *the urban fabric*, or tissue. The main task of a designer, according to Heeling, et al., is to combine these two in the best possible manner.

Conzen and Saverio Muratori describe the lot as the most conservative entity within a morphological complex.[54] Heeling, et al., on the other hand, focus more on the public street pattern and its relation to the private islands. As Erik Terlouw illustrates, the lots in most Western European towns founded in the twelfth and thirteenth centuries developed in a way known as the 'burgage cycle'.[55] The lots of the original layout (approximately 650 m²)[56] were divided lengthwise and the backside of lots and the alleyways, connecting the front- and backside, were developed resulting in smaller lots (of approximately 150 m²). The street

53
Heeling, et al., *Het ontwerp*, op. cit. (note 21).
54
Moudon, A.V., 'Getting to Know the Built Landscape: Typomorphology', in: K. Franck and L. Schneekloth (eds.), *Ordering Space: Types in Architecture and Design* (New York: Van Nostrand Reinhold, 1994), 289–311.
55
Terlouw, E., 'A House of One's Own', *OASE* 52 (1999), 32–77, 65–67.
56
Standard lot of 3 × 15 rods (= 11.30 × 56.50 m = 640 m²).

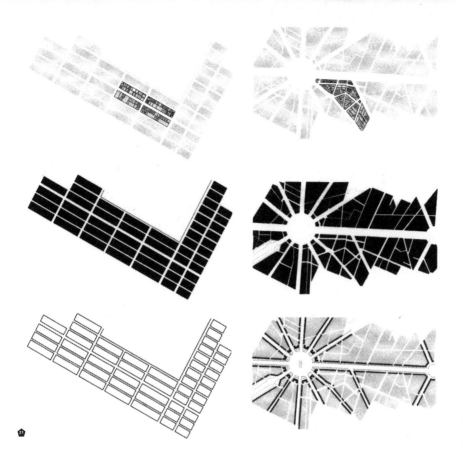

Entities of the
ground plan: lots,
islands and
network (Heeling,
et al. 2002: 102).

pattern, however, remained mostly intact and was more resistant than the lots. This robustness of the network (and the islands) makes it appropriate to view network and islands as the basic entities of the town plan.

The mutual dependence of streets and islands is important in understanding the ground plan. Street space, to use the words of Stephen Marshall, constitutes 'the basic core of all urban public space forming a contiguous network by which everything is linked to everything else. This continuum is punctured by lots of private land.'[57] For one, built floor space generates movements and causes flows (people, cars, etcetera) that need to be facilitated by the network. In addition, the open space of the network enables light to access the buildings and influences privacy, depending on the profile width and the size of the islands. Compactly developed islands can be compensated for by wide street profiles and vice versa. This whole interrelatedness of network, islands and building bulk should thus be at the core of a new definition of density.

Much has been researched and written on the role and character of the network in the urban landscape at different scale levels.[58] One perspective can be historical or morphological, another more technical (traffic engineering), or more concerned with the function of the network as a public space. Connectivity, pattern form, hierarchies, and so

57
Marshall, S., *Streets & Patterns* (Oxon: Spon Press, 2005), 13.
58
See e.g. Bach, B., et al., *Urban Design and Traffic; A Selection from Bach's Toolbox/Stedebouw en verkeer; een selectie uit de gereedschapskist van Bach* (Ede: Crow, 2006); Calabrese, L.M., *Reweaving UMA: Urbanism, Mobility, Architecture* (Rotterdam: Optima Grafische Communicatie, 2004), Marshall, *Streets & Patterns*, op. cit. (note 57); Meyer, H., F. de Josselin de Jong and M.J. Hoekstra (eds.), *Het ontwerp van de openbare ruimte* (Amsterdam: SUN, 2006); Rofé, Y., 'Space and Community: The Spatial Foundations of Urban Neighborhoods', *Berkeley Planning Journal* 10 (1995), 107–125.

forth are all aspects that must be considered when designing and analysing the network. Here it is important to note, however, that we do not aspire in this research to provide any exhaustive description of the form and/or function of the urban network, but to focus on its primary measurements and its relation to built density.

The function of the public (street) network in a city or town is two-fold. For one, it facilitates the different modes of movement taking place in the urban fabric and provides access to the islands. It also defines the urban layout by dividing land into public and private land. We follow here the line of reasoning employed by Leslie Martin and Lionel March, Heeling, et al. and Marshall.[59] They argue that the street grid (network) and the ground plan are the framework for urbanization.

The measurements of the network and the grain of the urban fabric, as mentioned by Manuel de Solà-Morales are decisive in establishing the relationship between general form and built content: smaller blocks (or islands) provide the greatest proportion of public ways and overall exposure ratio (façade length to area).[60] Jacobs argues for small blocks to stimulate city liveliness.[61] Amis Siksna underlines Jacob's arguments in the article *The Effects of Block Size and Form in North American and Australian City Centres*.[62] He argues that in cities with small- or medium-sized blocks, the street layout remains intact, whereas in cities with large initial blocks, the layout is modified by the addition of streets and alleys, creating smaller blocks and sub-blocks. Size thus matters, and the most fundamental measurements in the urban plan are related to the network.

Adding network density as a primary indicator of the density concept increases the latter's capacity to indicate important primary measurements of the urban landscape and describe important aspects of urban form. We demonstrate later that combining the network and built density allows us to introduce measures to an otherwise scale-less density concept. In addition, it enables the analysis of a range of properties that are characterized by the relation between serviced and served, between network and islands, lots and buildings.

Network density at the level of the urban fabric can be viewed as a specific example of a general *transition density* concept. With transition density we refer to the level of concentration of borders of different entities in a certain area. A border demarcates two locations. A fundamental change takes place when this border is crossed. The intensity of transitions in an area can be described as transition density. In a dwelling, the walls separating different rooms constitute the borders of transition, in a building these are the façades, in a building block these transitions are the borders of the lots. At the level of the urban fabric this can be defined as the public network (a zone of transition), and at the level of a district, the edges of the urban fabric that constitute the district define the transitions between one fabric and another (precise definitions of the different scales follow later in this chapter). In this research we focus on the transition density on the level of the urban fabric, that is, network density.

MULTIVARIABLE DEFINITION OF DENSITY

We suggest that a multivariable density concept consisting of the three fundamental indicators intensity (FSI), compactness (GSI) and network density (N) can offer a method that is specific enough to allow for the defi-

59
Martin, L. and L. March (eds.), *Urban Space and Structures* (Cambridge: Cambridge University Press, 1972), 6–27; Heeling, et al., *Het ontwerp*, op. cit. (note 21); Marshall, *Streets & Patterns*, op. cit. (note 57).
60
Solà-Morales, M. de, 'Towards a Definition: Analysis of Urban Growth in the Nineteenth Century', *Lotus*, 19 June 1978, 28–36.
61
Jacobs, *The Death and Life*, op. cit. (note 37), 178–186.
62
Siksna, A., 'The Effects of Block Size and Form in North American and Australian City Centres', *Urban Morphology* 1 (1997), 19–33.

nition of urban types, as well as economic enough to ensure that excessive amounts of data can be managed without drowning in too many over-detailed definitions. We maintain that this multivariable density model is a balanced concept that can be positioned between the too detailed – and thereby non-generic – and the too abstract – and thereby too inclusive – representations, and can distinguish between basic spatial properties. If this is the case, as we will try to demonstrate in the next chapter, then a method has been developed that is both effective enough to be able to differentiate (by constructing types), and economic enough to fit the adagio of Occam's razor: whenever something can be described in more fundamental terms, it should be done so.[63]

To be able to compare areas and plans, and to define the performance of different types of density, it is important to agree upon accurate definitions. Much confusion can be avoided by using definitions that are generally accepted. In this section, we describe the variables of the indicators and suggest a consistent set of definitions that can be used in this multivariable density approach.

FOUR VARIABLES TO CALCULATE DENSITY

The four variables needed to calculate the basic indicators FSI, GSI and N, are:
— Base Land Area (A);
— Network length (l);
— Gross floor area (F);
— Built up area, or footprint (B).

In the following sections we formulate workable definitions for these variables.

Base land area (A)

The boundaries of a plan area can be defined in various ways. The method of establishing boundaries is of particular importance in cases where areas are to be compared or used as references and when correlations, or associations, between two indicators are tested. There are roughly three ways of defining area boundaries:

— *Administrative boundaries*, such as cadastral boundaries, postal areas[64] or agreed upon boundaries, such as municipal boundaries registered by the Dutch Land Registry Office (*Kadaster*), and neighbourhood boundaries (*wijken* and *buurten*), defined by the Dutch municipalities;
— *Projected boundaries*, such as an arbitrary grid of pixels or circles, often used in GIS applications;
— *Generated boundaries* based on morphological characteristics.

One of the positive aspects of formal boundaries is that most statistical data is available for these areas. That was the reason that VROM, the Ministry of Housing, Spatial Planning and the Environment, recently used the four-digit postal code areas to identify *probleemwijken*, neighbourhoods judged as having a lot of socioeconomic and physical problems.[65] This method can be criticized as inadequate, as postal areas and neigh-

63
Stanford Encyclopedia of Philosophy, author's interpretation.

64
Postal areas are defined by the Dutch postal service; CBS, *Kerncijfers postcodegebied 2004* (The Hague: Statistics Netherlands, 2006).

65
Kamerstuk 24 april 2007, Ministry of Housing, Spatial Planning and the Environment.

bourhoods often do not coincide. The system of postal codes was developed in 1978 to economize the sorting of letters. Today, it is also used to analyse postal areas as in the example mentioned. However, area measurements such as the four-digit postal code areas, have an inbuilt 'ecological fallacy' well known in geography as 'The Modified Area Unit Problem' (MAUP), which basically means that statistics are arbitrary since the definition of the 'area' is subjective.[66] MAUP occurs when point-based measures of spatial phenomena are aggregated into districts, because the resulting summary values are influenced by the choice of these boundaries. If, instead of postal areas, neighbourhoods had been chosen in the case of the *probleemwijken*, the selection would probably have looked very different. Postal areas and neighbourhoods (*buurten* and *wijken*) in the Netherlands do not correspond and the summary results of these aggregates thus differ. Furthermore, the methods used to define neighbourhoods (and municipal borders) differ from one municipality to the other.[67] In rural areas, neighbourhood boundaries mostly follow the topography of the landscape; in urban areas socioeconomic criteria are more important for determining the boundaries of neighbourhoods.

Projected and generated boundaries have the same problem, but are at least more open to be adjusted in accordance to the research. The main difference between the two is that the first, the projected boundary, aims to control the geography and its content 'top-down', while the second, the generated boundary, analyses it 'bottom-up'.

In our opinion, the third method of drawing boundaries is more suitable when relating density to spatial properties. By letting the matter itself generate its boundaries, the artificial straightjacket forced upon that which is analysed is minimized. This requires, however, a sensitivity to local morphology and changes in density gradients when establishing the boundaries. Definitions of boundary entities (walls, cadastral borders or networks), and of the amount of homogeneity required of the components that make up the aggregation at hand, can help guide the demarcation. Such rules can also be translated into algorithms used by GIS, and could thus substitute the handicraft with a computerized scan of the urban landscape, dividing it into different geographical entities.

It is important to clarify another aspect: the difference in density at different scale levels. In his dispersal and concentration theory, Taeke De Jong paid particular attention to the nature of different scales.[68] The larger the area and the greater the variation in parts of the area, the more statistical in nature the index (dwellings per hectare or FSI) will become. In addition, the more variation is lost in the calculation, the more abstract and less formally relevant the result is. It is for this reason that a study by the University of Geneva defines an upper and lower range for the size of an urban fabric: between 0.5 and 8 hectares.[69] In the BYGG report of 1962, this range was set between 1 and 3 hectares.[70] We do not use such limits as our conclusions depend more on the consistency, or homogeneity, of the urban fabric than on the size of the area. The Bijlmermeer example discussed earlier, for instance, measures more than 30 hectares, but consists of only two large high-rise slabs in a park surrounded by streets. It would be incorrect to exclude this example solely because it is considered to be too big. Working with densities means accepting the arrogance of the average – because of its productive

66
Ståhle, A., *Compact Sprawl: Exploring Public Open Space and Contradictions in Urban Density* (Stockholm: KTH, 2008).

67
Meer, A.J. van der, *Gemeentegrenzen Nederland 1795 – heden*, dissertation OTB Research Institute, Delft University of Technology, 2007.

68
Jong, T. de and D.J.M. van der Voordt (eds.), *Ways to Study and Research Urban, Architectural and Technical Design* (Delft: DUP Science, 2002).

69
CETAT, *Indicateurs morphologiques pour l'amenagement: Analyse de 50 périmetres batis situes sur le canton de Geneve* (Geneva: Departement des traveaux publics, 1986), 23.
70
Rådberg, *Doktrin*, op. cit. (note 12), 11.

advantages – but at the same time elaborating on the (more or less) divers characteristics of the components that constitute this average.

Knowledge of the differences in density at different scale levels is of great importance. When working at a small scale, for instance at the scale of a building or lot, or at a larger scale, such as the whole city or region, new components can be constructed as aggregates of smaller components. In most cases this is accompanied by the addition of a certain surplus, or tare space. Tare space is commonly defined as the difference between gross and net areas. Later we provide a definition of tare space which is solely characterized by densities at different scale levels. We will later also return to ways to gauge homo- and heterogeneity on different levels of scale.

The aggregations we use in this book, illustrated by two schemes representing respectively a traditional closed perimeter building block (left) and a modernist open building block (right) ✿, are as follows:

Building The area of the building is the same as the built area or footprint. The borders of the built area are defined by the edges of the building footprint. We use the definitions as published in the Dutch standard NEN 2580.[71]

Lot The area of the lot (also referred to as parcel or plot) is the sum of built and non-built (predominately private) areas designated for building. The non-built area is the tare space between *building* and *lot*. In residential areas, these non-built areas are mostly used for gardens. In some cases, the lots comprise built areas only and thus correspond to the building; no tare space is added. The borders of the lots are defined by the legal boundaries specified in the cadastre.

Island The area of an island,[72] also referred to in the traditional city as an urban block, comprises the lots and, in some cases, non-built space not designated for building. These non-built spaces constitute the tare space between the *lot* and *island*. Some examples include playing fields, small squares or parking areas. The border of an island is defined by the surrounding public streets. When there is no bordering street, the periphery of the island is set by the lot boundaries.

Fabric The area of the fabric is similar to the scale and definitions used for a *plan unit,* as described by Conzen, and the *tessuto,* as used by Gianfranco Caniggia.[73] The urban fabric consists of a collection of islands, as well as the network that surrounds these islands and is required as access to the islands. These access streets primarily serve to access the private lots and buildings.[74] Circulation streets on the other hand are primarily used to move from one urban fabric to the other or across the city. When linear green or water elements such as the canals in the Grachtengordel in Amsterdam are part of the street pattern, these are considered as part of the network as well. The network area constitutes the tare space between *island* and *fabric*. The boundaries of the fabric are drawn in the middle of the access streets. In circumstances where there is no street, the boundaries of the fabric are set by the lot boundaries. The size of the fabric is determined by the level of homogeneity (spread) of the different islands within that fabric.

71
NEN, *NEN 2580: Areas and Volumes of Buildings – Terms, Definitions and Methods of Determination* (Delft: NEN, 2007).

72
According to Panerai, P., 'De schaal van het bouwblok', in: S. Komossa et al., *Atlas van het Hollandse bouwblok* (Bussum: Uitgeverij THOTH, 2002), 11–14, the ancient Romans called their urban blocks *insulae*, or island, reflecting the topological containment of buildings and land parcels (lots) within a continuum of public space primarily constituted by the system of public streets.
73
Moudon, 'Getting to Know', op. cit. (note 54).
74
'Access streets' are defined following Buchanan, C.D., *Mixed Blessing: The Motor in Britain* (London: Leonard Hill, 1958).

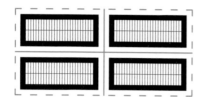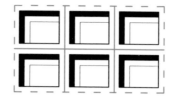

— — Exterior network

——— Interior network

Interior and exterior
streets of two
urban fabrics.

District The area of the district is similar to the *town plan* introduced by Conzen or the neighbourhood (*buurt*) defined by Van Lohuizen. The district is composed of a collection of fabrics and large-scale non-built areas not included in the fabric itself, such as circulation streets,[75] parks, sports fields and larger water areas. These constitute the tare space between *fabric* and *district*. The boundaries of the district are drawn in the middle of the circulation streets. In cases where the access streets are also used for circulation, the boundary of the district coincides with that of the fabric.

75
'Circulation streets' are defined following Buchanan, *Mixed Blessing*, op.cit. (note 74).

Network Length (l)

At the scale of an architectural object, the network of, for instance, a multifunctional high-rise tower consists of stairs, corridors, elevators and other spaces needed for pedestrian circulation within the building. At the scale of the district, the network consists of circulation streets, rails, roads, canals and so forth. At the scale of the urban fabric, which is the focus of this study, the network is the access street. In its most traditional form the access street coincides with the circulation street. In functionalist plans, different modalities are often separated and access streets do not coincide with circulation streets. A common characteristic of physical networks is that they function as access to the areas served. In the case of the urban fabric the street (that is, network) gives access to an island, in the case of a building the corridor (that is, network) gives access to a dwelling or a room. The network can be defined for all sorts of modalities, each of them taken separately or all together. It is important, however, to make the selection explicit, whatever modalities are used. For the samples of this book the car network was used to define network length.

In addition, one must differentiate between internal and external networks. 'Internal network' ● refers to all networks that do not coincide with any fabric demarcation. 'External network' refers to the network divided in half by a fabric demarcation. Only half of the external network contributes to the fabric as the other half 'belongs' to the surrounding fabrics. In practice, this implies that the entire network length inside a sample is measured and to this measure is added half of the network that circumscribes the sample.

Gross Floor Area (F)

The definition used here is taken from the Dutch standard NEN 2580.[76] The basic rule is that the gross floor area of a building is the sum of all surfaces, measured per floor, along the perimeter of the partitions that

76
NEN, *NEN 2580*, op. cit. (note 71).

Building

- Boundary line
- Tare space
- Built space
- Open space

Tare 60%

Tare 45%

Lot

Tare 0%

Tare 50%

Island

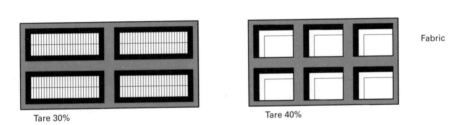

Fabric

Tare 30%

Tare 40%

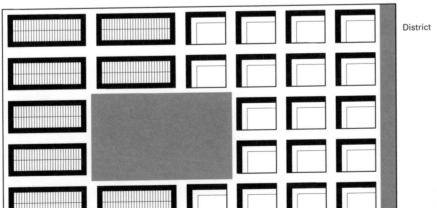

District

Tare space of the areas at each level of aggregation.

Tare 20%

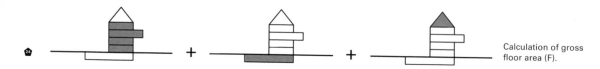

Calculation of gross floor area (F).

surround the building, including underground floor area and floor area under a pitched roof. ✿ Voids and wells are not included as long as the area is greater than 4 m². Occasional niches or recesses and irregular protrusions do not have to be taken into account, as long as the area is less than 0.5 m². Exterior spaces, such as loggias, balconies, uncovered walkways, roof terraces, etcetera are not included in the gross floor area calculation of a building. In addition, open fire escapes and emergency stairways are not included when calculating the gross floor area.

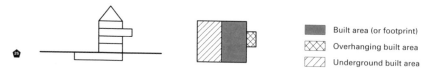

■ Built area (or footprint)
⊠ Overhanging built area
▨ Underground built area

Calculation of built area (B).

Built Area or Footprint (B)
When establishing the built area of buildings, the same definitions outlined above for gross floor area are used. The built area is defined as the floor area, measured at ground level along the perimeter of the dividing partitions of the building, and thus excludes overhanging or underground built areas. ✿

77
For an extensive
argumentation of the
construction of the
functions, see ◆.

NETWORK DENSITY (N)

The density of the network, N, refers to the concentration of networks in an area, in this case the fabric. The density of a network is defined as network length per square metre of base land area (m/m²), and is calculated as the sum of the whole internal network and half of the length of the network used to demarcate the base land area. The unit of the outcome is metre of network per square metre of fabric area.

◆ $$N_f = \frac{l_i + \frac{l_e}{2}}{A_f}$$

l_i length of interior network (m)
l_e length of edge network (m)
A_f area of fabric (m²)

BUILDING INTENSITY (FSI)

FSI reflects the building intensity independently of the programmatic composition and is calculated as follows for all levels of scale as described earlier:

F_x gross floor area (m²)
A_x area of aggregation x (m²)
x   aggregation (lot (l), island (i), fabric (f), or district (d))

◆ $$FSI_x = \frac{F_x}{A_x}$$

This index uses the unit m²/m².

COVERAGE (GSI)

GSI, or coverage, demonstrates the relationship between built and non-built space and is calculated as follows for all levels of scale as described earlier:

B_x footprint (m²)
A_x area of aggregation x (m²)
x   aggregation (lot (l), island (i), fabric (f), or district (d))

◆ $$GSI_x = \frac{B_x}{A_x}$$

This index uses the unit m²/m².

DERIVED INDICATORS

We can derive a series of indicators by using the basic
ones defined earlier, FSI, GSI and N. These will contribute
to describing the spatial properties of urban areas and
explore the potential of densities in relation to urban
form and performance. We elaborate on these issues in
the following chapter, using the indicators introduced
here. The derived indicators point to an abstract quality
and should not be interpreted in a literal way. The first
two we will discuss are building height and spaciousness
and both concern the relation between the built and non-
built space.

BUILDING HEIGHT (L)

The average number of storeys (or layers), L, can be
arrived at by ascertaining the intensity and coverage or,
FSI and GSI, for the aggregation x. If more floor area is
developed in a certain area, without changing the
footprint, L will increase. If the building height should
remain constant, then FSI and GSI have to increase.

◆ $$L = \frac{FSI_x}{GSI_x} \quad x \quad \text{aggregation } x$$

SPACIOUSNESS (OSR)

The variable OSR, or spaciousness, is a measure of the
amount of non-built space at ground level per square
metre of gross floor area. This figure provides an
indication of the pressure on non-built space. If more
floor area is developed in an area (with the same
footprint), the OSR decreases and the number of people
who will use the non-built space increases. The unit of
OSR is m^2/m^2.

$$\diamond \quad OSR = \frac{1-GSI_x}{FSI_x}$$

x   aggregation x

TARE (T)

One important feature of density is its characteristics at different levels of scale. The difference in base land area (A_x) between two levels of scale define the tare (T_x), also often described as the difference between net and gross. If T describes the tare between, for instance, fabric (x) and island (x–1), then T can be arrived at through:

$$\diamond \quad T_x = \frac{A_x - A_{x-1}}{A_x}$$

x   aggregation x
x–1   level of scale of the components of
        which aggregation x is composed

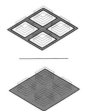

If the coverage or intensity is known for both fabric and island, then tare can be defined purely through density indicators. In the case of the fabric, the following applies:

$$\diamond \quad T_f = 1 - \frac{GSI_f}{GSI_i}$$

$$\diamond \quad T_f = 1 - \frac{FSI_f}{FSI_i}$$

The relationship between tare and built densities on different levels of scale can be generalized as follows:

$$\diamond \quad T_x = 1 - \frac{GSI_x}{GSI_{x-1}}$$

x   aggregation x
x–1   level of scale of the components of which
        aggregation x is composed

$$T_x = 1 - \frac{FSI_x}{FSI_{x-1}}$$

x   aggregation x

x–1 level of scale of the components of which aggregation x is composed

As the amount of privately issued land, PIL (*uitgeefbaar terrein*) is the negative, or the remaining part, of tare, PIL can be expressed as follows:

$$PIL = 1 - T_f$$

$$PIL = 1 - \frac{GSI_f}{GSI_i}$$

$$PIL = 1 - \frac{FSI_f}{FSI_i}$$

MESH AND PROFILE WIDTH (w and b)
Network density can be used to calculate an indicative mesh size (w), or the distance from street to street in a square grid of the urban fabric, using the following formula:

$$w = \frac{2}{N_f}$$

A high network density (N) corresponds to a small mesh of the urban layout and a low N to a large mesh. Combined with the tare of the fabric (T_f), one can arrive at the profile width (b). The relationship between these variables can be described as:

$$b = \frac{2(1 - \sqrt{1 - T_f})}{N_f}$$

or, combined with ◆:

◈ $$b = \frac{2\left(1 - \sqrt{\dfrac{GSI_f}{GSI_i}}\right)}{N_f}$$

DERIVATION OF FORMULAE

Derivation of ◆:

$L=F/B$

$L=(F/A)/(B/A)$

$FSI=F/A$ (def)

$GSI=B/A$ (def)

$L=FSI/GSI$

Derivation of ◆:

$FSI=F/A$ (def)

$F=FSI·A$

$GSI=B/A$ (def)

$B=GSI·A$

$OSR=(A−B)/F$ (def)

$OSR=(A−A·GSI)/(A·FSI)$

$OSR=(1−GSI)/FSI$

The construction of OSR gradients in the Spacemate:

$OSR=(1−GSI)/FSI$

$FSI(GSI)=1/OSR−GSI/OSR$

$GSI(FSI)=1−OSR·FSI$

Intersection with y-axis: $FSI(0)=1/OSR$

Intersection with x-axis: $GSI(0)=1$

Derivation of ◆ and ◆:

$GSI_f=B/A_f$ (def)

$A_f=B/GSI_f$

$GSI_i=B/\sum A_i$ (def)

$\sum A_i=B/GSI_i$

$T_f=(A_f−\sum A_i)/A_f$ (def)

$T_f=1−(B/GSI_i)/(B/GSI_f)$

$T_f=1−GSI_f/GSI_i$

◆ is derived in the same way, but B is substituted for by F

Derivation of ◆ and ◆:

$T_f=1−GSI_f/GSI_i$ (def)

$1−T_f=GSI_f/GSI_i$

$PIL=1−T_f$ (def)

$PIL=GSI_f/GSI_i$

◆ is derived in the same way, but GSI_f and GSI_i are substituted for by FSI_f and FSI_i

Derivation of ◆:

$N_f=(\sum l_i+(\sum l_e)/2)/A_f$ (def)

For a grid with n squares with a mesh-size of w:

$(\sum l_i+(\sum l_e)/2)=2n·w$

$A_f=n·w^2$

$N_f=2n·w/(n·w^2)$

$N_f=2/w$

$w=2/N_f$

Derivation of ◆:

$T=(A_f−\sum A_i)/A_f$ (def)

$A_f=w^2$

$A_i=(w−b)^2$

$T_f=(w^2−(w−b)^2)/w^2$

$T_f=1−(w−b)^2/w^2$

$(w−b)^2/w^2=1−T_f$

$1−b/w=\mathrm{root}(1−T_f)$

$b=w(1−\mathrm{root}(1−T_f))$

$w=2/N_f$

$b=2(1−\mathrm{root}(1−T_f))/N_f$

Derivation of ◆:

$b=2(1−\mathrm{root}(1−T_f))/Nf$ ◆

$T_f=1−GSI_f/GSI_i$

$b=2(1−\mathrm{root}(GSI_f/GSI_i))/N_f$

Derivation of Φ:

$b = 2(1 - \text{root}(1 - T_f))/N_f$ ◆

$b \cdot N_f/2 = 1 - \text{root}(1 - T_f)$

$\text{root}(1 - T_f) = 1 - b \cdot N_f/2$

$1 - T_f = (1 - b \cdot N_f/2)2$

$T_f = 1 - (1 - b \cdot N_f/2)^2$

Derivation of ◆:

$T_f = 1 - (1 - b \cdot N_f/2)^2$ ◆

$1 - T_f = (1 - b \cdot N_f/2)^2$

$PIL = 1 - T_f$ (def)

$PIL = (1 - b \cdot N_f/2)^2$

Deviation from a square grid (☎ page 186)

derivation of ◆:

$N_f = (\sum l_i + (\sum l_e)/2)/A_f$ (def)

$N_f = (w_x + w_y)/(w_x \cdot w_y)$

$w_x = n \cdot w_y$

$w_y = (n + 1)/(n \cdot N_f)$

$T_f = (A_f - \sum A_i)/A_f$ (def)

$T_f = 1 - A_i/A_f$

$A_i = (w_x - b)(w_y - b)$

$A_f = w_x \cdot w_y$

$T_f = 1 - (w_x - b)(w_y - b)/(w_x \cdot w_y)$

$T_f = 1 - (n \cdot w_y - b)(w_y - b)/(n \cdot w_y^2)$

$w_y = (n + 1)/(n \cdot N_f)$

$T_f = 1 - (1 - b \cdot N_f/(n+1))(1 - n \cdot b \cdot N_f/(n+1))$

From this last, b can be derived through:

$b = (n+1)^2/(2n \cdot N) -$

$\text{root}((n+1)^4/(4n^2 \cdot N^2) - T \cdot (n+1)^2/(n \cdot N^2))$

Derivation of ◆:

$N_p = l_p/A_f$ (def) where

$l_p = 4(w - b)/2$

$N_p = 2(w - b)/w^2$

$w = 2/N_f$ ◆

$N_p = 2(2/N_f - b)/(2/N_f)^2$

$N_p = N_f(1 - b \cdot N_f/2)$

Derivation of ◆:

$N_p = N_f(1 - b \cdot N_f/2)$ ◆

$b = 2(1 - \text{root}(1 - T_f))/N_f$ ◆

$b \cdot N_f/2 = 1 - \text{root}(1 - T_f)$

$N_p = N_f(1 - (1 - \text{root}(1 - T_f)))$

$N_p = N_f \cdot \text{root}(1 - T_f)$

Derivation of ◆:

$PIL = 1 - T_f$ (def)

$N_p = N_f \cdot \text{root}(1 - T_f)$ ◆

$N_p = N_f \cdot \text{root}(PIL)$

Derivation of ◆:

$DPI_0 = x_0 \cdot 2 \cdot 100/d$

$x_0/h = (l - d + x_0)/(L \cdot h)$

$x_0 = (l - d)/(L - 1$

$DPI_0 = (l - d) \cdot 200/(d \cdot (L - 1))$

$DPI_0 = 200 \cdot (l/d - 1)/(L - 1)$

$GSI = d/l$

$L = FSI/GSI$ ◆

$DPI_0 = 200 \cdot (1/GSI - 1)/(FSI/GSI - 1)$

$DPI_0 = 200 \cdot GSI(1/GSI - 1)/(FSI - GSI)$

$DPI_0 = 200 \cdot (1 - GSI)/(FSI - GSI)$

Derivation of ◆:

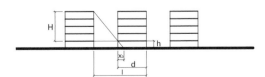

$x_0/h_n=(l-d)/H$

$x_0=h_n(l-d)/H$

$DPI_0=x_0 \cdot 2 \cdot 100/d$

$DPI_0=200 \cdot h_n(l-d)/(d \cdot H)$

$DPI_0=200 \cdot h_n(l/d-1)/H$

$DPI_0=200 \cdot h_n(1/GSI-1)/H$

Derivation of ◆:

$DF_e=50 \cdot (\cos\alpha_{e1}+\cos\alpha_{e2})$

$\alpha_{e1}=\alpha_{e2}$

$\cos\alpha_{e1}=\cos\alpha_{e2}=\cos\alpha_e$

$DF_e=50 \cdot (\cos\alpha_{e1}+\cos\alpha_{e2})$

$DF_e=50 \cdot (\cos\alpha_e+\cos\alpha_e)$

$DF_e=100 \cdot \cos\alpha_e$

Derivation of ◆:

$\tan\alpha_e=2h \cdot L/(l-d)$

$\tan\alpha_e=2h \cdot L/(d(l/d-1))$

$\tan_e=(2h/d)(FSI/GSI)/(1/GSI-1)$

$\tan\alpha_e=(2h/d) \cdot (FSI/(1-GSI))$

$\tan\alpha_e=2h/(d \cdot OSR)$

Derivation of ◆:

$OSR_f=(1-GSI_f)/FSI_f$ ◆

$GSI_f=B/A_f$ (def)

$FSI_f=F/A_f$ (def)

$OSR_f=(1-B/A_f)/(F/A_f)$

$OSR_f=(A_f-B)/F$

$A_f=F \cdot OSR_f+B$

$OSR_i=(1-GSI_i)/FSI_i$ ◆

$GSI_i=B/\sum A_i$ (def)

$FSI_i=F/\sum A_i$ (def)

$OSR_i=(1-B/\sum A_i)/(F/\sum A_i)$

$OSR_i=(\sum A_i-B)/F$

$\sum A_i=F \cdot OSR_i+B$

$\Delta OSR=(A_f-\sum A_i)/F$ (def)

$\Delta OSR=((F \cdot OSR_f+B)-(F \cdot OSR_i+B))/F$

$\Delta OSR=(F \cdot OSR_f+B-F \cdot OSR_i-B))/F$

$\Delta OSR=OSR_f-OSR_i$

Derivation of ◆:

Connectivity Ratio = c/A_f (def) where

c = amount of crossing per hectare

Every square in a grid has 4 corners with each

¼ of a crossing. In a grid of n squares:

$c=n \cdot 4 \cdot 1/4$

$A_f=n \cdot w^2$

$w=2/N_f$ ◆

Connectivity Ratio = $(n \cdot 4 \cdot 1/4)/(n \cdot w^2)$

Connectivity Ratio = $1/w^2$

Connectivity Ratio = $N_f^2/4$

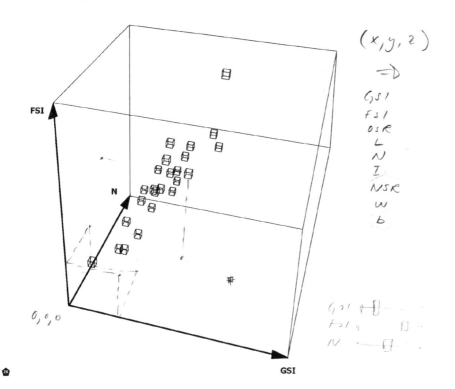

FSI

(x, y, z)

$\Rightarrow$

GSI

FSI

OSR

L

N

I

NSR

W

b

N

0,0,0

GSI

Spacematrix. The FSI on the z-axis gives an indication of the intensity in an area and the GSI on the x-axis reflects its compactness. The N on the y-axis provides us with information concerning the area's network.

REPRESENTATION OF DENSITY

SPACEMATRIX

To be able to simultaneously assess the three main indicators FSI, GSI and N, a three-dimensional diagram has been constructed, the Space-matrix: FSI on the z-axis expresses the built intensity of a certain area, GSI on the x-axis is an indicator of the compactness of the built environment, and N on the y-axis describes the network density, and is as such an indicator of size of the urban layout. ● For every selection of an urban landscape, all entities of its composition can be positioned in the Space-matrix. The position of a district, for instance, is composed of a cluster of fabrics, which are composed of a series of islands, and so on. All the necessary information of the derived indicators described above is present through the position of all parts (absolute and relative). This means that an area can be represented by many mediators, such as maps, photos or text, but also through its density fingerprint, expressed as a series of positions in the Spacematrix. This spatial DNA of an area offers much data (absolute and relative) to analyse and make explicit certain spatial properties of the area. These can serve as input for the understanding of and speculation on other, non-spatial properties.

SPACEMATE AND NETWORK PROPERTIES

Separate projections of the Spacematrix are in the present context necessary due to limitations in data management and representation (and thus communication) of the results. The ones that have proven productive

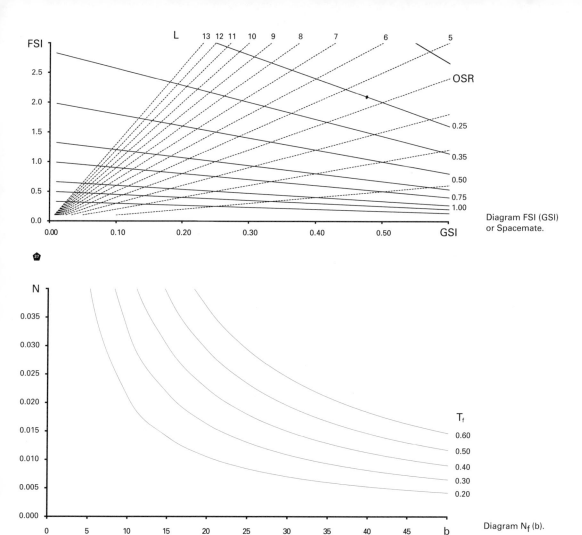

Diagram FSI (GSI)
or Spacemate.

Diagram N$_f$ (b).

are FSI (GSI) and FSI (N). The projection FSI (GSI) in the Spacematrix, the Spacemate, is shown in ☉. Here FSI on the y-axis gives an indication of the built intensity in an area and GSI on the x-axis reflects the coverage, or compactness, of the development. The OSR and L are gradients that fan out over the diagram. OSR describes the spaciousness (or pressure on the non-built space), and L represents the average number of storeys.

The projection FSI (N) is used to describe the parking performance of different urban environments (Chapter 5). Again, FSI shows on the y-axis, but here N on the x-axis gives an indication of the density of the network in the area. Gradients can be constructed here that indicate the pressure (in terms of floor space) on the network.

Based on ☉, another diagram can be constructed with network density (N$_f$), profile width (b) and tare space (T$_f$) as shown in ☉. The N$_f$ on the y-axis denotes the network density of the urban layout, and b on the x-axis the profile width of the streets. The tare space as a percentage of

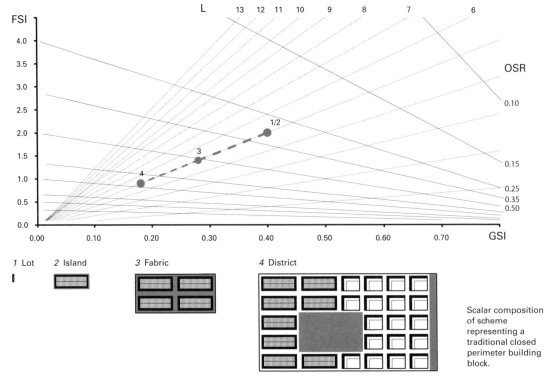

1 Lot   2 Island   3 Fabric   4 District

Scalar composition of scheme representing a traditional closed perimeter building block.

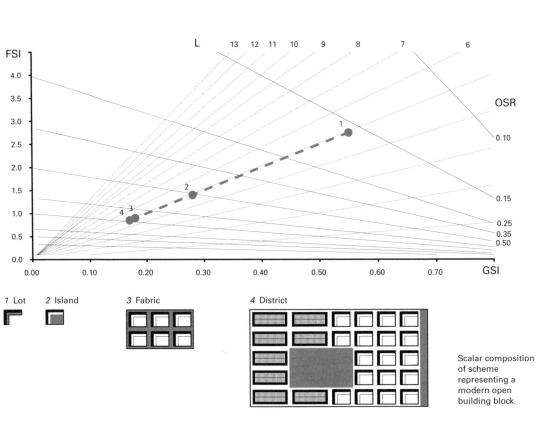

1 Lot   2 Island   3 Fabric   4 District

Scalar composition of scheme representing a modern open building block.

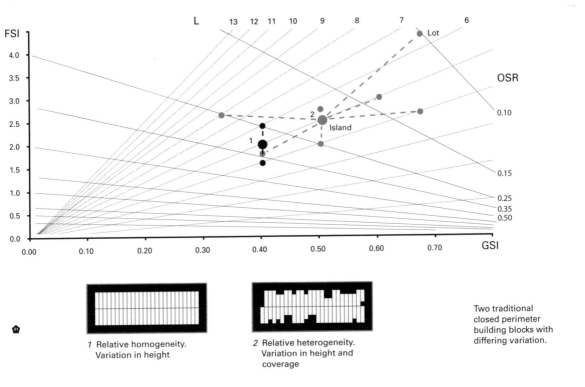

1 Relative homogeneity.
Variation in height

2 Relative heterogeneity.
Variation in height and
coverage

Two traditional
closed perimeter
building blocks with
differing variation.

public space in a fabric is shown as gradients in the diagram. With two
known indicators the third can be derived from the diagram.

$$T = 1 - \left(1 - \frac{b \cdot N_f}{2}\right)^2$$

$$PIL = \left(1 - \frac{b \cdot N_f}{2}\right)^2$$

SCALE AND VARIATION

Two aspects of the urban landscape that can be gauged with the help of
the Spacematrix are scale and homogeneity. The multivariable density of
the different aggregations – building, lot, island, fabric and district – convey not only absolute values of the different aggregations, but also the
relative values in the form of tare. A fabric composed of a certain amount
of islands will be positioned at a position closer to the origin of the diagram (lower GSI and FSI) than the average of the islands. ⊕ ⊕ The (relative)
distance between the two describes the amount of tare present as network in the fabric. In fabrics composed of high-density islands and
scarce public network (narrow alleys and large blocks), the resulting fabric will have a position relatively close to that of the islands. In a case
where islands are surrounded by a vast space of (modern) infrastructure,

Grachtengordel

De Pijp

Two examples:
Grachtengordel and
De Pijp.

the positions will be further apart. In the first example little tare is added to the islands as in the second a large amount is added. This is true at all levels of scale.

Besides the scalar composition that can be gauged through the Spacematrix (and the Spacemate), the amount of homogeneity versus heterogeneity of the aggregations can be represented. Every aggregation can be represented both as an average of its components and with specific values for every single component that form the aggregation. The average is the density value of a certain level of scale, the specific values of the components form a larger or smaller cluster around this centre of gravity. In the case of pure repetition, and thus absolute homogeneity, the positions of every component and the average coincide. The heterogeneity of an area is represented by the size of the spread, or cluster, of components. The character of the spread can of course differ in pattern, from a single deviation from a large bulk of relative homogeneity, to a symmetrical and balanced spread of the components. ◉

The complete data picture can thus be said to form the DNA, or spatial fingerprint, of a specific area. A fabric will in the Spacematrix be characterized both by the average values determining the positions of the different scale levels (district, fabric, island, lot and building), and by the size of the spread of the individual components. Some of the indicators are directly present through positions in the Spacematrix. Examples of these are GSI, FSI, N, L, OSR and w. Others achieve their value through the relative values of the different levels of scale. Examples of these are tare and profile width (T and b).

DENSITY CALCULATIONS OF FOUR EXAMPLES
To illustrate the differentiating potential of Spacematrix, we can use four of the samples from Amsterdam discussed earlier: Grachtengordel, De Pijp, Betondorp and Zuidwest Kwadrant.◉ ◉ ◉

Betondorp

Zuidwest Kwadrant (Osdorp).

Two examples:
Betondorp and
Zuidwestkwadrant.
(Osdorp).

GRACHTENGORDEL AND DE PIJP

The Grachtengordel (1613) and De Pijp (1875) are both examples of fabrics with traditional building blocks composed of many individual lots. In the case of the Grachtengordel, these lots were developed individually, while in De Pijp building developers sought to pack as many dwelling units as possible into relatively small blocks. The Grachtengordel was developed as an extension of the medieval city, which, due to the economic growth at the end of the sixteenth century, had become overcrowded. The urban fabric is characterized by an orthogonal and rational layout of streets, canals and blocks and is not based on the underlying landscape or the adjacent older fabric. De Pijp, on the other hand, was shaped by the existing landscape. This resulted in a smaller grain, and because of speculation, a lack of canals or other costly elements. Despite the similarities in building type, the network patterns are rather different in terms of size: measurement of the islands and the width of the street profile differ significantly.

The residential density in Grachtengordel is 65 dwellings per hectare and in De Pijp 165 dwellings per hectare.[78] This confirms the conclusion that dwelling density has a weak relation to building type. The Spacemate density (FSI and GSI) of the Grachtengordel and De Pijp is, however, fairly similar. Both have an FSI_f of approximately 2.0 and, with almost 50 per cent of the fabric built upon, a GSI_f of 0.50. At the scale of the island the values are similar as well.[79] As the built densities (FSI and GSI) are similar at the scale of the fabric and the island, the tare space is the same in both cases: approximately 35 per cent of the fabric is used for access streets. In the case of the Grachtengordel, this public (tare) space is concentrated in a few wide streets (including canals). In De Pijp the tare space is evenly distributed over the fabric, resulting in a lot of narrow streets. This difference becomes clear when network densities and profile widths are compared. In the Grachtengordel N is 0.012 and b

78
Based on statistics from O+S, Amsterdam. Available online at www.os.amsterdam.nl (2007).

79
FSI_i=3.00 and GSI_i=0.74 for Grachtengordel and FSI_i=2.84 and GSI_i=0.75 for De Pijp.

is 32 m, while in De Pijp N is twice as high and b more narrow (0.023 and 18 m respectively).[80] Both morphological similarities and differences can thus be expressed using the three indicators FSI, GSI and N.

BETONDORP AND ZUIDWEST KWADRANT

Betondorp was developed in the early 1920s when Amsterdam was struggling with a housing shortage. The dwelling density of this low-rise development is similar to the Grachtengordel, with 70 dwellings per hectare. The Spacemate density, however, is much lower: the FSI_f is 0.58 and thus almost a fourth of the FSI_f in the Grachtengordel and De Pijp. In Zuidwest Kwadrant in Osdorp, the closed (perimeter) blocks of the inner city have been transformed into half-open blocks that allow light, air and green space to penetrate the islands and the buildings. The dwelling density of 50 dwellings per hectare is lower than in Betondorp. The FSI_f is, however, higher: 0.75. As both areas, Betondorp and Zuidwest Kwadrant, are rather monofunctional (housing), this can only be explained by the difference in dwelling size. The coverage (GSI) in Betondorp is 0.30 while in Zuidwest Kwadrant only 0.15, leaving large amounts of non-built space. The lower coverage in Zuidwest Kwadrant is compensated for by the higher buildings that create a higher FSI than in Betondorp. Again, the multivariable approach is valuable when discussing urban form. When looking at network density, it is interesting to note that Betondorp and De Pijp have similar values, indicating that the grain of the urban layout is similar in both cases. Betondorp, however, has narrower streets (11 m). The Grachtengordel and Zuidwest Kwadrant both have larger islands and wider streets. Although the building types are different here, the street patterns show structural similarities in terms of mesh size and street width.

In the following chapter, the Spacematrix method and its definitions are used to investigate the correlation between density and urban form. With the use of empirical material (empirical research) and mathematical analysis (explorative research) we show that this multivariable approach can be used to define urban types in terms of density.

80
The mesh size of the two samples is 164 m in the Grachtengordel and 87 m in De Pijp.

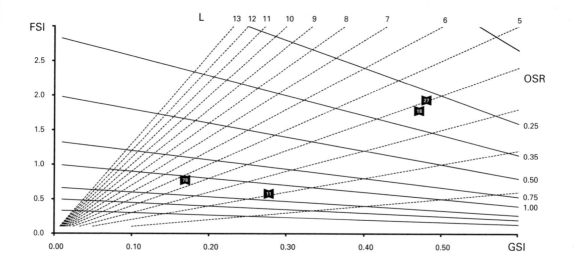

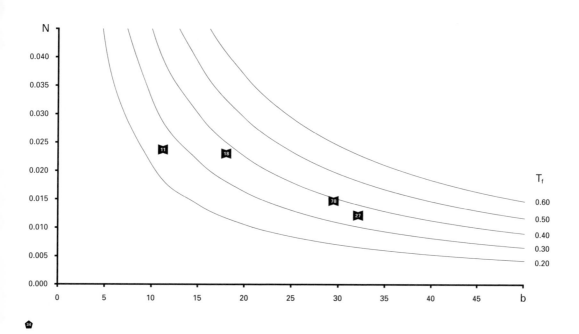

Four examples in the two diagrams: FSI (GSI) or Spacemate and N_f (b).

■
SAMPLES FROM THE NETHERLANDS,
GERMANY (BERLIN) AND SPAIN (BARCELONA)

WWW.SPACECALCULATOR.NL

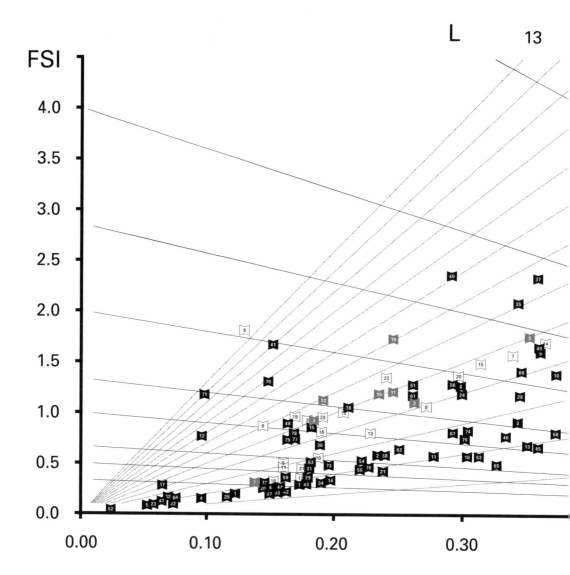

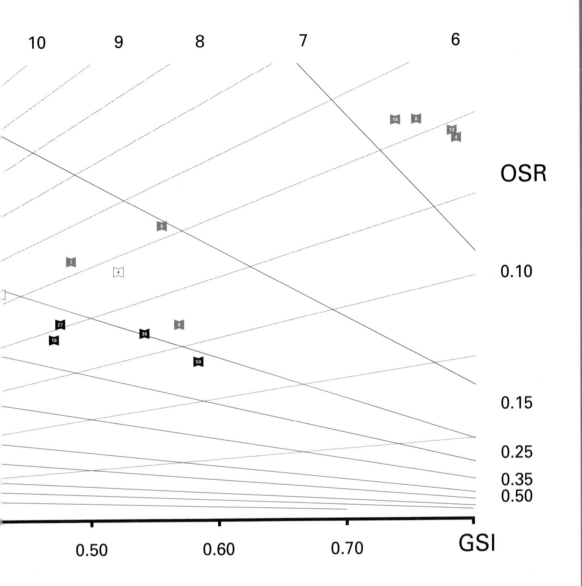

10   9   8   7   6

OSR

0.10

0.15

0.25

0.35
0.50

0.50   0.60   0.70   GSI

◼ The Netherlands

▢ Germany (Berlin)

◼ Spain (Barcelona)

◨1 ACHTERBOS

De Ronde Venen

	ISLAND		FABRIC
A	15.7 ha	A	16.4 ha
FSI	0.21	FSI	0.20
GSI	0.13	GSI	0.12
OSR	4.25	OSR	4.45
L	1.60	L	1.60
		N	0.005 /m
		w	385 m
		b	8 m
		T	4 %

◨2 AMSTELDORP 1

Amsterdam

	ISLAND		FABRIC
A	2.1 ha	A	3.2 ha
FSI	0.88	FSI	0.59
GSI	0.35	GSI	0.23
OSR	0.74	OSR	1.30
L	2.50	L	2.50
		N	0.033 /m
		w	60 m
		b	11 m
		T	33 %

◨3 AMSTELDORP 2

Amsterdam

	ISLAND		FABRIC
A	3.5 ha	A	5.0 ha
FSI	1.33	FSI	0.92
GSI	0.50	GSI	0.34
OSR	0.38	OSR	0.72
L	2.66	L	2.66
		N	0.026 /m
		w	76 m
		b	13 m
		T	31 %

◀ ANLOO

Aa en Hunze

ISLAND		FABRIC	
A	15.7 ha	A	18.4 ha
FSI	0.18	FSI	0.16
GSI	0.11	GSI	0.10
OSR	4.86	OSR	5.81
L	1.62	L	1.62
		N	0.013 /m
		w	158 m
		b	12 m
		T	15 %

☐ ARNIMPLATZ

Berlin

ISLAND		FABRIC	
A	5.7 ha	A	8.1 ha
FSI	2.97	FSI	2.09
GSI	0.57	GSI	0.40
OSR	0.15	OSR	0.29
L	5.23	L	5.23
		N	0.010 /m
		w	198 m
		b	32 m
		T	30 %

◼ BALLOO

Aa en Hunze

ISLAND		FABRIC	
A	22.1 ha	A	24.2 ha
FSI	0.09	FSI	0.08
GSI	0.06	GSI	0.05
OSR	10.7	OSR	11.8
L	1.51	L	1.51
		N	0.007 /m
		w	275 m
		b	12 m
		T	9 %

▮₁ BARCELONETA

Barcelona

ISLAND		FABRIC	
A	1.0 ha	A	2.0 ha
FSI	5.12	FSI	2.55
GSI	0.97	GSI	0.48
OSR	0.01	OSR	0.20
L	5.27	L	5.27
		N	0.070 /m
		w	28 m
		b	8 m
		T	50 %

▮₆ BERGEN 1

Bergen

ISLAND		FABRIC	
A	5.1 ha	A	6.9 ha
FSI	0.37	FSI	0.27
GSI	0.20	GSI	0.15
OSR	2.13	OSR	3.11
L	1.84	L	1.84
		N	0.019 /m
		w	106 m
		b	15 m
		T	27 %

▮₇ BERGEN 2

Bergen

ISLAND		FABRIC	
A	4.0 ha	A	5.0 ha
FSI	0.39	FSI	0.31
GSI	0.22	GSI	0.18
OSR	2.03	OSR	2.68
L	1.75	L	1.75
		N	0.017 /m
		w	119 m
		b	13 m
		T	20 %

⬛8 BERLAGE PLAN ZUID 1

Amsterdam

ISLAND	FABRIC
A 7.7 ha	**A** 14.5 ha
FSI 2.41	**FSI** 1.28
GSI 0.56	**GSI** 0.30
OSR 0.18	**OSR** 0.55
L 4.27	**L** 4.27
	N 0.017 /m
	w 117 m
	b 32 m
	T 47 %

⬛9 BERLAGE PLAN ZUID 2

Amsterdam

ISLAND	FABRIC
A 5.6 ha	**A** 10.4 ha
FSI 2.99	**FSI** 1.61
GSI 0.67	**GSI** 0.36
OSR 0.11	**OSR** 0.40
L 4.44	**L** 4.44
	N 0.022 /m
	w 91 m
	b 24 m
	T 46 %

⬛10 BERLAGE PLAN ZUID 3

Amsterdam

ISLAND	FABRIC
A 4.3 ha	**A** 7.2 ha
FSI 2.33	**FSI** 1.39
GSI 0.63	**GSI** 0.37
OSR 0.16	**OSR** 0.45
L 3.71	**L** 3.71
	N 0.021 /m
	w 95 m
	b 22 m
	T 41 %

² BESOS

Barcelona

ISLAND		FABRIC	
A	7.2 ha	A	9.7 ha
FSI	1.48	FSI	1.11
GSI	0.35	GSI	0.26
OSR	0.44	OSR	0.67
L	4.21	L	4.21
		N	0.011 /m
		w	174 m
		b	24 m
		T	25 %

¹¹ BETONDORP

Amsterdam

ISLAND		FABRIC	
A	8.8 ha	A	11.7 ha
FSI	0.77	FSI	0.58
GSI	0.37	GSI	0.28
OSR	0.82	OSR	1.24
L	2.09	L	2.09
		N	0.024 /m
		w	84 m
		b	11 m
		T	25 %

¹² BIJLMER OUD

Amsterdam

ISLAND		FABRIC	
A	30.8 ha	A	33.4 ha
FSI	0.83	FSI	0.76
GSI	0.10	GSI	0.10
OSR	1.08	OSR	1.18
L	7.92	L	7.92
		N	0.004 /m
		w	546 m
		b	22 m
		T	8 %

🏴13 BLOKZIJL

Steenwijk

ISLAND		FABRIC	
A	4.1 ha	A	5.4 ha
FSI	0.90	FSI	0.69
GSI	0.46	GSI	0.35
OSR	0.60	OSR	0.94
L	1.95	L	1.95
		N	0.036 /m
		w	55 m
		b	7 m
		T	24 %

🏴3 BORRELL I SOLIER

Barcelona

ISLAND		FABRIC	
A	1.4 ha	A	1.9 ha
FSI	1.21	FSI	0.90
GSI	0.24	GSI	0.18
OSR	0.63	OSR	0.91
L	4.96	L	4.96
		N	0.016 /m
		w	122 m
		b	16 m
		T	25 %

🏴14 BORSELE

Borsele

ISLAND		FABRIC	
A	4.7 ha	A	5.3 ha
FSI	0.38	FSI	0.34
GSI	0.22	GSI	0.20
OSR	2.03	OSR	2.37
L	1.71	L	1.71
		N	0.015 /m
		w	130 m
		b	8 m
		T	12 %

15 BUURT NEGEN

Amsterdam

	ISLAND		FABRIC	
A	2.1 ha	A	3.3 ha	
FSI	1.35	FSI	0.86	
GSI	0.29	GSI	0.18	
OSR	0.53	OSR	0.95	
L	4.71	L	4.71	
		N	0.027 /m	
		w	73 m	
		b	15 m	
		T	37 %	

---

2 CHAMISSOPLATZ

Berlin

	ISLAND		FABRIC	
A	3.3 ha	A	4.7 ha	
FSI	3.21	FSI	2.24	
GSI	0.62	GSI	0.43	
OSR	0.12	OSR	0.26	
L	5.22	L	5.22	
		N	0.017 /m	
		w	120 m	
		b	20 m	
		T	30 %	

---

4 CIUTAT VELLA

Barcelona

	ISLAND		FABRIC	
A	2.0 ha	A	2.3 ha	
FSI	4.33	FSI	3.75	
GSI	0.91	GSI	0.79	
OSR	0.02	OSR	0.06	
L	4.77	L	4.77	
		N	0.030 /m	
		w	66 m	
		b	5 m	
		T	13 %	

16 COLIJNSPLAAT

Noord-Beveland

ISLAND		FABRIC	
A	3.9 ha	A	5.0 ha
FSI	0.74	FSI	0.58
GSI	0.39	GSI	0.30
OSR	0.81	OSR	1.21
L	1.89	L	1.89
		N	0.022 /m
		w	89 m
		b	11 m
		T	23 %

5 CONGRES

Barcelona

ISLAND		FABRIC	
A	3.5 ha	A	5.8 ha
FSI	2.88	FSI	1.76
GSI	0.58	GSI	0.35
OSR	0.15	OSR	0.37
L	4.99	L	4.99
		N	0.020 /m
		w	99 m
		b	22 m
		T	39 %

17 DE BERG ZUID

Amersfoort

ISLAND		FABRIC	
A	9.2 ha	A	10.7 ha
FSI	0.33	FSI	0.28
GSI	0.08	GSI	0.07
OSR	2.78	OSR	3.28
L	4.34	L	4.34
		N	0.011 /m
		w	183 m
		b	14 m
		T	14 %

18 DE PIJP

Amsterdam

ISLAND		FABRIC	
A	3.3 ha	A	5.2 ha
FSI	2.84	FSI	1.78
GSI	0.75	GSI	0.47
OSR	0.09	OSR	0.30
L	3.79	L	3.79
		N	0.023 /m
		w	87 m
		b	18 m
		T	37 %

19 DE VESTE

Helmond

ISLAND		FABRIC	
A	1.0 ha	A	1.4 ha
FSI	1.59	FSI	1.16
GSI	0.53	GSI	0.39
OSR	0.30	OSR	0.53
L	3.00	L	3.00
		N	0.025 /m
		w	81 m
		b	12 m
		T	27 %

20 DOUVE WEIEN

Heerlen

ISLAND		FABRIC	
A	5.2 ha	A	6.2 ha
FSI	0.33	FSI	0.27
GSI	0.18	GSI	0.15
OSR	2.53	OSR	3.16
L	1.85	L	1.85
		N	0.015 /m
		w	131 m
		b	12 m
		T	17 %

21 DREISCHOR

Schouwen-Duiveland

ISLAND	FABRIC
A 3.9 ha	A 4.8 ha
FSI 0.53	FSI 0.43
GSI 0.29	GSI 0.24
OSR 1.33	OSR 1.77
L 1.81	L 1.81
	N 0.029 /m
	w 69 m
	b 7 m
	T 19 %

22 DWARSGRACHT

Steenwijkerland

ISLAND	FABRIC
A 11.7 ha	A 12.5 ha
FSI 0.13	FSI 0.12
GSI 0.08	GSI 0.07
OSR 7.10	OSR 7.60
L 1.70	L 1.70
	N 0.004 /m
	w 550 m
	b 17 m
	T 6 %

6 EIXAMPLE

Barcelona

ISLAND	FABRIC
A 12.1 ha	A 18.8 ha
FSI 4.50	FSI 2.89
GSI 0.86	GSI 0.56
OSR 0.03	OSR 0.15
L 5.20	L 5.20
	N 0.014 /m
	w 144 m
	b 29 m
	T 36 %

23 EMMER-ERFSCHEIDENVEEN

Emmen

	ISLAND		FABRIC
A	8.9 ha	A	10.4 ha
FSI	0.12	FSI	0.10
GSI	0.07	GSI	0.06
OSR	8.07	OSR	9.61
L	1.64	L	1.64
		N	0.007 /m
		w	302 m
		b	24 m
		T	15 %

24 FEYENOORD

Rotterdam

	ISLAND		FABRIC
A	2.4 ha	A	4.1 ha
FSI	2.07	FSI	1.19
GSI	0.52	GSI	0.30
OSR	0.23	OSR	0.59
L	3.98	L	3.98
		N	0.023 /m
		w	88 m
		b	21 m
		T	42 %

7 FINESTRELLES

Barcelona

	ISLAND		FABRIC
A	12.3 ha	A	15.7 ha
FSI	0.39	FSI	0.31
GSI	0.18	GSI	0.14
OSR	2.10	OSR	2.80
L	2.24	L	2.24
		N	0.014 /m
		w	147 m
		b	17 m
		T	22 %

25 GEES

Coevorden

	ISLAND		FABRIC	
A	2.9 ha	A	3.5 ha	
FSI	0.20	FSI	0.17	
GSI	0.14	GSI	0.12	
OSR	4.26	OSR	5.24	
L	1.45	L	1.45	
		N	0.020 /m	
		w	98 m	
		b	8 m	
		T	16 %	

26 GOEDEREEDE

Goedereede

	ISLAND		FABRIC	
A	2.4 ha	A	2.9 ha	
FSI	1.04	FSI	0.86	
GSI	0.51	GSI	0.42	
OSR	0.48	OSR	0.68	
L	2.06	L	2.06	
		N	0.032 /m	
		w	62 m	
		b	6 m	
		T	17 %	

8 GOTIC

Barcelona

	ISLAND		FABRIC	
A	6.0 ha	A	7.2 ha	
FSI	4.80	FSI	3.95	
GSI	0.92	GSI	0.76	
OSR	0.02	OSR	0.06	
L	5.23	L	5.23	
		N	0.022 /m	
		w	91 m	
		b	8 m	
		T	18 %	

27 GRACHTENGORDEL

Amsterdam

ISLAND		FABRIC	
A	7.1 ha	A	11.0 ha
FSI	3.00	FSI	1.94
GSI	0.73	GSI	0.48
OSR	0.09	OSR	0.27
L	4.08	L	4.08
		N	0.012 /m
		w	164 m
		b	32 m
		T	35 %

1 GRACIA

Barcelona

ISLAND		FABRIC	
A	3.0 ha	A	3.8 ha
FSI	2.47	FSI	1.92
GSI	0.73	GSI	0.57
OSR	0.11	OSR	0.22
L	3.38	L	3.38
		N	0.025 /m
		w	80 m
		b	9 m
		T	22 %

3 GRAZER DAMM

Berlin

ISLAND		FABRIC	
A	8.7 ha	A	11.7 ha
FSI	1.21	FSI	0.90
GSI	0.24	GSI	0.18
OSR	0.62	OSR	0.91
L	5.00	L	5.00
		N	0.012 /m
		w	165 m
		b	23 m
		T	25 %

4 HACKESCHE HÖFE

Berlin

	ISLAND		FABRIC
A	3.9 ha	A	4.5 ha
FSI	2.84	FSI	2.45
GSI	0.60	GSI	0.52
OSR	0.14	OSR	0.20
L	4.70	L	4.70
		N	0.011 /m
		w	181 m
		b	13 m
		T	13 %

---

28 HEEMRAADSSINGEL

Rotterdam

	ISLAND		FABRIC
A	6.9 ha	A	11.5 ha
FSI	1.98	FSI	1.18
GSI	0.58	GSI	0.35
OSR	0.21	OSR	0.55
L	3.42	L	3.42
		N	0.017 /m
		w	116 m
		b	26 m
		T	40 %

---

29 HEVEADORP

Doorwerth

	ISLAND		FABRIC
A	10.1 ha	A	12.2 ha
FSI	0.44	FSI	0.37
GSI	0.22	GSI	0.18
OSR	1.76	OSR	2.24
L	2.04	L	2.04
		N	0.020 /m
		w	102 m
		b	9 m
		T	18 %

⬛³⁰ HOLENDRECHT 1

Amsterdam

ISLAND		FABRIC	
A	11.8 ha	A	21.9 ha
FSI	1.27	FSI	0.69
GSI	0.36	GSI	0.19
OSR	0.51	OSR	1.18
L	3.57	L	3.57
		N	0.013 /m
		w	152 m
		b	40 m
		T	46 %

⬛³¹ HOLENDRECHT 2

Amsterdam

ISLAND		FABRIC	
A	2.0 ha	A	4.1 ha
FSI	0.92	FSI	0.45
GSI	0.37	GSI	0.18
OSR	0.69	OSR	1.82
L	2.50	L	2.50
		N	0.019 /m
		w	103 m
		b	31 m
		T	51 %

⬛³² HOOG SOEREN

Apeldoorn

ISLAND		FABRIC	
A	7.4 ha	A	8.1 ha
FSI	0.14	FSI	0.13
GSI	0.08	GSI	0.07
OSR	6.39	OSR	7.06
L	1.88	L	1.88
		N	0.014 /m
		w	140 m
		b	6 m
		T	9 %

5 HUFEISENSIEDLUNG

Berlin

	ISLAND		FABRIC	
A	16.8 ha	A	20.7 ha
FSI	0.59	FSI	0.48
GSI	0.20	GSI	0.16
OSR	1.37	OSR	1.76
L	2.98	L	2.98
		N	0.014 /m
		w	147 m
		b	15 m
		T	19 %

33 HUISDUINEN

Den Helder

	ISLAND		FABRIC	
A	1.6 ha	A	2.0 ha
FSI	0.33	FSI	0.27
GSI	0.19	GSI	0.15
OSR	2.41	OSR	3.20
L	1.75	L	1.75
		N	0.031 /m
		w	64 m
		b	7 m
		T	21 %

34 IJLST

Wymbritseradeel

	ISLAND		FABRIC	
A	6.1 ha	A	7.5 ha
FSI	0.39	FSI	0.31
GSI	0.23	GSI	0.19
OSR	1.99	OSR	2.59
L	1.65	L	1.65
		N	0.008 /m
		w	259 m
		b	26 m
		T	19 %

35 JAVA ISLAND

Amsterdam

ISLAND		FABRIC	
A	4.7 ha	A	6.2 ha
FSI	2.72	FSI	2.09
GSI	0.45	GSI	0.34
OSR	0.20	OSR	0.31
L	6.08	L	6.08
		N	0.014 /m
		w	140 m
		b	17 m
		T	23 %

36 JORDAAN

Amsterdam

ISLAND		FABRIC	
A	4.7 ha	A	6.5 ha
FSI	2.54	FSI	1.84
GSI	0.75	GSI	0.54
OSR	0.10	OSR	0.25
L	3.40	L	3.40
		N	0.021 /m
		w	96 m
		b	14 m
		T	28 %

6 KARL-MARX-ALLEE II

Berlin

ISLAND		FABRIC	
A	9.9 ha	A	14.5 ha
FSI	1.28	FSI	0.87
GSI	0.21	GSI	0.14
OSR	0.62	OSR	0.98
L	6.03	L	6.03
		N	0.011 /m
		w	186 m
		b	32 m
		T	32 %

⬚ KLAUSENERPLATZ

Berlin

ISLAND		FABRIC	
A	4.3 ha	A	5.9 ha
FSI	2.14	FSI	1.57
GSI	0.46	GSI	0.34
OSR	0.25	OSR	0.42
L	4.63	L	4.63
		N	0.012 /m
		w	165 m
		b	24 m
		T	27 %

37 KNSM ISLAND

Amsterdam

ISLAND		FABRIC	
A	3.3 ha	A	5.8 ha
FSI	4.17	FSI	2.34
GSI	0.64	GSI	0.36
OSR	0.09	OSR	0.27
L	6.50	L	6.50
		N	0.024 /m
		w	83 m
		b	21 m
		T	44 %

38 KOLENKIT

Amsterdam

ISLAND		FABRIC	
A	1.8 ha	A	3.5 ha
FSI	2.08	FSI	1.06
GSI	0.42	GSI	0.21
OSR	0.28	OSR	0.75
L	5.00	L	5.00
		N	0.020 /m
		w	102 m
		b	29 m
		T	49 %

39 NOORDERHOF

Amsterdam

ISLAND		FABRIC	
A	2.4 ha	A	3.2 ha
FSI	1.42	FSI	1.03
GSI	0.54	GSI	0.39
OSR	0.33	OSR	0.59
L	2.65	L	2.65
		N	0.025 /m
		w	79 m
		b	12 m
		T	27 %

---

8 LANDSBERGER TOR

Berlin

ISLAND		FABRIC	
A	2.7 ha	A	3.8 ha
FSI	1.52	FSI	1.07
GSI	0.39	GSI	0.27
OSR	0.40	OSR	0.68
L	3.92	L	3.92
		N	0.018 /m
		w	110 m
		b	18 m
		T	30 %

---

40 LANDTONG

Rotterdam

ISLAND		FABRIC	
A	2.8 ha	A	4.5 ha
FSI	3.72	FSI	2.36
GSI	0.46	GSI	0.29
OSR	0.15	OSR	0.30
L	8.10	L	8.10
		N	0.021 /m
		w	96 m
		b	20 m
		T	37 %

41 LANGSWATER

Amsterdam

ISLAND		FABRIC	
A	2.9 ha	A	3.2 ha
FSI	1.86	FSI	1.67
GSI	0.17	GSI	0.15
OSR	0.45	OSR	0.51
L	11.1	L	11.1
		N	0.009 /m
		w	222 m
		b	11 m
		T	10 %

10 MAR BELLA

Barcelona

ISLAND		FABRIC	
A	1.2 ha	A	2.2 ha
FSI	3.11	FSI	1.73
GSI	0.44	GSI	0.25
OSR	0.18	OSR	0.44
L	7.03	L	7.03
		N	0.013 /m
		w	148 m
		b	38 m
		T	44 %

9 MÄRKISCHES VIERTEL

Berlin

ISLAND		FABRIC	
A	16.1 ha	A	17.9 ha
FSI	2.02	FSI	1.81
GSI	0.14	GSI	0.13
OSR	0.42	OSR	0.48
L	14.0	L	14.0
		N	0.005 /m
		w	394 m
		b	21 m
		T	10 %

42 MOLENAARSGRAAF

Graafstroom

ISLAND		FABRIC	
A	9.5 ha	A	11.6 ha
FSI	0.30	FSI	0.25
GSI	0.20	GSI	0.16
OSR	2.67	OSR	3.40
L	1.54	L	1.54
		N	0.010 /m
		w	195 m
		b	18 m
		T	18 %

11 MONTBAU

Barcelona

ISLAND		FABRIC	
A	4.7 ha	A	6.3 ha
FSI	1.63	FSI	1.21
GSI	0.33	GSI	0.25
OSR	0.41	OSR	0.62
L	4.92	L	4.92
		N	0.027 /m
		w	74 m
		b	10 m
		T	26 %

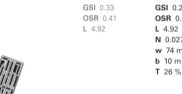

43 NAGELE

Noordoostpolder

ISLAND		FABRIC	
A	3.4 ha	A	4.3 ha
FSI	0.37	FSI	0.30
GSI	0.22	GSI	0.18
OSR	2.07	OSR	2.76
L	1.68	L	1.68
		N	0.016 /m
		w	124 m
		b	13 m
		T	20 %

⚑ NIEHOVE

Groningen

ISLAND		FABRIC	
A	4.7 ha	A	5.7 ha
FSI	0.31	FSI	0.26
GSI	0.19	GSI	0.16
OSR	2.61	OSR	3.30
L	1.64	L	1.64
		N	0.020 /m
		w	102 m
		b	9 m
		T	18 %

⚑ NIEUWPOORT

Liesveld

ISLAND		FABRIC	
A	2.7 ha	A	3.4 ha
FSI	0.84	FSI	0.67
GSI	0.45	GSI	0.36
OSR	0.66	OSR	0.96
L	1.86	L	1.86
		N	0.020 /m
		w	98 m
		b	10 m
		T	20 %

⚑ NIEUW SLOTEN

Amsterdam

ISLAND		FABRIC	
A	4.3 ha	A	6.9 ha
FSI	1.24	FSI	0.77
GSI	0.54	GSI	0.33
OSR	0.38	OSR	0.86
L	2.31	L	2.31
		N	0.028 /m
		w	70 m
		b	15 m
		T	38 %

47 NIMRODPARK

Hilversum

	ISLAND		FABRIC
A	14.8 ha	A	19.4 ha
FSI	0.16	FSI	0.12
GSI	0.08	GSI	0.06
OSR	5.76	OSR	7.75
L	1.88	L	1.88
		N	0.014 /m
		w	146 m
		b	19 m
		T	24 %

48 NOLENSTRAAT

Amsterdam

	ISLAND		FABRIC
A	2.8 ha	A	3.9 ha
FSI	1.25	FSI	0.89
GSI	0.23	GSI	0.16
OSR	0.62	OSR	0.94
L	5.47	L	5.47
		N	0.019 /m
		w	105 m
		b	16 m
		T	28 %

49 NOORDEREILAND

Rotterdam

	ISLAND		FABRIC
A	2.7 ha	A	5.2 ha
FSI	3.16	FSI	1.65
GSI	0.69	GSI	0.36
OSR	0.10	OSR	0.39
L	4.59	L	4.59
		N	0.027 /m
		w	75 m
		b	21 m
		T	48 %

⑩ ONKEL-TOM-SIEDLUNG 1

Berlin

ISLAND		FABRIC	
A	20.0 ha	A	25.0 ha
FSI	0.70	FSI	0.56
GSI	0.23	GSI	0.19
OSR	1.09	OSR	1.45
L	2.98	L	2.98
		N	0.013 /m
		w	153 m
		b	16 m
		T	20 %

⑪ ONKEL-TOM-SIEDLUNG 2

Berlin

ISLAND		FABRIC	
A	18.3 ha	A	22.8 ha
FSI	0.61	FSI	0.49
GSI	0.20	GSI	0.16
OSR	1.32	OSR	1.72
L	3.04	L	3.04
		N	0.013 /m
		w	154 m
		b	16 m
		T	20 %

⑤⁰ OUDE BOTERINGE

Groningen

ISLAND		FABRIC	
A	3.1 ha	A	4.2 ha
FSI	2.13	FSI	1.56
GSI	0.79	GSI	0.58
OSR	0.10	OSR	0.27
L	2.70	L	2.70
		N	0.030 /m
		w	66 m
		b	10 m
		T	27 %

⏚ PARKSIEDLUNG SPRUCH

Berlin

ISLAND		FABRIC	
A	4.1 ha	A	4.4 ha
FSI	0.86	FSI	0.80
GSI	0.25	GSI	0.23
OSR	0.87	OSR	0.96
L	3.52	L	3.52
		N	0.006 /m
		w	353 m
		b	13 m
		T	7 %

⏚ PEDRALBES

Barcelona

ISLAND		FABRIC	
A	2.3 ha	A	2.8 ha
FSI	1.42	FSI	1.13
GSI	0.24	GSI	0.19
OSR	0.54	OSR	0.71
L	5.92	L	5.92
		N	0.011 /m
		w	174 m
		b	19 m
		T	20 %

⏚ PEPERKLIP

Rotterdam

ISLAND		FABRIC	
A	2.6 ha	A	4.5 ha
FSI	2.20	FSI	1.28
GSI	0.45	GSI	0.26
OSR	0.25	OSR	0.58
L	4.89	L	4.89
		N	0.014
		w	144 m
		b	34 m
		T	42 %

13 RAUCHSTRASSE

Berlin

	ISLAND		FABRIC	
A	1.9 ha	A	2.6 ha	
FSI	1.36	FSI	1.01	
GSI	0.28	GSI	0.21	
OSR	0.53	OSR	0.79	
L	4.87	L	4.87	
		N	0.014 /m	
		w	143 m	
		b	20 m	
		T	26 %	

13 RAVAL

Barcelona

	ISLAND		FABRIC	
A	1.4 ha	A	1.6 ha	
FSI	4.47	FSI	3.83	
GSI	0.91	GSI	0.78	
OSR	0.02	OSR	0.06	
L	4.89	L	4.89	
		N	0.027 /m	
		w	74 m	
		b	6 m	
		T	14 %	

14 RIBERA

Barcelona

	ISLAND		FABRIC	
A	1.2 ha	A	1.5 ha	
FSI	4.88	FSI	3.94	
GSI	0.92	GSI	0.74	
OSR	0.02	OSR	0.07	
L	5.33	L	5.33	
		N	0.057 /m	
		w	35 m	
		b	4 m	
		T	19 %	

⌗14 RIEHMERS HOFGARTEN

Berlin

ISLAND	FABRIC
A 4.3 ha	**A** 6.1 ha
FSI 2.42	**FSI** 1.71
GSI 0.52	**GSI** 0.37
OSR 0.20	**OSR** 0.37
L 4.67	**L** 4.67
	N 0.008 /m
	w 244 m
	b 39 m
	T 29 %

⬛52 ROSENGAARDE

Dalfsen

ISLAND	FABRIC
A 21.6 ha	**A** 22.1 ha
FSI 0.04	**FSI** 0.04
GSI 0.02	**GSI** 0.02
OSR 24.4	**OSR** 24.9
L 1.63	**L** 1.63
	N 0.004 /m
	w 461 m
	b 5 m
	T 2 %

⌗15 RUDESHEIMER PLATZ

Berlin

ISLAND	FABRIC
A 4.8 ha	**A** 6.3 ha
FSI 1.97	**FSI** 1.50
GSI 0.41	**GSI** 0.31
OSR 0.30	**OSR** 0.46
L 4.76	**L** 4.76
	N 0.014 /m
	w 139 m
	b 18 m
	T 24 %

16 SIEMENSSTADT

Berlin

ISLAND		FABRIC	
A	14.1 ha	A	16.5 ha
FSI	0.96	FSI	0.82
GSI	0.22	GSI	0.19
OSR	0.81	OSR	0.99
L	4.30	L	4.30
		N	0.008 /m
		w	254 m
		b	20 m
		T	15 %

53 SLOTEN

Gaasterland-Sloten

ISLAND		FABRIC	
A	3.6 ha	A	5.0 ha
FSI	0.79	FSI	0.57
GSI	0.43	GSI	0.31
OSR	0.73	OSR	1.20
L	1.83	L	1.83
		N	0.033 /m
		w	60 m
		b	9 m
		T	27 %

54 SLOTERMEERLAAN

Amsterdam

ISLAND		FABRIC	
A	2.8 ha	A	4.8 ha
FSI	0.85	FSI	0.50
GSI	0.38	GSI	0.22
OSR	0.74	OSR	1.57
L	2.24	L	2.24
		N	0.038 /m
		w	52 m
		b	12 m
		T	41 %

■ 55 SLOTERMEER NOORD

Amsterdam

ISLAND		FABRIC	
A	3.3 ha	A	4.6 ha
FSI	0.64	FSI	0.46
GSI	0.31	GSI	0.22
OSR	1.09	OSR	1.71
L	2.07	L	2.07
		N	0.030 /m
		w	67 m
		b	10 m
		T	28 %

▨ 17 STAAKEN

Berlin

ISLAND		FABRIC	
A	6.5 ha	A	8.9 ha
FSI	0.44	FSI	0.32
GSI	0.24	GSI	0.17
OSR	1.74	OSR	2.57
L	1.83	L	1.83
		N	0.014 /m
		w	143 m
		b	21 m
		T	27 %

■ 56 STADSTUINEN

Rotterdam

ISLAND		FABRIC	
A	5.8 ha	A	11.0 ha
FSI	2.46	FSI	1.28
GSI	0.57	GSI	0.29
OSR	0.18	OSR	0.55
L	4.35	L	4.35
		N	0.020 /m
		w	101 m
		b	28 m
		T	48 %

57 STAPHORST

Staphorst

ISLAND		FABRIC	
A	19.4 ha	A	20.5 ha
FSI	0.22	FSI	0.21
GSI	0.16	GSI	0.15
OSR	3.83	OSR	4.08
L	1.39	L	1.39
		N	0.005 /m
		w	392 m
		b	11 m
		T	5 %

58 STEVENSWEERT

Maasgouw

ISLAND		FABRIC	
A	3.0 ha	A	4.4 ha
FSI	1.20	FSI	0.80
GSI	0.56	GSI	0.37
OSR	0.37	OSR	0.78
L	2.15	L	2.15
		N	0.038 /m
		w	53 m
		b	10 m
		T	33 %

18 TEMPELHOFER FELD

Berlin

ISLAND		FABRIC	
A	6.9 ha	A	9.0 ha
FSI	0.42	FSI	0.32
GSI	0.20	GSI	0.15
OSR	1.90	OSR	2.62
L	2.12	L	2.12
		N	0.013 /m
		w	151 m
		b	19 m
		T	23 %

⊠19 THERMOMETERSIEDLUNG

Berlin

	ISLAND		FABRIC
A	8.6 ha	A	9.8 ha
FSI	1.09	FSI	0.96
GSI	0.19	GSI	0.17
OSR	0.74	OSR	0.87
L	5.66	L	5.66
		N	0.008 /m
		w	262 m
		b	17 m
		T	12 %

⊠20 TIERGARTEN DREIECK

Berlin

	ISLAND		FABRIC
A	2.9 ha	A	4.9 ha
FSI	2.35	FSI	1.37
GSI	0.51	GSI	0.30
OSR	0.21	OSR	0.51
L	4.63	L	4.63
		N	0.010 /m
		w	210 m
		b	49 m
		T	41 %

59 TROELSTRALAAN

Amsterdam

	ISLAND		FABRIC
A	2.6 ha	A	3.7 ha
FSI	0.50	FSI	0.36
GSI	0.23	GSI	0.16
OSR	1.54	OSR	2.33
L	2.22	L	2.22
		N	0.022 /m
		w	92 m
		b	14 m
		T	28 %

VAILLANTLAAN

The Hague

ISLAND		FABRIC	
A	1.3 ha	A	2.4 ha
FSI	2.60	FSI	1.42
GSI	0.64	GSI	0.35
OSR	0.14	OSR	0.46
L	4.10	L	4.10
		N	0.021 /m
		w	94 m
		b	25 m
		T	46 %

VENSERPOLDER

Amsterdam

ISLAND		FABRIC	
A	7.3 ha	A	12.2 ha
FSI	1.97	FSI	1.17
GSI	0.44	GSI	0.26
OSR	0.28	OSR	0.63
L	4.49	L	4.49
		N	0.016 /m
		w	129 m
		b	29 m
		T	40 %

VIJFHUIZEN

Haarlemmermeer

ISLAND		FABRIC	
A	1.0 ha	A	1.4 ha
FSI	0.86	FSI	0.64
GSI	0.34	GSI	0.25
OSR	0.76	OSR	1.17
L	2.54	L	2.54
		N	0.018 /m
		w	109 m
		b	15 m
		T	26 %

⬛15 VILA OLIMPICA

Barcelona

ISLAND		FABRIC	
A	9.3 ha	A	15.8 ha
FSI	2.02	FSI	1.19
GSI	0.40	GSI	0.23
OSR	0.30	OSR	0.64
L	5.08	L	5.08
		N	0.013 /m
		w	159 m
		b	37 m
		T	41 %

⬛21 GRUNEWALD

Berlin

ISLAND		FABRIC	
A	9.0 ha	A	11.4 ha
FSI	0.57	FSI	0.45
GSI	0.22	GSI	0.18
OSR	1.36	OSR	1.81
L	2.59	L	2.59
		N	0.013 /m
		w	151 m
		b	17 m
		T	21 %

⬛63 VOGELWIJK

The Hague

ISLAND		FABRIC	
A	5.3 ha	A	7.5 ha
FSI	0.71	FSI	0.50
GSI	0.26	GSI	0.18
OSR	1.05	OSR	1.64
L	2.73	L	2.73
		N	0.017 /m
		w	120 m
		b	19 m
		T	30 %

64 VONDELPARK

Amsterdam

	ISLAND		FABRIC	
A	4.5 ha	**A**	7.0 ha	
FSI	2.86	**FSI**	1.84	
GSI	0.62	**GSI**	0.40	
OSR	0.13	**OSR**	0.33	
L	4.61	**L**	4.61	
		N	0.021 /m	
		w	97 m	
		b	19 m	
		T	36 %	

65 VREEWIJK

Rotterdam

	ISLAND		FABRIC	
A	1.7 ha	**A**	2.1 ha	
FSI	0.63	**FSI**	0.50	
GSI	0.42	**GSI**	0.33	
OSR	0.93	**OSR**	1.35	
L	1.52	**L**	1.52	
		N	0.024 /m	
		w	85 m	
		b	10 m	
		T	21 %	

66 WAGENINGEN-HOOG

Wageningen

	ISLAND		FABRIC	
A	12.0 ha	**A**	15.1	
FSI	0.18	**FSI**	0.14	
GSI	0.10	**GSI**	0.08	
OSR	5.12	**OSR**	6.62	
L	1.84	**L**	1.84	
		N	0.015 /m	
		w	138 m	
		b	15 m	
		T	21 %	

22 WASSERSTADT 1

Berlin Spandauersee

ISLAND		FABRIC	
A	3.8 ha	A	5.4 ha
FSI	1.93	FSI	1.35
GSI	0.34	GSI	0.24
OSR	0.34	OSR	0.56
L	5.61	L	5.61
		N	0.020 /m
		w	100 m
		b	16 m
		T	30 %

23 WASSERSTADT 2

Berlin Spandauersee

ISLAND		FABRIC	
A	2.2 ha	A	2.6 ha
FSI	1.16	FSI	0.96
GSI	0.23	GSI	0.19
OSR	0.66	OSR	0.85
L	5.00	L	5.00
		N	0.014 /m
		w	141 m
		b	13 m
		T	18 %

67 WATERGRAAFSMEER 1

Amsterdam

ISLAND		FABRIC	
A	8.8 ha	A	15.7 ha
FSI	1.44	FSI	0.81
GSI	0.52	GSI	0.29
OSR	0.33	OSR	0.87
L	2.77	L	2.77
		N	0.020 /m
		w	99 m
		b	25 m
		T	44 %

68 WATERGRAAFSMEER 2

Amsterdam

ISLAND	
A	4.0 ha
FSI	1.54
GSI	0.63
OSR	0.24
L	2.44

FABRIC	
A	10.4 ha
FSI	0.59
GSI	0.24
OSR	1.30
L	2.44
N	0.021 /m
w	96 m
b	37 m
T	62 %

69 WEENA

Rotterdam

ISLAND	
A	3.1 ha
FSI	6.19
GSI	0.72
OSR	0.05
L	8.59

FABRIC	
A	5.7 ha
FSI	3.32
GSI	0.39
OSR	0.18
L	8.59
N	0.017 /m
w	116 m
b	31 m
T	46 %

70 WILDEMANBUURT

Amsterdam

ISLAND	
A	2.6 ha
FSI	1.96
GSI	0.22
OSR	0.40
L	8.78

FABRIC	
A	4.0 ha
FSI	1.30
GSI	0.15
OSR	0.65
L	8.78
N	0.021 /m
w	97 m
b	18 m
T	34 %

71 WILHELIMINAPLEIN

Amsterdam

ISLAND		FABRIC	
A	1.5 ha	A	1.6 ha
FSI	1.33	FSI	1.18
GSI	0.11	GSI	0.10
OSR	0.67	OSR	0.77
L	12.0	L	12.0
		N	0.010 /m
		w	193 m
		b	12 m
		T	12 %

72 WOLVESCHANS 1

Leek

ISLAND		FABRIC	
A	4.7 ha	A	6.1 ha
FSI	0.41	FSI	0.31
GSI	0.19	GSI	0.15
OSR	1.99	OSR	2.72
L	2.15	L	2.15
		N	0.019 /m
		w	108 m
		b	13 m
		T	23 %

73 WOLVESCHANS 2

Leek

ISLAND		FABRIC	
A	2.8 ha	A	3.7 ha
FSI	0.64	FSI	0.48
GSI	0.26	GSI	0.20
OSR	1.17	OSR	1.67
L	2.46	L	2.46
		N	0.023 /m
		w	87 m
		b	11 m
		T	24 %

YPENBURG 1

The Hague

ISLAND	FABRIC
A 2.0 ha	**A** 2.6 ha
FSI 1.07	**FSI** 0.83
GSI 0.39	**GSI** 0.30
OSR 0.56	**OSR** 0.84
L 2.72	**L** 2.72
	N 0.013 /m
	w 158 m
	b 19 m
	T 23 %

YPENBURG 2

The Hague

ISLAND	FABRIC
A 2.6 ha	**A** 3.6 ha
FSI 1.06	**FSI** 0.74
GSI 0.43	**GSI** 0.30
OSR 0.54	**OSR** 0.94
L 2.46	**L** 2.46
	N 0.020 /m
	w 101 m
	b 16 m
	T 30 %

YPENBURG 3

The Hague

ISLAND	FABRIC
A 4.5 ha	**A** 4.9 ha
FSI 0.54	**FSI** 0.49
GSI 0.25	**GSI** 0.23
OSR 1.40	**OSR** 1.59
L 2.15	**L** 2.15
	N 0.017 /m
	w 118 m
	b 6 m
	T 9 %

77 ZUIDWEST KWADRANT 1

Amsterdam

ISLAND		FABRIC	
A	4.0 ha	A	6.9 ha
FSI	1.28	FSI	0.75
GSI	0.29	GSI	0.17
OSR	0.56	OSR	1.11
L	4.47	L	4.47
		N	0.017
		w	120 m
		b	28 m
		T	41 %

78 ZUIDWEST KWADRANT 2

Amsterdam

ISLAND		FABRIC	
A	4.9 ha	A	8.0 ha
FSI	1.28	FSI	0.78
GSI	0.28	GSI	0.17
OSR	0.57	OSR	1.06
L	4.62	L	4.62
		N	0.015 /m
		w	136 m
		b	30 m
		T	39 %

79 ZUIDWEST KWADRANT 3

Amsterdam

ISLAND		FABRIC	
A	4.0 ha	A	6.9 ha
FSI	1.27	FSI	0.75
GSI	0.29	GSI	0.17
OSR	0.56	OSR	1.12
L	4.47	L	4.47
		N	0.023 /m
		w	88 m
		b	21 m
		T	41 %

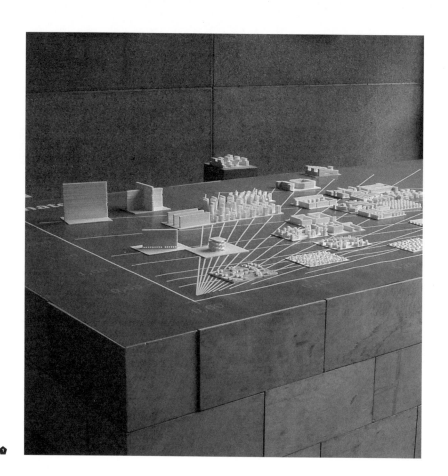

Exhibition
'Dwelling on
Density', Delft
University of
Technology, Faculty
of Architecture,
2004.

4
DENSITY AND URBAN FORM

In this chapter we will use the definition of density as developed in the previous chapter to establish a plausible relationship between urban form and density. Our assumption is that urban density exercises limitations that to a significant degree determine the conditions for urban form. These limitations develop in the context of constraints. Some are geometrical and physical, others are individual (preferences, biography and talents of the designers), or collective (professional doctrines) and many are societal (rules, laws, levels of material wealth and acceptable standards).

The multivariable approach to define density suggested in the previous chapter, in combination with the constraints present at a certain place and moment in time, exert specific limitations on the potential possibilities for urban form. This occurs to such an extent that it is possible to predict the urban fabric types that are most likely to occur under given density conditions.[1]

Some important critical questions, however, need to be posed before defining urban fabric types. These questions include: Is it possible, in the event of hybridization (the melting away of types) to define formal types? And are not the frequently used traditional types too image oriented and activity based? The solution could be to opt for purely performance-oriented urban types. We propose to construct a description of urban fabrics based purely on density in which formal characteristics could then also be viewed as a performance. To get there we aim to demonstrate that density can assume a leading role in describing urban fabric types. A number of formal types will be examined to provide a context for developing our arguments.

This chapter starts with an introduction to the two methods that have been used to investigate the relationship between urban form and density. These methods are exploratory and empirical research. Later, these methods will be used to discuss *network types* based on the relationship between network density and certain aspects of urban form, and on the other hand to define *building types* based on the relationship between built density and built form. The combination of the two enables us to define *urban fabric types* and link different performances, such as parking, daylight access and urbanity to urban density, issues which will be discussed in Chapter 5.

RESEARCH METHOD

The relationship between density and form has a different character depending on which side of this relationship is being examined. *Prescribing* density is a situation in which the designer is forced to design to given density conditions so that density is first formulated and form subsequently emerges. This describes the way the density concept has at times been used in practice. Building codes and schemes for the garden city at the beginning of the twentieth century are examples of this. The opposite is true with the use of density when *describing* a specific part of the urban landscape. The form already exists and density is a descriptive

1
An urban (or architectural) type is a summary (concept) of urban (or architectural) designs with common characteristics (Jong, T. de and H. Engel, 'Typological Research', in: T.M. de Jong and D.J.M. van der Voordt (eds.), *Ways to Study and Research Urban, Architectural and Technical Design* (Delft: DUP Science, 2002), 103–106, 103). These can be formal or functional: organic form types (tree, flower), geometric form types (pyramid, cube), function type (railway station, shopping centre).

outcome. The analysis and diagnosis of the congested city by the *Society for improving the condition of the labouring classes*, discussed in Chapter 2, are examples of such a descriptive use.

When prescribing density the point of departure is specific (density) and the outcome is open (built form). This is less the case if a range of densities, prescribed as a limited space in the Spacematrix (or a limited surface in the Spacemate), is used. The most specific density is characterized by one position in the diagram, but how open is the outcome? This is an important question. How much variation in built form is possible under specific density conditions? This of course depends on what is viewed as variation and on the extent to which it is discernible. When each bay window is seen as a variation, an unlimited number of options are present within each density condition. Information that is too detailed distracts from the primal structural properties that are of importance, particularly in the early stages of urban planning. On the other hand, if the resolution is not sharp enough we risk losing important spatial information and ending up with statistics. However, wrong selections do not exist, and it is merely a question of levels of resolution and their usefulness. If the hypothesis holds, prescribing density in the context of existing constraints imposes sufficient limitations on the resulting composition of urban layouts that fabric types can be differentiated.

When density is applied to describe (map, represent) a part of the urban landscape, we begin with a specific instance of built form (empirical or virtual) to arrive through the use of accepted definitions at an abstract and specific representation. If there is a significant correlation between density and form, then one would expect to find regularities and clusters through which types can be defined. When using the concept of density to describe (part of) the urban landscape one has to remember that density always works with averages. This means that individual variations of the entities that are analysed will be lost when presenting the average. This is less of a problem when the entities are similar. The problem becomes more serious when there is a great variety between them. Any concept describing objects and phenomena around us runs this risk.

A car trip is illustrative of the tension between reality and representation, diversity and average. If the speed of a car trip is recorded one has to choose the relevant time frame. If the journey is not divided into shorter trajectories one ends up with one figure, representing the average speed for the whole trip. On the other end of the representation spectrum, such a detailed account of every change of speed throughout the whole journey is provided that it is merely reconstructed, with all its particular incidents. The key is to define the appropriate level of detail for the analysis that will be applied. In the case of describing density, spread and variation can be described at a variety of scales as was proposed in Chapter 3.

EXPLORATIVE AND EMPIRICAL RESEARCH

Two methods have been used in this chapter to investigate the relation between density and urban form and to examine the way results can be prescriptively and descriptively used: explorative and empirical research.

Explorative research is based on deductive reasoning and concerns the geometrical and physical properties of built form and the influences that invented and real world constraints can have on built form. The use of formulas to capture basic geometries not only allows one to make comparisons between different cases, the use of variables also means that the trends are made visible. How does the measurement of network influence the relationship between private and public land? How does concentration of building mass compare to a peripheral distribution? What are the characteristics of such different distributions, under the same density conditions, in terms of building depth, exposure and accessibility? The method resembles the work of Leslie Martin and Lionel March, L.H.J. Angenot and A. Heimans discussed in earlier chapters, and allows great freedom to define, combine and experiment, but is very rigid in its deductive principles of logical reasoning and mathematical precision.

Empirical research can be described as inductive. Here empirical data is used that by definition has been affected by all kinds of real-world constraints. The samples used have specific, historical, geographical, cultural, political and ideological contexts. Changing uses, new standards of acceptance or economic pressure might have led to ex- or intensification. The existence of unique examples is dependent upon there being some interpretative system covering generic concepts. A plethora of individual objects and events constitute the urban realm which is communicated using general concepts. Our empirical research uses typomorphological research undertaken by M.R.G. Conzen and SAR, but places less emphasis on the detail and contingent properties of the urban landscape. We believe that generic knowledge can be found in the empirical evidence and that at times too much emphasis has been placed on details that detract from key issues.

Applying both of these research methods can tell us about the influence of design and planning conventions and the changes that they have gone through. A historical, geographical and cultural interpretation of the empirical material can help to explain what constraints have been important to the structuring of the urban environment, and the changes in their influence over time. Chapter 2 to a large extent illustrates this interpretation of empirical material. Empirical research yields a historical view of individual and collective knowledge accumulated in the urban landscape. Explorative research is able to look beyond the constraints of the present and explore new insights on possible urban forms.

SELECTION CRITERIA OF SAMPLES
The (empirical) samples used in this research have been selected on the basis of representing a broad spectrum of morphological patterns. These have been influenced by a variety of constraints, regulations and preferences from one period to the next (historical spread) and from one country to the other (geographical spread). To limit the number of samples and constraints, we have focused primarily on samples dominated by housing.

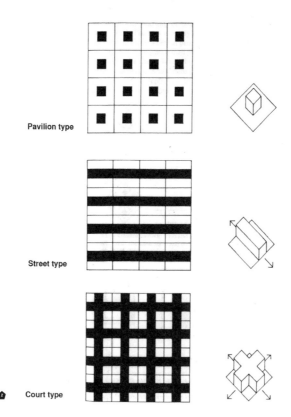

Pavilion type

Street type

⬠ Court type

'Pavilion', 'street' and 'court' types (Martin and March 1972: 36).

Three criteria for the selection of samples include:
1 Samples should represent different *morphological patterns*;
2 All *historical periods* should be represented, from medieval to present-day urban environments;
3 Samples should have a certain *geographical and cultural spread*, allowing an investigation into structural similarities and possible differences.

Morphological Spread

To represent a broad range of morphological patterns different building types have to be represented. For this purpose we use the three basic types described by Martin and March: the 'pavilion', the 'street', and the 'court' type.[2] ⬠ These are also called *point* (or nucleated) development, *strip* (or linear) development and *block* (or peripheral) development, descriptions that will be used in the following discussion. All three can be found in low-rise, mid-rise and high-rise solutions. This results in a matrix of nine morphological categories.

A wide range of network patterns should also be included. Here we rely on the work of Manuel de Solà-Morales and Amis Siksna. De Solà-Morales states that the measurements of the urban pattern are decisive for the relationship between general form (street pattern) and built content.[3] Siksna distinguishes three categories of block (or island) size in his study of the robustness of the city layout of North American and Australian city centres.[4] They are small blocks (less than 10,000 m²), medium sized blocks

2
Martin, L., L. March et al., 'Speculations', in: L. Martin and L. March, (eds.), *Urban Space and Structures* (Cambridge: Cambridge University Press, 1972), 28–54, 35–37.
3
Solà-Morales, M. de, 'Towards a Definition: Analysis of Urban Growth in the Nineteenth Century', *Lotus*, 19 June 1978, 28–36.
4
Siksna, A., 'The Effects of Block Size and Form in North American and Australian City Centres', *Urban Morphology* 1 (1997), 19–33, 20.

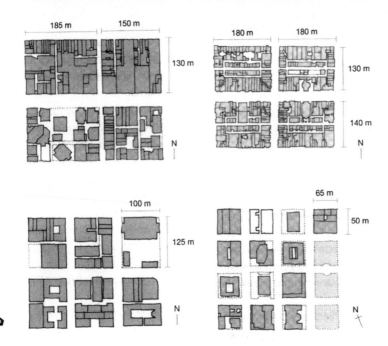

Compositional variations of the 'grid' (Marshall 2005: 224).

(between 10,000 and 20,000 m²) and large blocks (larger than 20,000 m²). In general, European blocks are smaller and therefore a category of blocks with a size of less than 5,000 m² has been added to Siksna's categories to match the European context.

Historical Spread

In Chapter 2, four periods in Dutch history of urban developments were described. The selection of empirical samples is based on the same periods. A subdivision of the third period (1900–1970) has been made to achieve a better representation of this turbulent period, characterized by huge contrasts in doctrines and resulting urban form. The first part covers the period just after the introduction of the *Housing Act* in 1901 and can be characterized as a period in which plans no longer were merely pragmatic land-division plans for the development of the commodity housing. Social, political and aesthetical ideals started to play a greater role. The second part begins after the Second World War with the rebuilding of the Netherlands. It is defined by a state-coordinated realization of the modern ideals expressed in the 1930s by CIAM.

The described periods, covering the time from 1350 to 2000, generally coincide with a cross section of Dutch cities. It includes their first extension areas from the inner city during the seventeenth century, the nineteenth-century expansions and the twentieth-century move to the outskirts. The selection of empirical samples is aimed at having a wide representation of different morphological and network patterns within each historical period, but this was not always possible for the simple reason that not all patterns were present in each period.

Geographical and Cultural Spread

To allow us to compare Dutch practice with other geographical and cultural points of reference, we have compared Amsterdam to two other European cities: Berlin in Germany and Barcelona in Spain. In the first period until around 1850, both Amsterdam and Berlin experienced periods of intensification, city growth and stagnation. Barcelona, on the other hand, did not grow in terms of territory until 1860 when the construction of an expansion plan was started. At that time Barcelona had one of the highest population densities in Europe, double that of Amsterdam: 850 inhabitants per hectare in Barcelona compared to 400 inhabitants per hectare in Amsterdam.[5] During the second period (1815–1900) all three cities expanded to accommodate population growth and the rural-urban migration that fuelled increasing industrialization. Around this period, the layout of Berlin developed under very liberal planning policies that encouraged land and building speculation. This resulted in notorious housing conditions in the so called *Mietkasernenstadt*, which acquired the dubious reputation of having the worst living conditions in Europe.[6] The same laissez-faire politics was dominant in Amsterdam, but because the characteristics of land and urban layout were to a large extent influenced by natural factors such as existing ditches, rather small and narrow city blocks were the outcome. The city expansion in the same period in Barcelona was again very different. A detailed survey preceded a master plan by engineer Ildefonso Cerdà that consisted of a street layout with large square blocks. Joan Busquets describes in his book *Barcelona, the Urban Evolution of a Compact City* the outstanding nature of this plan by Cerdà and suggests that Cerdà should be included in the list of 'founders' of modern urban planning along with Reinhard Baumeister, Joseph Stübben and Raymond Unwin.[7]

INTRINSIC PROPERTIES OF THE ISLAND

EXPLORATIVE RESEARCH

Prior to the empirical search for regularities and correlations between Spacematrix density and urban form, some questions should be formulated about the range of possible solutions under certain density conditions. How many possible solutions, or actualizations, can be expected under specific density conditions? And if density can be seen as a condition that limits the amount of possible solutions (internal constraint), what other conditions (external constraints) can be named that further diminish the amount of solutions that are probable to be actualized in the real world under certain density conditions?

As mentioned earlier, it is commonly accepted that there is little to no correlation between density and urban form. This presupposes that under a certain density (prescribed or registered) the building mass can take any form: 'Anything goes.' This misconception, in our opinion, is partly caused by the too rough resolution of existing and commonly used density definitions. Using one variable, such as dwellings per hectare or FSI, relies on a far too blunt instrument to make enough sharp differentiations which can be used to construct types or classes. This means that

5
Busquets, J., *Barcelona, the Urban Evolution of a Compact City* (Rovereto: Nicolodi, 2005), 117. For Amsterdam population density, see Berghauser Pont, M. and P. Haupt, *Space Density and Urban Form* (Delft: 2009), 235–271.
6
Taverne, E., *De wortels van de contemporaine stad*, Reader Architectuur- en Stedenbouwgeschiedenis (Groningen: Rijksuniversiteit Groningen, 2000), 39.

7
Busquets, *Barcelona*, op. cit. (note 5), 122–133.

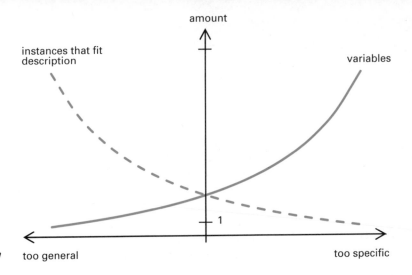

amount

instances that fit description

variables

1

too general

too specific

Tension between (too) general and (too) specific.

too many examples, or instances, fall under one density value (for example 40 dw/ha), and important differences in properties (such as basic urban form) are drowned. At the other extreme of the spectrum, attempts to capture the complexity of reality that are too detailed run into the opposite problem. The huge respect for difference demands an almost endless amount of properties to be registered. In the end, only very few instances fit a singular compound of descriptions, and the amount of classes approaches infinity. Descriptions that are too detailed reproduce a complex reality and leave little space for type constructions and generic conclusions. The balance between the type descriptions and the amount of variables is at stake here. ⬠ One reason that the Spacematrix method is appropriate for the purpose of differentiating between basic urban forms could be that the quantity of indicators used and their content fits nicely with the quantity of commonly used descriptions of urban landscapes. This speculative assumption would turn into a reasonable explanation if the empirical investigation shows significant correlations between this multivariable density and urban form.

To investigate these conditioning aspects of density on the options for urban form, two experiments were set up. First, a series of workshops were organized with students from Delft University of Technology, Masters in Architecture and Urbanism.[8] Many models were produced exemplifying various density conditions.[9] Secondly, combinatorics was used to illustrate the deflation of the space of solutions.

Workshops with Students
The models produced by students during the workshops ranged from transparent (dominated by voids) to compact (dominated by mass), from low-rise to high-rise, and from empty to dense. Without specifying any additional constraints this resulted in a pure geometrical system of forms in which only mass could be distinguished from open space. However, the constraint of the material and individual preferences in all cases limited the formal solutions.

8
In collaboration with professor Rudy Uytenhaak (2004).
9
Unfortunately, on 13 May 2008 the models were destroyed during the fire that hit the Faculty of Architecture in Delft.

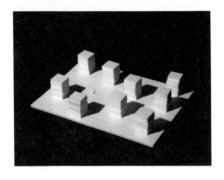
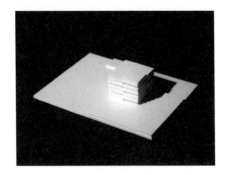
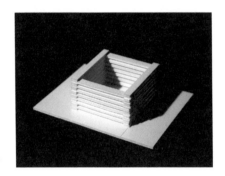
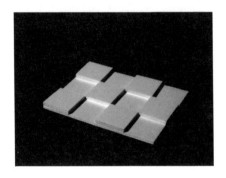

Student models
with identical FSI
of 1.0 (student work
MSc3, Delft
University of
Technology, 2004).

The students were initially asked to design models with FSI 1.0, resulting in spatial solutions ranging from a concentrated tower of ten storeys to an evenly spread-out mass of one storey. ◗ In other words, the FSI was achieved by working between the extremes of concentrating the building mass or dispersing the same amount of mass. The first strategy resulted in a very low coverage, while in the second no open space remained. In a second step, the students produced models based on a given FSI and GSI, in this case 1.0 and 0.2 respectively. The models demonstrate that plans with the same compactness still show considerable variation in building mass configuration. This is mostly due to the scale of individual buildings. ◗ The building mass becomes dominant when using small dimensions as it is spread over the model, particularly if the GSI increases. ◗ The building mass is concentrated, as is the open space, when smaller building units are combined into bigger blocks.

Even with the shrinking of the bandwidth to a smaller interval (for instance from 'FSI between 0.5 and 1.0' to 'FSI between 0.5 and 0.6'), or to a specific value ('FSI of 0.55') *and* with the addition of more indicators, such as GSI, the possible actualizations of designs still seems infinite. Surely, with a hypersensitivity to differences – every different position of a bay window means a unique actualization, for example – the possibilities are indeed infinite. However, few, many, or no bay windows are not relevant here; such variation does not upset the predefined types, and all fall neatly into a category independently of these – for this purpose – minor differences. Still, even with a rougher typological resolution, a huge

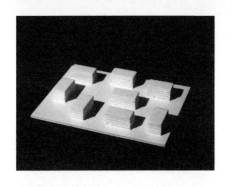
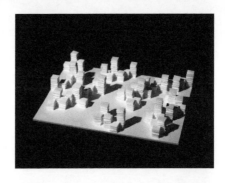
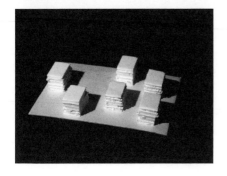
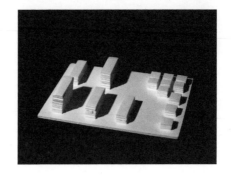

Student models
with identical FSI
of 1.0 and GSI 0.2
(student work
MSc3, Delft
University of
Technology, 2004).

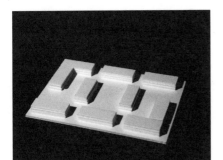
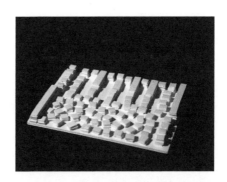

Student models
with identical FSI
of 1.0 and GSI 0.4
(student work
MSc3, Delft
University of
Technology, 2004).

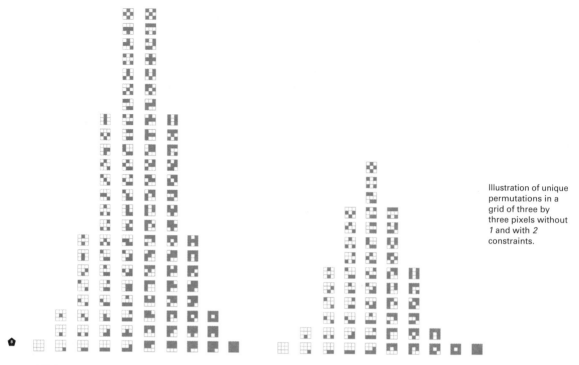

Illustration of unique permutations in a grid of three by three pixels without 1 and with 2 constraints.

1 Unique permutations without constraints.

2 Unique permutations with constraints.

amount of possibilities remains. Theoretically, even if 'not everything goes', an infinite amount of solutions can be actualized. However, the size of the 'space of solutions' is further narrowed by what were earlier termed *external* constraints. The reality of measures and real-world constraints cuts away many theoretically possible solutions. Among other things, physical, economic, social and aesthetical requirements limit the possible solutions under a specific density value or bandwidth. One can compare this to the possible solutions for the amount of buttons on a shirt. Everything from one to 100 buttons would work. However, in most cases we find between five and eight buttons on produced and worn shirts. In the same way, theoretically, a closed perimeter block is possible to design, build and inhabit with a very low density if the building depth is 1 m instead of the 10 to 15 m usually encountered at our latitude. However, the extreme costs and the inconvenience of the plan puts an end to the option before it even gets the chance to be formulated. In reality, the existence of such a case is statistically insignificant, as are many other possibilities on the periphery of that which is possible. The reality of spatial requirements (plan organization, access); urban physics (daylight, ventilation, noise); social organization (size of development unit, property structure, regulations); and preferences and acceptance (privacy, view), just to mention a few, quickly shrink the space of solutions.

As the workshop described above progressed, the students were confronted with external constraints such as minimum and maximum building depths, minimum distances between buildings, degrees of variation, etcetera. A total of more than 100 models were developed that demonstrated a narrowing of (structural) variation as a result of the pre-scribed constraints. What took place during the workshops could be described as the transition from a situation without limitations to a more detailed set of rules spelling out the requirements. The initial, deliberately prescribed, conditions were formulated in terms of FSI and GSI. These con-stituted two basic conditions that limit the primary distribution of building mass. In a world where no other guiding principles would be present these conditions seem to be very open, as the models indeed showed. We could then rightly claim that 'almost anything goes'. In the real sociospatial ma-terial world, however, numerous constraints exist. The workshops showed that imposing some simplified versions of these real-world requirements generated solutions that structurally and formally moved closer to each other in the direction of recognizable urban types.

Combinatorics
Variations in GSI can be used to illustrate the tension between the num-ber of solutions and constraints. The variety of solutions with one GSI value (amount of coverage) can be analysed in an abstract and deductive way through combinatorics. Combinatorics is a branch of pure mathe-matics that studies combinations of objects belonging to a finite set in accordance with certain constraints.[10] It can be used to investigate the number of ways that a specified array of units can be combined. An ex-ample of a problem that can be approached by combinatorics is: In how many different combinations can a deck of 52 distinct playing cards be ordered? The answer is 52! (52 factorial), which is equal to $8.0658*10^{67}$.

To illustrate a situation with somewhat more limited possibilities, we can use a square cut into nine equal parts. In a grid of nine pixels (3*3), each pixel can be black or white, symbolizing mass or void. The amount of possible configurations can be described as $C(n,p)=n!/(p!*(n-p)!)$, where n is the number of possible positions (in this case nine) and p the number of black pixels that are to be distributed. In terms of coverage, GSI can be described as p/n. The grid turns from white to black step by step and at every stage all permutations can be drawn and calculated. The level of resolution and precision defines the number of permuta-tions. For example, a fictive building block of 40 × 40 m, divided into pixels of 20*20m, 10*10m or 5*5m, can have for a coverage of 25 per cent respectively 4, 1,820, and $2,75*10^{10}$ possible layouts. This is known as a combinatoric explosion.

When the first pixel is turned black (GSI=1/9), nine possibilities exist of which only three are unique. A 'unique permutation' means cases that can-not be achieved through mirroring or rotating one of the other permutations. For C(9,1) this means that there are three unique permutations: the black pixel positioned in the centre, the corner and in the middle of one side. Two black pixels can be arranged in 36 mutations, of which 8 are unique, three pixels in 84 mutations of which 16 are unique, etcetera. In ⬯, the left drawing shows the number of unique permutations for every GSI value (or C(n,p)). Maximum variations occur with a coverage of 4/9 and 5/9.[11]

The number of permutations decreases when two constraints are added: maximum depth of the mass (relates to usability and microcli-mate) and adjacency to the outer contour of the grid (accessibility), are

10
Concise Oxford English Dictionary, Eleventh Edition.

11
If we would have used 2 × 2 pixels, 4 × 4, or any even amount, we would have arrived at an optimum where the coverage is 0.5.

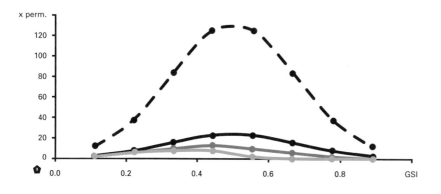

- - ● - - All perm
—●— Unique perm
—●— Access and depth
—●— >= 3-Sided

Comparison
between the
amount of unique
permutations
without any
constraints and
with constraints.

added.  The number of possibilities decreases even more rapidly when more pixels are filled in. In other words, fewer permutations occur with a higher GSI. This means that without any constraints most permutations have a coverage of 0.5. With tighter requirements, however – for instance the requirement that a minimum of three sides are non-built to guarantee privacy, view and daylight – the number of permutations decreases quickly for coverage between 4/9 and 5/9, and is reduced to zero for high coverage.

These experiments show that within the theoretical logic of empty space and mass, most differentiation can be found when 50 per cent of the matrix is white (or void) and the other 50 per cent is black (or mass). Imposed real-world constraints, however, change the trend by decreasing the number of possibilities in general and shift the point for maximum permutations towards layouts with less coverage. Could it be that constraints of the kinds discussed here limit the options to such an extent that we can recognize formal similarities and speak of types? If this is the case the theoretical combinatoric explosion of possibilities might be mitigated by:

1   Intrinsic density conditions (geometrical);
2   External real world constraints;
3   Our conceptual ability to recognize similarities, ignore differences and define types.

Whether there is enough *significant clustering of formal features* to define types with the use of Spacematrix will be discussed later in this chapter when we analyse the empirical material. But based on the experiments described above, it becomes clear that permutations with higher coverage result in more peripheral dispositions, while in the permutations with more open space other possibilities occur. Varying the composition of the mass when a maximum depth is specified is easier when the coverage is low.

The work of the Master students and the combinatorial experiments show that reality (models with constraints) is less diverse than the infinite theoretical possibilities of a specific density might suggest. In the following paragraph the empirical material collected in the Netherlands and abroad will be analysed to examine to what extent there is a correlation between formal similarities (type) and ranges of density in the real world.

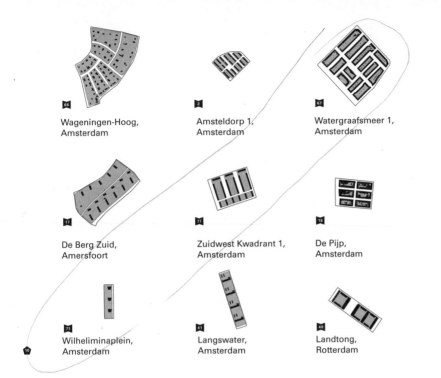

68 Wageningen-Hoog, Amsterdam	2 Amsteldorp 1, Amsterdam	67 Watergraafsmeer 1, Amsterdam
17 De Berg Zuid, Amersfoort	77 Zuidwest Kwadrant 1, Amsterdam	18 De Pijp, Amsterdam
71 Wilheliminaplein, Amsterdam	41 Langswater, Amsterdam	40 Landtong, Rotterdam

Nine archetypical samples (see ⬛ ⬛ for positions in Spacemate and Nf(b)-diagram).

EMPIRICAL RESEARCH

A series of areas in the Netherlands has been analysed in this research to investigate whether formal similarities within certain densities can be found in the real world.[12] For the classification of the samples, the morphological types as described earlier in this chapter have been used: point (or nucleated), block (or peripheral) and strip development, which all can be found in low-rise, mid-rise and high-rise solutions. For the following section, a sample has been chosen as an archetype for each category to illustrate the general type. The values have been calculated for the scale of the island.

As can be seen in the Spacemate, each archetype has its own unique position. ⬛ The low-rise point type is represented by the villas of Wageningen Hoog (⬛ in ⬛ ⬛); Amersfoort ⬛ with mid-rise apartment buildings in green surroundings represents the mid-rise point type; and Koningin Wilhelminaplein ⬛, an area with 12-storey flats, is chosen to represent the high-rise point type. For the strip type, Amsteldorp ⬛, Zuidwest Kwadrant ⬛ and Langswater ⬛, with building heights of respectively two, five and 11 storeys, have been selected. The (perimeter) block types Watergraafsmeer ⬛, De Pijp ⬛ and Landtong ⬛, with two, five, and eight storeys respectively, have the highest building coverage (GSI). The archetypical samples are shown on the following pages. Interesting to note is that Watergraafsmeer, with the lowest FSI among the block types, is, in terms of FSI, comparable to the mid-rise strip type represented by Zuidwest Kwadrant and the high-rise point type, Koningin Wilhelminahof. In terms of FSI, these samples are similar, but in terms of GSI,

12
All samples can be found in ⬛

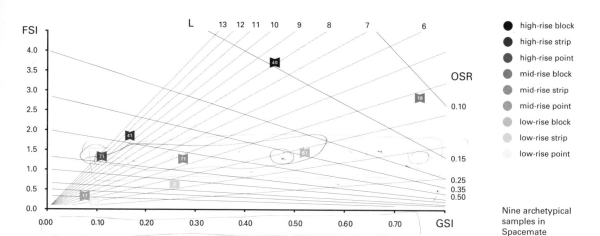

Nine archetypical samples in Spacemate (scale: island). Numbers referring to samples in ⑩.

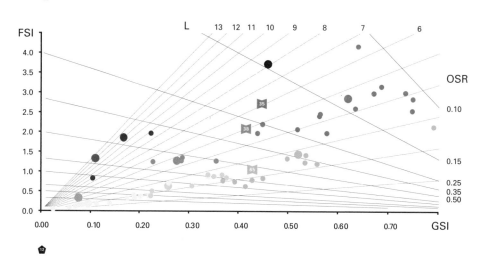

All Dutch samples in Spacemate (scale: island). Numbers referring to samples in ⑩.

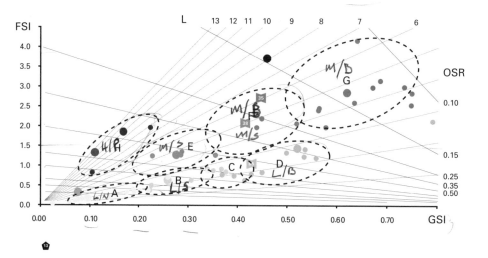

A low-rise point type

B low-rise strip type

C hybrid low-rise strip/block type

D low-rise block type

E mid-rise strip type

F hybrid mid-rise strip/block type

G mid-rise block type

H hybrid high-rise point/strip type

Clusters of building types in Spacemate (scale: island).

high-rise block
high-rise strip
high-rise point
mid-rise block
mid-rise strip
mid-rise point
low-rise block
low-rise strip
low-rise point

Kolenkit,
Amsterdam

Java island,
Amsterdam

Vreewijk,
Rotterdam

Three examples of
'in-between' types
(see ⬟ for position
in Spacemate).

building height and OSR, the differences are great. In other words, building types can be distinguished from one another in terms of density, but
only when a multivariable density concept is used.

In ⬟ all the Dutch samples have been added to the diagram. Although
not all types are equally represented, it is obvious that clusters can be
drawn in the diagram. Within the low-rise samples, point types such as
Wageningen Hoog have a lower GSI and FSI than strip types, such as Amsteldorp, which again have a lower density (GSI and FSI) than the block
types. Mid-rise samples show the same logic although in general the
density is higher. However, although the differences between the clusters are clear, distinctions between one type and another are sometimes
difficult to define. They tend to slowly transcend from one type into another, with all kinds of hybrid forms occurring in between.

Kolenkit (▨ in ⬟ ⬟) represents a good example of a hybrid form. Mor-
phologically speaking it can be defined as strip type but in Spacemate it
is located in close proximity to a cluster of block types. Kolenkit is one of
the first examples in Amsterdam whereby the closed perimeter block
was opened up. It was transformed into an open block by having only the
short ends removed. Two strips of buildings define one island surrounded by streets. In comparison to other strip types in Osdorp with
more space in between, or examples of 'real' strip types with only one
building per island, the density of this sample is higher. In other words
the first is an example of a hybrid type – the open block type – suspended
between the strip and the block type.

Another sample, Java island ▨ in ⬟ ⬟, characterized as a block type,
has a rather low coverage (GSI) when compared to the other block types.
Here, the large size of the inner courts and, therefore, the size of the islands explain the relatively low GSI. It accounts for the deviation from
the core of the block type cluster. The same can be said about the group
of samples situated between the low-rise block type and low-rise strip
type. Some samples in this position have transformed from a more strip-
like type through intensification of the islands towards a block type.
Others have deliberately been designed as a semi-block type with parts
of the perimeter of the block left open (Vreewijk ▨ in ⬟ ⬟).

Based on the empirical material we can conclude that building types
on the scale of islands can be clustered in Spacemate. ⬟ Because not all
types had enough representatives, only six of them are drawn: low-rise
point, strip and block type; mid-rise strip and block type and high-rise
strip type. In addition we found out that each of the clusters close to
their borders are surrounded by hybrid forms. Three 'in-between' types
can be identified in the diagram.

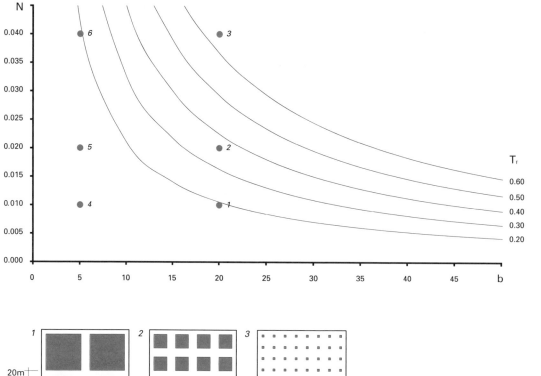

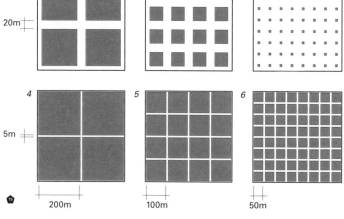

Six schemes with varying network density and profile width, positioned in the $N_f(b)$ diagram.

These vague edges of type clusters, indicating a hybridization of types as was discussed in the beginning of this chapter, also occurs in other positions in the diagram. It could, therefore, be worthwhile, and maybe even necessary, to move towards a purely performance-based description of building types. A Spacematrix description could then replace the more conventional, formal types. This would mean that the above described empirical research serves more as a temporary ladder, necessary to make an argument, but which at a certain point is disposed of. Instead of attaching the conventional professional terminology to the suggested clusters, the position(s) – absolute and relative – in itself works as a description that, combined with performance, can be both productive and purged of associative distractions. It is thus possible to imagine a situation where a multivariable density description supplants the limited traditional concepts used to describe the built environment. Whether or not this is desirable is another question. A both/and approach is probably the most realistic and productive: Spacematrix as a spatial DNA, loaded with information about spatial and other associated properties *and* traditional classifications with commonsense connotations. The advantages of a pure density description are also its weakness as the terminology of the professional language game conveys much meaning that is absent in a more technical, instrumental description.

The results of the explorative research discussed earlier in this chapter (combinatorics and experiments with Master students) match the outcome of the empirical analysis. The expectations created by deductive and geometrical exercises did not suddenly become invalidated by totally unexplained clustering (or lack of it) in the empirical data. In fact the opposite is the case. To date, the multivariable density seems to be highly suited to account for structural differences in urban form. The concept is not too statistical and general, or too detailed and specific. We can conclude that analysis using multivariable density works at the level of the island in conveying structural similarities of building types.

INTRINSIC PROPERTIES OF THE URBAN GROUND PLAN

EXPLORATIVE RESEARCH

To demonstrate the interrelation between some indicators introduced earlier, six schemes of very different nature can be compared. ◉ The first two schemes (1 and 4) represent a small mesh size of 50 m (N=0.04), the second two (2 and 5) have a mesh of 100 m (N=0.02), and the last two (3 and 6) a mesh of 200 m (N=0.01). In combination with a street profile width of 5 and 20 m respectively, the sizes of the islands range from 10 to 190 m. The amount of network space, or fabric tare space, is lowest where a very wide mesh size (large islands) is combined with narrow streets (scheme 3), and highest where a very fine mesh (small islands) and wide streets are present (scheme 4).

N_f, b and T_f are all measurable entities that could quite easily be collected from maps. This, however, demands that there is an existing fabric or a drawn design to study. The relationship between these variables expressed in the ◆ in the previous chapter, and represented in the diagram in ◉, can help monitor the trade-offs of certain combinations to define some fundamental properties of urban form. Analysing with the use of variables instead of unique examples makes it possible to understand the general trends hidden in the relation between network density, street profile and tare space.

The possible combinations of network density and profile width can be determined in the diagram based on, for instance, the assumption that a minimum of 60 per cent of privately issued land (PIL) is required and that subsequently a maximum of 40 per cent is available for network space.[13] This means that the network density may not be higher than approximately 0.015 when combined with a wide profile of 30 m. For a smaller mesh size than this, but with the same profile width (30 m), the amount of private land quickly falls below 60 per cent. On the other hand, with a narrow street profile, for instance 15 m, the critical level defined as 60 per cent private land will be reached only when the network density becomes higher than 0.030.

13
Of all the Amsterdam samples, three quarters have more than 60 per cent privately issued land, and none less than 50 per cent.

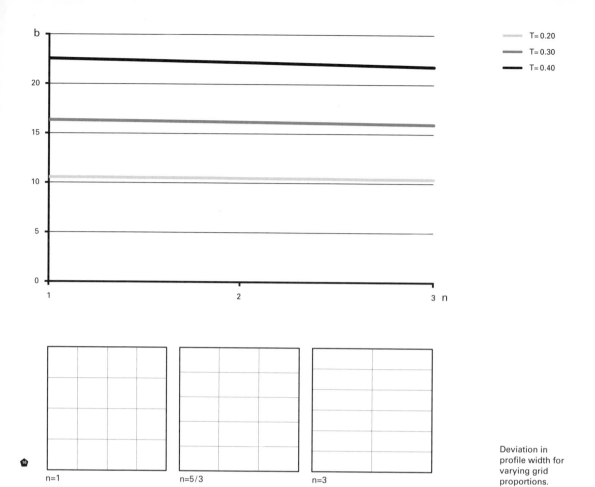

b

	T= 0.20
	T= 0.30
	T= 0.40

n=1   n=5/3   n=3

Deviation in
profile width for
varying grid
proportions.

Up to now the grid has been treated as a symmetrical grid where the islands are conceptualized as squares. Although it might be assumed that this offers sufficient accuracy, considerable deviations from real values might make this analysis rather crude. A comparison between the rectangular grid patterns and the square ones used so far in this section may offer some clues about the extent of the deviation. The proportion of the two directions of a grid can be called n. In a square mesh n=1, and in the rectangular islands the longer side is n times the shorter side. If the ◆ is adapted to this variation in proportions, the deviation of street width can be monitored for different values of n.[14] If the value of N is set at 0.020, the diagram in ◐ shows how the profile width changes for three different tares (0.20, 0.30, and 0.40) when the grid transforms from a square (n=1) to a rectangular one (n=3). The deviation is no more than between 1.4 per cent for n=5/3 and 3.4 per cent for n=3. This can be regarded as negligible for present purposes. Of course, other performances change when squared blocks are transformed into rectangular ones, but the relationship between profile width, tare space and network density remains more or less the same.

14
$T_r(n)=1-(1-b\cdot N_f/(n+1))(1-b\cdot n\cdot N_f/(1+n))$. For further details, see ⬛.

186

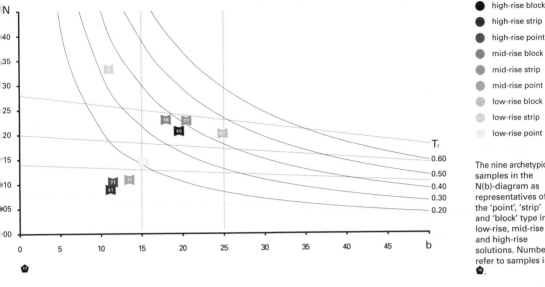

high-rise block
high-rise strip
high-rise point
mid-rise block
mid-rise strip
mid-rise point
low-rise block
low-rise strip
low-rise point

The nine archetypical samples in the N(b)-diagram as representatives of the 'point', 'strip' and 'block' type in low-rise, mid-rise and high-rise solutions. Numbers refer to samples in ⓮.

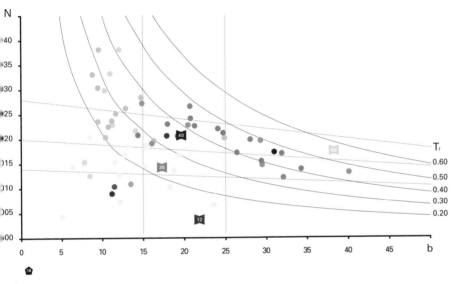

All Dutch samples in the N(b)-diagram. Numbers refer to samples in ⓮.

EMPIRICAL RESEARCH

⓮ shows the $N_f(b)$–diagram, introduced earlier in this chapter, with the nine archetypical samples. (⓮, page 181) To investigate whether regularities can be found within certain network density conditions, all the Dutch samples have been positioned in the diagram. ⓮ The wide representation of network densities (or mesh sizes) can be seen in the spread of the samples along the y-axis ranging between 0.004 and 0.040 or, in terms of meshes, from 50 to 500 m. The most common network densities fall between 0.01 and 0.03, which correspond to a mesh from 65 to 200 m. Based on the block size categories discussed in an earlier paragraph, four zones can be distinguished in the diagram. These can be further divided into three categories of different street widths.

Landtong

Bijlmer (see Figure 18 for positions in Spacemate).

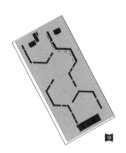

Watergraafsmeer 2

Java island

Four samples with different network properties. (see 🔟 for positions in $N_f(b)$-diagram).

What becomes clearly visible from the diagram with all of the Dutch samples is that the variety in profile widths, represented by the x-axis, is larger when the network density is lower. ☻ Therefore, when a fine-meshed urban plan is drawn, narrow streets are apparently needed to ensure enough private land to make the island usable and the plan feasible. We can compare this to the building depth discussed in the previous paragraph. Buildings of 5 m deep are theoretically possible but not likely as these are less functional and more costly. Of course, solutions with wider streets are theoretically possible but they are not probable as the practical feasibility diminishes as the size of the islands shrink. With larger mesh sizes the streets can be wider and still have reasonably sized islands.

The samples with the finest grain mostly have narrow streets and the islands contain low-rise buildings. Small- and medium-size islands have larger profile widths, ranging from 5 to 40 m. It can be observed that the samples with narrow streets mostly occur in combination with low-rise building types. Wider streets are often accompanied by higher buildings, especially mid-rise strip and block types.

High-rise types seem to show the least dependency on the size of the islands and the width of the streets. However, when taking a closer look at the samples it becomes clear that some high-rise samples are similar to mid-rise samples in terms of network pattern. These samples, such as Landtong ▨ in ☻ ☻ in Rotterdam, have a network density similar to their surroundings and can, from this point of view, be regarded as well-integrated in the urban context. One difference, though, is that instead of four to five storeys, the buildings have more than seven storeys. Samples from downtown New York or Seattle can also be found in these categories. The other high-rise samples with larger-sized network patterns, mostly built in the 1960s, are different. They have their own internal logic in which streets and buildings are disintegrated, in line with ideals of the functionalist city as promoted by CIAM. The Bijlmer ▨ in ☻ ☻ in Amsterdam is a good example in the Netherlands of this kind of urban planning.

Some of the samples seem to contradict the conclusions described above. Watergraafsmeer ▨ in ☻ ☻ in Amsterdam, for example, is the only low-rise block type with relatively wide streets. One reason might be that this area was realized in a period (the 1930s) when public space was regarded as extremely important. Most low-rise samples, however, do not have such a large amount of tare space, probably due to economic constraints. The amount of network tare space per square metre of gross floor space (network ratio, or ΔOSR; we will return to this indicator in the next chapter) in Watergraafsmeer is extremely high and, therefore, quite costly. Another example is Java Island ▨ in ☻ ☻, a mid-rise block type that, in comparison to the other samples within this category, has a rather low network density. Large islands in combination with relatively narrow streets are uncommon in the Netherlands, but, as we will discuss later, more common abroad. It is furthermore interesting to note that in the case of the Dutch samples, building types with higher built densities (mid-rise strip and block types) have more tare space (network) than building types with lower built densities (low-rise point, strip and block types). The higher built density is compensated for by a larger amount of public space.

Based on these findings one can conclude that by defining the density of the network (N), a large amount of building types are still 'suitable'. A higher N is often combined with low-rise types, but this is not always the case. However, by combining building and network densities, the performance of an area, in terms of daylight access, public parking, urbanity, privacy and crowdedness changes radically and as such the combination of the two, building and network density, convey more about the performance of an urban fabric than when they are merely treated in isolation.

URBAN FABRIC TYPES

An urban fabric type can be viewed as consisting of a specific combination of, on the one hand, a network type (defined by N, b, and T) which describes the basic layout of the ground plan and the accompanying series of islands, and on the other hand the building type (defined by FSI, GSI, OSR and L), which describes the infill of the islands.

The amount of network needed to access the islands is incorporated in the density figures on the scale of the urban fabric. The difference between island and fabric density is an indicator of the amount of network space (T_f) needed to access the islands. In order to grasp the consequences of adding network to the islands, the nine archetypes that were discussed earlier are positioned again in the Spacemate, but this time adding the density calculations on the level of the fabric. ❀ The GSI and FSI values on the scale of the fabric are all lower than on the scale of the island because of the added tare space. But the different building types still retain unique positions in the diagram, and, when all other Dutch samples are included, the clusters can again be discerned to represent the different building types. ❀

The scale of the network, however, is not represented through the amount of network tare space. This can only be grasped using N. Two Amsterdam examples with identical built densities and the same network tare space illustrate this. The Grachtengordel is composed of large islands (N=0.012) and wide street profiles, while De Pijp, which has the same built density, has small islands (N=0.023) and narrow streets. Based on one building type, in this case the block type, we can thus arrive at different urban fabric types, because of the different network densities. The position in the three-dimensional Spacematrix model is therefore different. However, to cluster urban fabric types within this model is complex and demands further development of computerized software to manage and analyse data, and to represent the outcome. Therefore we have chosen to use projections here, conveying partial information of the Spacematrix.

The basic spatial properties of an area can be conveyed using all the indicators by which the urban fabric type is characterized. These include intensity (FSI), coverage (GSI) and network density (N), as well as the derived indicators spaciousness (OSR), building height (L) and street width (b). In Chapter 5 these will be used to link urban density to performances other than urban form.

COMPARATIVE RESEARCH

In order to investigate the validity of the clusters defined with the Spacematrix method outside the Netherlands, the Dutch situation – especially Amsterdam – has been compared with Berlin in Germany and Barcelona

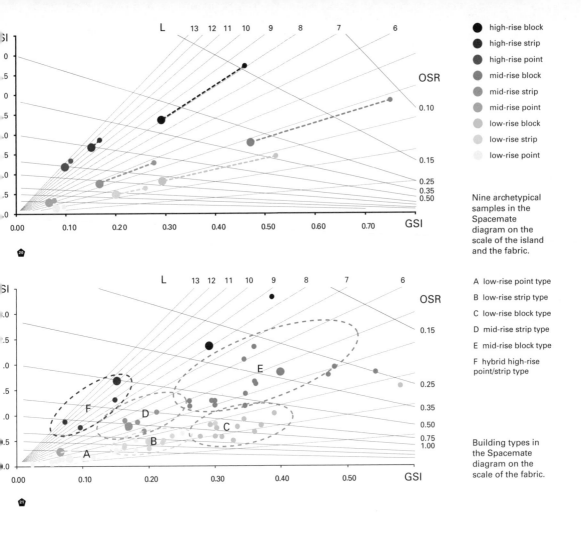

Legend:
- ● high-rise block
- ● high-rise strip
- ● high-rise point
- ● mid-rise block
- ● mid-rise strip
- ● mid-rise point
- ○ low-rise block
- ○ low-rise strip
- ○ low-rise point

Nine archetypical samples in the Spacemate diagram on the scale of the island and the fabric.

A low-rise point type
B low-rise strip type
C low-rise block type
D mid-rise strip type
E mid-rise block type
F hybrid high-rise point/strip type

Building types in the Spacemate diagram on the scale of the fabric.

in Spain. Next to this, some changes in density through history have also been investigated to sketch the influence of state interventions (building ordinances, standards, etcetera) and changing ideologies (Garden City Movement, CIAM, etcetera). A comparison with more European fabrics and fabrics from other continents would certainly be interesting, but is beyond the scope of this research.

AMSTERDAM, BERLIN AND BARCELONA

When comparing the samples from Berlin and Barcelona with those from Amsterdam, one can initially conclude that the clustering of building types remains valid. ⚉ A closer look at the areas developed between the seventeenth and the beginning of the twentieth century – a period in which the mid-rise block type was predominant – shows that the Cerdà grid in Barcelona, Eixample, ▣ ⚉ ⚉ has the highest intensity (FSI$_f$=2.89), followed by the Chamissoplatz ▣ in ⚉ ⚉ in Berlin (FSI$_f$=2.24). Samples from Amsterdam, such as the Jordaan ▣ in ⚉ ⚉ (FSI$_f$=1.84) and De Pijp ▣ in ⚉ ⚉ (FSI$_f$=1.78) have lower building intensities. In the three cities the coverage of the block type is similar, between 0.4 and 0.6. The reason for

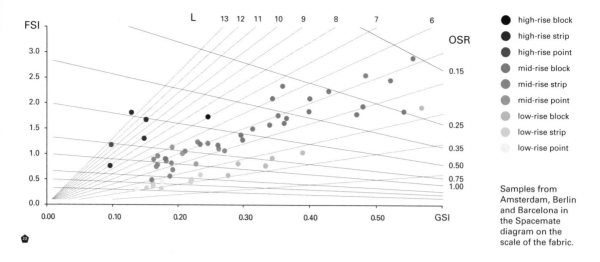

FSI

L   13 12 11   10   9   8   7   6

OSR

Samples from
Amsterdam, Berlin
and Barcelona in
the Spacemate
diagram on the
scale of the fabric.

- high-rise block
- high-rise strip
- high-rise point
- mid-rise block
- mid-rise strip
- mid-rise point
- low-rise block
- low-rise strip
- low-rise point

the difference in built density can thus be found in the height of the buildings, approximately four storeys in Amsterdam, while in Berlin and Barcelona the average building height is five storeys. Berlin's *Mietkasernenstadt* is often described as representing some of the worst housing conditions in Europe. Based on the density figures we can conclude that the reasons for this cannot be found in the physical structure of the *Mietkasernen*. More probably, as was the case in the Jordaan in Amsterdam, simply too many people lived in too little space.

Furthermore, the urban layout of Berlin, compared to that of Amsterdam, in general shows larger islands. All samples from Berlin have network densities of less than 0.020 with a mesh size larger than 100 m. The majority of these samples have a street profile width of 15 to 25 m. The samples are, therefore, all concentrated in two clusters in the N(b) diagram. As a result, all samples have less tare space than the Dutch samples. Although it might seem difficult to intensify such large islands as the access to the buildings becomes problematic (large depth of islands), some of the Berlin samples have different kinds of alleys that enable access to the interior of the islands. The islands are in other words subdivided into smaller sub-islands. This is especially the case in the areas with the highest built intensities. Hackesche Höfe ⌶ in, for example, has a network density of 0.011 (which is comparable to the Grachtengordel) and a street width of 13 m (comparable to that of the Jordaan). A closer examination of the island shows that it has numerous entrances to the buildings in the interior of the island, and four pedestrian routes crossing it. This kind of subdivision is described by Siksna in his comparison between American and Australian city centres.[15] He concludes that the larger blocks (islands) have in the course of history been eroded and split up into smaller units, while the smaller blocks remained intact. The same conclusion can be reached about Berlin, although in this case many blocks of this kind were originally designed with passages.

In 'economic' terms the Berlin samples with less street and more floor space can be described as being more optimized than the Dutch samples. But there are other factors that have contributed to the differences found.

15
Siksna, 'The Effects', op.
cit. (note 4).

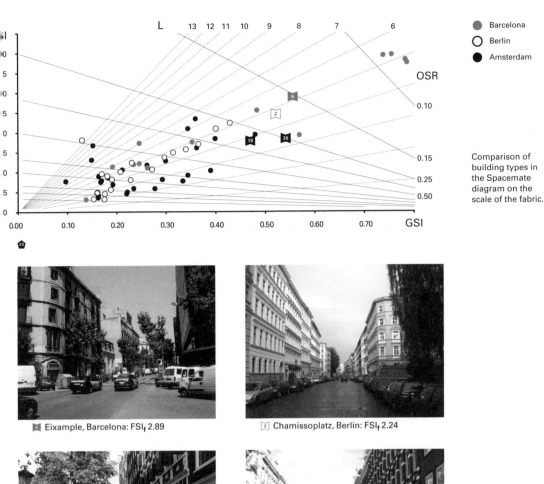

L 13 12 11 10 9 8 7 6

OSR

0.10

0.15
0.25
0.50

GSI

0.00 0.10 0.20 0.30 0.40 0.50 0.60 0.70

● Barcelona
○ Berlin
● Amsterdam

Comparison of building types in the Spacemate diagram on the scale of the fabric.

Eixample, Barcelona: FSI$_f$ 2.89

Chamissoplatz, Berlin: FSI$_f$ 2.24

Jordaan, Amsterdam: FSI$_f$ 1.84

De Pijp, Amsterdam: FSI$_f$ 1.78

Street view of four mid-rise block type samples from Barcelona, Berlin and Amsterdam (see for positions in Spacemate).

The existing pattern of canals and ditches in the Netherlands needed to manage water was often used as a basis for urban development. This water system often had a rather fine mesh size from the outset.

Java island in represents the only sample from Amsterdam that has similar large measures (N and b) to those frequently found in Berlin. The conditions of the site, being an island with a depth of 130 m, also affected this development. It was difficult to project two blocks within the depth of 130 m. Therefore, larger blocks were designed with extra buildings in the interior to arrive at a higher density.

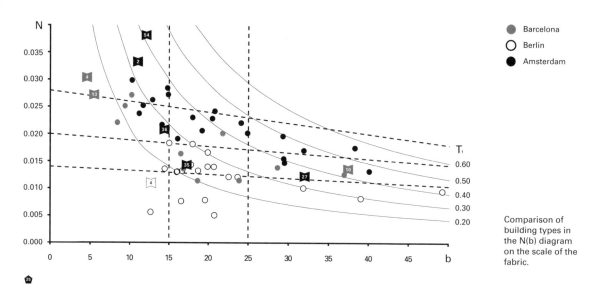

Comparison of building types in the N(b) diagram on the scale of the fabric.

Most of the samples from Barcelona, except for the medieval ones, also show lower network densities than the Dutch samples. As a consequence, the mesh size in general is larger. However, the spread in street profiles is much larger in Barcelona, ranging from Barceloneta ▨ in ⚫ ⚫ with less than 9 m to Mar Bella ▨ in ⚫ ⚫ with 40-m-wide streets. The fine-grained samples in Barcelona, all with narrow streets, are found in the oldest parts of the city such as Raval ▨ in ⚫ ⚫ and Ciutat Vella ▨ in ⚫ ⚫. Such fine-grained urban layouts are present in Amsterdam too, not only in the medieval core but also in areas of a more recent date (Amsteldorp ▨ in ⚫ ⚫ and Slotermeerlaan ▨ in ⚫ ⚫). Part of the dominant doctrine at that time was to realize housing with optimal daylight access. This often resulted in urban layouts whereby streets have entrances only on one of their sides in order to create gardens on the sunniest side. This requires a large amount of network and thus a high network density. With far lower built densities than the examples from Barcelona, however.

THE HISTORICAL DEVELOPMENT OF AMSTERDAM
The initial transition from liberal-competitive capitalism to state-managed capitalism at the turn of the twentieth century brought with it a greater emphasis on public space. This may be one of the reasons that during the latter period the amount of tare space shows a relative increase, mainly caused by wider streets. Although it is often presumed that the modernist plans of the 1950s and 1960s contain large amounts of green space, this is not to be found in the amount of network space on the scale of the urban fabric. However, on the lower scale of the island and the higher scale of the district, the amount of tare space is significantly higher during this period. This is found both in terms of green semi-public space within the islands and large parks in and between fabrics. The period from 1950 to 1970 shows a larger spread, with more extremes in network (tare) space. This might be a result of a greater variation in building types in the developments taking place in this period, ranging from fabrics with high-rise apartments to low-rise row housing developments.

Street view of ten mid-rise block type samples from Berlin, Barcelona and Amsterdam (see 24 for positions in the N(b) diagram).

4
Hackesche Höfe, Berlin: N_f 0.011 and b 12 m

27
Grachtengordel, Amsterdam: N_f 0.012 and b 32 m

36
Jordaan, Amsterdam: N_f 0.021 and b 14 m

35
Java island, Amsterdam: N_f 0.014 and b 17 m

11
Barceloneta, Barcelona: N_f 0.070 and b 8 m

10
Mar Bella, Barcelona: N_f 0.014 and b 37 m

13
Raval, Barcelona: N_f 0.027 and b 6 m

4
Ciutat Vella, Barcelona: N_f 0.030 and b 5 m

2
Amsteldorp, Amsterdam: N_f 0.033 and b 11 m

54
Slotermeerlaan, Amsterdam: N_f 0.030 and b 10 m

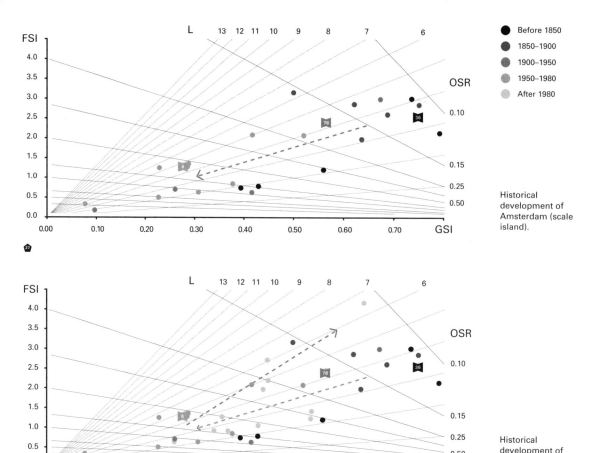

Historical
development of
Amsterdam (scale
island).

Historical
development of
Amsterdam (scale
island).

One can conclude that despite the different circumstances under which urban plans were designed and realized, the three main characteristics of the urban ground plan, network density, street profile and network (tare) space, do not show a significant change of trend.

Coverage on the scale of the islands, however, shows an immense variation throughout history. Until recently, GSI decreased at a somewhat constant pace from a coverage of more than 75 per cent in the seventeenth century to 60 per cent around 1900 and to less than 30 per cent during the modern extensions of the 1960s. ☻ Put another way, in this historical sequence we can identify a slow transition from compact to more spacious building layouts.

The reasons for this development are numerous and complex and have partly been discussed in Chapter 2. Until 1900 urban developments were driven mostly by pragmatic technical and economic forces, resulting in maximized floor space on the one hand, and, on the other, no more open space than absolutely necessary, mostly in the form of infrastructure. The growth of the population, combined with the absence of building regulations and the difficulties in controlling (illegal) constructions, made expansions of houses, small industries and other buildings in the courtyards a fact. This can be seen very clearly in the Jordaan. ⬛ in ⬢ Towards the end of the nineteenth century, the practice of city development was reformed. Public space became more important and through the *Housing Act* (1901) higher standards in terms of daylight access, fresh air and open space were (theoretically) assured. The results only gradually showed up in practice. Amsterdam Zuid ⬛ in ⬢, designed by Berlage and seen as one of the first examples of large-scale publicly generated housing in the Netherlands, shows a decrease in coverage, both at the level of the island and of the fabric.

The increase in public space (wider streets), larger green inner courts and stricter regulations for buildings resulted in a decrease in GSI. The developments after the Second World War, designed and built based on the CIAM doctrines of living and working in green and spacious environments, resulted in a further decline of the GSI. Compared to the Jordaan, the coverage in Zuidwest Kwadrant ⬛ in ⬢ (constructed in the 1960s) was less than a third (0.28 compared to 0.75). Since the 1970s, however, this trend has turned. ⬢ Economic pressure and a preference for more 'lively' urban environments have led to a decrease in the amount of green open space and a rise in building coverage. Still, due to other constraints, such as the demands of modern traffic (influencing street widths and necessary parking space), and acceptable standards for privacy and light access, coverage does not achieve the levels of the nineteenth century and earlier periods.

The development of the building intensity (FSI) through history shows roughly the same trend as the coverage (GSI). However, due to the differences in building height, there is a wider spread of building intensity within each historical period. Any clear trend for decreasing intensities, such as can be found for coverage, is therefore not evident when intensity is examined in isolation. When looking at the position of each sample in the Spacemate, however, a decrease of built intensity before the 1970s can be spotted for both the low-rise and the mid-rise types. Based on these findings one can conclude that the densities of low-rise and mid-rise types, in the Netherlands at least, have decreased both in terms of intensity as well as in terms of coverage. Only the recent samples have higher values, perhaps in response to functionalist doctrines being put aside for ideas on urbanity, and necessitated by a larger demand for economic efficiency.

SCALE AND ABSTRACTION
So far, the scale levels of the island and fabric have been studied and the correlation between density and urban form investigated. This has led to clusterings of building and urban fabric types. The higher aggregations (district, city and region) and the lower components (lot, building and cell) are outside the scope of this research. We can, however, speculate as to which approaches could be used to expand the current research strategy into other levels of scale. On the scales of district, city and region other types could be researched and defined. For these levels of scale, the notions of built form and urban form lose some of their relevance. Density variables become very statistical as much diversity is shred in the averages at those scales. This, however, means little since the properties on those

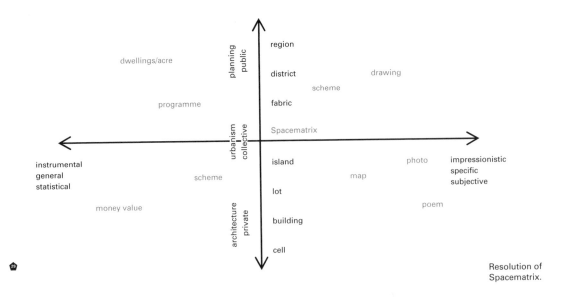

region

dwellings/acre

planning
public

district   drawing

scheme

programme   fabric

urbanism
collective   Spacematrix

instrumental   island   photo   impressionistic
general   scheme   map   specific
statistical   lot   subjective

money value   poem

architecture
private   building

cell

Resolution of
Spacematrix.

scales that are relevant to study have more to do with general intensities (built and network) and the distribution of tare (parks, agrarian land, nature, water, etcetera). Thus, the nature of tare, and the spread (variation) and properties of the components (for example fabrics, network) are probably the most important aspects that should be researched.

The 'spatial DNA', represented through the Spacematrix, connects all the levels of scale and conveys different information: absolute (the position of an island), relative (comparison to other islands constituting a fabric, district, etcetera), contextual (the fabric of which the island is a component) and composite (the components – lots and buildings – that make up the island). This 'Great Chain of Building' of the urban landscape through the scales can be reconnected to the earlier discussion on *resolution*. The horizontal axis in the diagram on page 175 can be combined with a vertical scale axis. The result can be viewed in ●. Along the horizontal axis, different representations (or descriptions) of the urban landscape can be arranged. The extremes of specific and general can then be substituted for by a series running from the subjective, for instance artistic expression, via a photo, through detailed and then more reduced maps, passing the Spacematrix representation, then through abstract schemes, and finally ending in statistics and pure numbers. The other axis moves from the smallest component to the larger aggregations. Earlier we maintained that the multivariable density method that has been constructed in this research has the proper resolution to differentiate between building and urban fabric types. The scale levels that have been investigated and show a significant correlation are island and fabric. The higher and lower levels of scale can be assumed to become either too blurred by statistical averages (district, city, region) or to be too specific to be relevant to an understanding of urban structural properties. Thus, the fit between resolution and scale can then be said to be at its greatest in the intersection where multivariable density and the scales of island and fabric intersect.

The matrix in ♟ can be further interpreted by assigning different attributes to the axes. The horizontal axis can be said to span the *statistical* and the *subjective*. The abstract left pole has an instrumental character, while the opposite pole leans towards impressionism and solipsism. The position of the Spacematrix representation somewhere in between has a *dialectic* quality; abstract and instrumental, but still deciphering specific spatial properties. Many morphologic analyses can be said to take place somewhere between this middle position and the right end of the horizontal axis, with the position varying depending on whether detailed or more abstract cartographic representations are used. The other axis, the scale hierarchy, coincides well with existing discipline demarcations: the lowest ones being the terrain of architecture; the middle level urbanism, constituting the framework for the first; and the higher scales constituting the field of planning. These levels combine well with the adjectives private (architecture), civic (urbanism) and collective (planning). Summarizing, one could propose that the multivariable density method that has been constructed here combines different dialectic positions; between too big and too small; between collective and private; between too general and too specific; and between planning and architecture. In other words, succinctly describing the dialectic character of urbanism.

Nevertheless, even if the above points to a central role of urbanism, the ideal approach includes, one would assume, an awareness of the totality along both axes, and requires a jumping, iterative way of working with different scales, resolutions and representations. To travel all these positions, one does need to be familiar with the many specific components, methods and techniques needed to assemble an integrated whole. Spacematrix should be one solid piece of ground in this complex matter.

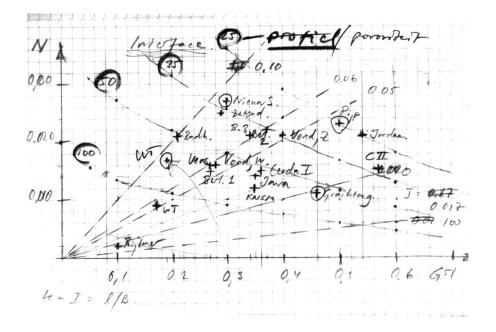

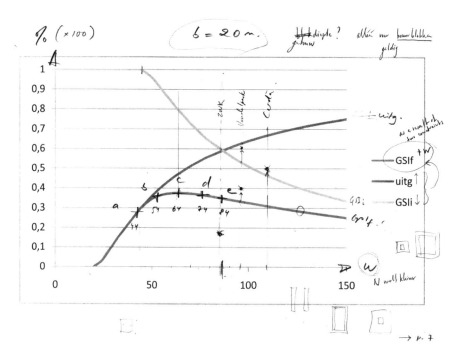

→ p. 7

Pursuing
performances.

5
THE PERFORMANCE OF DENSITY

Every aspect of density, high or low, has its advantages and disadvantages, depending on the context (place and time) in which it is assessed. Attempts to describe the 'best densities' or the 'good city' have a long history, but all tend towards highly prescriptive recommendations based on the subjective leanings of individual authors in specific contexts.[1] To be able to link negative or positive consequences to urban density we use the arguments of Kevin Lynch in his book *Good City Form*.[2] His arguments rely on the identification of measurable performance dimensions upon which a normative theory of appropriate densities can be built.

These performances are in most cases closely linked to constraints and requirements applied in the real world to secure certain qualities in our cities. At a meeting in Paris in 1905, the causes of health problems, such as cholera outbursts in the city, were discussed. Overcrowding and insufficient daylight in the bedrooms were identified as contributing factors.[3] As a result of these discussions, rules were defined throughout Europe that made street width and building height interdependent. They came to have a great impact on the resulting urban densities and the city development in general as these rules were enshrined by laws. Jonathan Barnett explains how in New York zoning laws, mainly aimed at controlling more abstract considerations of public health and welfare, unintentionally came to determine the basic design framework of the American city.[4] Rules stipulated the distance that high-rise building had to be set back to permit sunlight to fall on the streets and sidewalks and allow light and air into the interiors of the buildings. These rules were implemented, however, with little attention being paid to their design implications, although the impact on built form and densities was great. These are examples of how constraints imposed in a wider context came to affect the built environment. Later, regulations implemented to influence the development of cities also described densities more directly. The Garden City Movement is a good early example of this (Raymond Unwin's proposal of a maximum density of 12 dwellings to the acre, and the minimal requirement for spaciousness defined by Anton Hoenig).

The shifting attitudes towards urban density and its associated qualities not only show ideological changes, but are also very much related to the whole development of the city and the material wealth of its inhabitants. Poor people concentrated in inadequate houses that offer poor shelter and damp interiors, situated in narrow alleys with hardly any sanitation whatsoever in congested conditions, with rudimentary or no public services, whether it be in Amsterdam a century ago, or in Bangalore today, can hardly be described other than as inhumane. In contrast, well-educated twenty-first-century knowledge workers shopping and wining and dining next to well-designed public spaces, between high-standard offices and apartment buildings, occupying a similar density, is seen as constituting a 'vibrant urbanity'. Clearly, the level of material wealth and the availability of technical facilities that can take the edge

1
Larice, M. and E. Macdonald (eds.), *The Urban Design Reader* (Oxon: Routledge, 2007), 109.
2
Lynch, K., *A Theory of Good City Form* (Cambridge, MA: MIT Press, 1981).
3
Rådberg, J., *Doktrin och täthet i svenskt stadsbyggande 1875–1975* (Stockholm: Statens råd för byggnadsforskning, 1988).

4
Barnett, J., *An Introduction to Urban Design* (New York: Harper and Row, 1982).

off of physical inconveniences (electricity, water, sewer, air conditioning, insulation, etcetera) influence the ability to cope with high densities, both historically and at present.

It is necessary to define the relationship between density and performance, and the evaluation of these performances, in any discussion of 'appropriate' densities. This will enable us to understand how constraints influence city development. Performances can further produce important information about problems and possibilities to be expected under different density conditions. 'Problems' and 'possibilities' are of course formulated at a specific moment in time and space and the same performance (daylight access, for example) can be judged as inadequate (too hot) or more than adequate (plenty of daylight), depending on historical and geographical context. What we want to emphasize in what follows is the relative objectivity of performances and the contextuality of the judgement hereof. This is in line with the earlier discussion on the Spacematrix method as a universal interpretative and representative structure, filled with contingent content that is being contextually interpreted and acted on. Performances can be viewed as serving as extensions of the objective character of density into the physical realm of the urban landscape, to suspend the rhetoric, interests and preferences of accompanying judgements.

Let us return for a moment to the terms used by Ernest Alexander, mentioned at the beginning of Chapter 3.[5] Alexander distinguishes between physical density and perceived density. The same physical density can be perceived and evaluated in very different ways, by different people, in different cultures and locations, under different circumstances. We believe a flaw in this approach is that it moves too quickly from the physical to the subjective. Although Alexander makes clear that the perceived reaction is influenced not only by 'individual cognitive factors' but also by external 'sociocultural factors', a focus on the individual experience of density is at the centre of his analysis. We would prefer to linger a little longer on the physical by further investigating separate properties – sub-properties and composite properties – of the built environment in relation to density. The most fundamental sub-properties that have been discussed so far include the amount of built programme (intensity, or FSI), the primary distribution of this programme (coverage, height and spaciousness; or GSI, L and OSR) and the composition and measures of the urban ground plan (N_f, b, and T_f).

An example of a composite property is the relationship between N and FSI. The relationship between these properties, combined with the assumption of the number of cars per square metre of floor space, can be used to arrive at a parking performance. Performances can be arrived at in a deductive way through clear definitions of density, using Spacematrix, and standards (kengetallen). In the case of parking the standard might be an assumption of required cars per household, or a norm defined by the municipality. Based on a given density and parking norm, we can calculate the parking performance. In one case there may be more cars than parking spaces available along the streets, and in another case the streets remain almost empty. An evaluation of the situation (as acceptable or unacceptable) requires judgement based on the imagination and preferences of a person (professional or non-professional), which is

5
Alexander, E.R., 'Density Measures: A Review and Analysis', *Journal of Architectural and Planning Research* 10 (3) 1993, 181–202.

certainly conditioned by 'individual cognitive factors' and 'sociocultural factors'. However, the judgement can be temporarily suspended, making it possible to explore solutions and performances without over-hasty qualifications.

Using performances in this way we can engage with aspects of density without having to use qualifications such as 'too high' or 'too low'. This would enable professionals to better ground their decisions and the trade-offs made between performances. It is important to notice, however, that even if we might aim for neutral performance outcomes, the trade-offs taking place between them are, of course, highly value based. For instance, a choice for more programme at the cost of parking space comes after weighing the pros and cons, perhaps through valuing built intensity higher than car mobility.

We can now compare the series defined by Alexander (A) with the one suggested by us (B):

A Physical Density – Perceived Density
B Physical Density – Performances – Standards – Evaluation (Perceived Density)

In B, standards and evaluation represent the two moments when contextual values enter the equation. The standards are of a more collective character (regulations, the urban practice, group of professionals, etcetera), the second is individual. If A is a good characterization of the personal reaction to built density (good, bad, fear, pleasure, indifference), then B could be viewed as a scheme for the professional engagement with density during analysis and design. It is important to bear in mind that the properties of density have an objective character (for example, one metre of street to every metre of floor space), performances register variable trends, standards (contextually grounded in collective values) supply those variables with a temporarily fixed value (two parking spaces per household, for instance, or a certain amount of daylight prescribed by a norm), and, finally, the judgement of those performances is made by a person in a professional context with personal preferences.

An interesting question concerning performances is how they were judged and evaluated in the past in comparison to present judgements. In terms of evaluation many would agree to describe the transformation of De Pijp in Amsterdam that took place during the last century as one going from negative overcrowding in 1899 to a situation today of urbanity, with its positive connotations. At the same time, the once much appreciated peace and quiet in the Western Garden Cities of Amsterdam is today viewed as boring 'undercrowding',[6] not in tune with a consumer society where intensity (turnover), commercial interface and thresholds for services are considered to be of the utmost importance.

When designing our cities we often use existing built environments as a reference. Some qualities appeal to commissioners, consumers and designers while others do not. To also work with and think about the urban landscape in terms of performance can help to avoid inappropriate use of these references. When striving for a vibrant urbanity, the

6
Lozano, E., 'Density in Communities, or the Most Important Factor in Building Urbanity', in: Larice and Macdonald, *The Urban*, op. cit. (note 1), 312–327, 320–321.

values might to some be obvious (high densities, good accessibility, a mix of functions), but one must also remember that the original physical makeup of an area might not be acceptable today. For example, narrow streets and few cars might be incompatible with present norms of accessibility and two cars per household. Such conflicting aspirations might become more explicit through critically working with density and performances.

BASIC PERFORMANCES INDICATORS

In Chapter 3 a distinction was made between the variables used to measure density (base land area, network length, gross floor area and built area), the basic density indicators (FSI, GSI and N), and indicators that can be derived from these, such OSR, L, w and b. The most basic properties of a built environment can be said to already be present in these variables. On many occasions, such basic data as the amount of programme and the use of the ground surface can add to the understanding of an area in a first survey. Through their simplicity, however, they add little to the understanding of a professional familiar with a specific situation. The basic density indices have the ability to convey more than the rather obvious. Building intensity and compactness of an area can be achieved through the density variables and, in combination, a Spacemate description of probable types can be made. The third group, the derived indicators, can actually be considered as the most basic performance indicators that have the ability to add information to these descriptions, not by adding new variables, but through combining and extracting from the predefined ones.

The very first derived indicator, introduced on page 108, is a description of a property of the built environment, namely its height (L=FSI/GSI). It is an abstract description as it represents an average of a chosen selection and has no intention to be specific to any individual building. As a matter of fact, this indicative property of average descriptions is present on any level of scale. Even for an individual building, an often useful description such as 'six floors' usually fails to respect partial basements, setbacks and accents. Still, we keep using it because of its pragmatic ability to focus on the main issue, temporarily ignoring specificities. This drowning of the particular in the tide of an averaging description is not – as we have earlier emphasized – a specific characteristic of the use of density, but of every representation (drawing, language, and so forth). The indicators derived through density must thus be treated as abstract approximations and used with the knowledge of its indicative and not literal character. Those derived indicators are valuable in comparisons and for gauging trends, not as descriptions of individual components.

Next to the very basic notion of building height introduced in the previous chapter, indicators that depict spaciousness (OSR), and differences between levels of scale (T, or tare) were introduced. Also, two indicators of measurement were suggested that produce an abstract representation of mesh size (w) and profile width (b) of a fabric. Other combinations and performances can through creativity and investigation be derived or constructed with the use of the basic density indices FSI, GSI and N.

A quick analysis of constraints and bottlenecks in contemporary practice – which by no means is exhaustive – can provide an overview of relevant performances. Many constraints come from the field of urban physics, some of which have been imposed through building legislation. Examples of such issues are daylight access, sunlight, air pollution and wind. Energy consumption is another performance in this series which will, due to peak oil, climate change and CO_2 reduction targets, become increasingly urgent in the near future. Performances that are relevant to the urban practice as they determine the feasibility of projects to a large extent are parking, the ratio between public and private land, and commercial exposure. Performances that deal more with the perception of an area are, for instance, urbanity, privacy and circulation convenience. We will explore three performances: parking, daylight access and urbanity. This approach could also be extended and applied to many other performances. In all cases, the investigation into the relation between density and performance should always focus on the *conditional* character of density for the performance of the urban landscape. In some cases this conditionality is rather direct and obvious (for example user intensity), in other cases more concealed (daylight access), sometimes controversial and tainted by vested interests (crime and happiness), and in some others probably not even worth the effort to pursue (infertility). The amount of daylight, for instance, is pretty straightforward. Even if weather, pollution and interior decoration affect the final daylight penetration, the urban layout plays an important role in conditioning the access of daylight. In many other cases, density might participate as a minor condition in a complex set of physical, social and psychological factors. In such cases there is a danger of assigning this minor factor an exaggerated role, and even regarding it as a simple cause (for instance: high-rise living causes depression, à la Christopher Alexander[7]).

It is important to emphasize here that the calculations and examples that follow are only intended to identify such conditionalities and uncover trends, and should not be interpreted as directly applicable values. Every concrete situation necessitates a tailor-made approach to take complexity into account. Nevertheless, the formulas and values can be used to support explorative design processes.

PARKING

In the current practice of urban planning, parking is often one of the critical bottlenecks. Friction between parking, property and profit is present early in the design process. The point at which it is feasible to opt for a built parking solution instead of public parking on the street is very important as the costs for built parking solutions are generally high and profits are rather low. Furthermore, the potential to create high-quality public pedestrian space in a dense urban setting is dependent on the number of cars on the streets, both moving and parked. Alexander defines a threshold density of 75 parking places per hectare, which means that about 10 per cent of the land is consumed by parking.[8] The basic question posed here is in what way the conditions created by the urban layout (network density and street width) and the amount of building bulk (FSI) determine the parking performance on public streets and on private islands.

7
Alexander, C., et al., *A Pattern Language: Towns, Buildings, Construction* (New York: Oxford University Press, 1977), 115.

8
Alexander, 'Density Measures', op. cit. (note 5), 121.

Zuidwest Kwadrant 3	Zuidwest Kwadrant 2	Parksiedlung Spruch
Amsterdam	Amsterdam	Berlin
FSI_f 0.75	FSI_f 0.75	FSI_f 0.80
N_f 0.023	N_f 0.015	N_f 0.006

Three samples with the same FSI, but different network density (N) that illustrate the difference in parking performance.

An initial rough estimate of the parking performance of an area can be undertaken if we relate total programme (FSI_f) to the amount of network (N_f). The first, programme, generates a need for parking, while the second, network, can accommodate all or a part of this need. Three examples are used to help explain the logic of this relation. ✿ All three areas have the same FSI on the scale of the fabric but have been realized within different network layouts. In the first example much of the network is used to access the buildings. In the second example, less network is available, and the last example has only a quarter of the amount of network of the first one.

The general parking performance under different density conditions can thus be described in terms of the capacity of the network to accommodate parked cars. This Parking Performance Index (PPI) can be defined as the amount of the parking capacity of the network that is needed for parking:

$$\diamond \quad PPI = \frac{\text{Parking need}}{\text{Parking capacity}}$$

A PPI larger than 1.0 means that the capacity is insufficient and a PPI less than 1.0 that the need can be accommodated for by the network. In what follows we will define the two components, capacity and need, more precisely to arrive at a variable description of the parking performance that can be used to assess plans and reveal trends.

CAPACITY OF THE NETWORK

First, the capacity of the network has to be determined. Depending on the length and the width of the network, a certain number of cars can, in theory, be parked in this network. The logic of this relationship is rather simple: a fabric with the network density N_f has a certain street length with the average width, b, that can accommodate the parking need generated by the floor space, F, of the same area, A. Two issues are of importance for the capacity of the network: the number of crossings and the possible parking layouts. A specific area has a certain amount of network, described by its network density, N_f. The higher the network density, the more street length is present in that area. Not all of this network, however, can be used for parking. For every crossing the potential parking length is reduced. The resulting density of the network with a potential for parking, N_p, can be described as follows

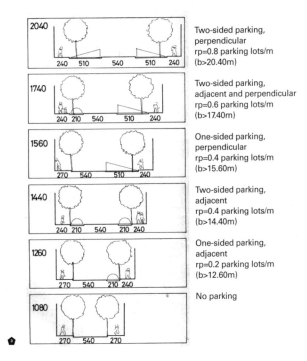

2040		Two-sided parking, perpendicular rp=0.8 parking lots/m (b>20.40m)
1740		Two-sided parking, adjacent and perpendicular rp=0.6 parking lots/m (b>17.40m)
1560		One-sided parking, perpendicular rp=0.4 parking lots/m (b>15.60m)
1440		Two-sided parking, adjacent rp=0.4 parking lots/m (b>14.40m)
1260		One-sided parking, adjacent rp=0.2 parking lots/m (b>12.60m)
1080		No parking

Threshold values for different r_p values; based on starting points defined by SAR in *Deciding on Density* (SAR 1977: 50).

$$N_p = \frac{l_p}{A_s}$$

l_p network with parking potential (m)

N_p can be expressed in terms of network density and profile width, tare and privately issued land (PIL), as follows (see ◆ for details):

$$N_p = N_f - \left(1 - \frac{b \cdot N_f}{2}\right)$$

$$N_p = N_f - \sqrt{1 - T_f}$$

$$N_p = N_f \sqrt{PIL}$$

The capacity of the remaining network to accommodate parked cars depends furthermore on the chosen parking solution. For instance, a layout where cars are parked on one side along the street can accommodate 0.2 cars per metre of network.[9] We can call this the minimum option. The maximum option consists of cars parked on both sides of the street, perpendicular to the street. This results in a maximum capacity of 0.8 cars per metre of network.[10] This varying form factor, r_p, determines

[9]
Parking space 2.5*5 m, i.e. one parking space in 5 m: 1/5=0.2 /m.
[10]
Parking space 2.5*5 m, i.e. two parking spaces in 2.5 m: 2.5/2=0.8 /m.

the parking capacity on the micro scale. It must of course be chosen bearing the total street width, b, in mind. A maximum solution with double perpendicular parking lots demands a profile width of at least 20.4 m.[11] On the other hand, with only one line of parked cars along the street, the total width might be as little as 12.6 m. The threshold values for r_p used here come from the Stichting Architectuur Research.[12] ⬠

11
For this example, the profile studies by Stichting Architectuur Research have been used. See Stichting Architectuur Research, *Deciding on Density: An Investigation into High Density Allotments with a View to the Waldeck Area, The Hague* (Eindhoven, 1977).
12
Ibid., 50.

Parking layout:
One sided, adjacent
    $r_p = 0.2$ parking lots/m (b > 12.60m)
Two sided, adjacent
    $r_p = 0.4$ parking lots/m (b > 14.40m)
One sided, perpendicular
    $r_p = 0.4$ parking lots/m (b > 15.60m)
Two sided, one adjacent, one perpendicular
    $r_p = 0.6$ parking lots/m (b > 17.40m)
Two sided, perpendicular
    $r_p = 0.8$ parking lots/m (b > 20.40m)

The capacity of the public network to accommodate parked vehicles, expressed as the potential amount of parking lots per m² of a plan area (/m²) can now be described as:

⬠   Parking capacity $(/m^2) = r_p \cdot N_f \sqrt{1-T_f}$

or

⬠   Parking capacity $(/ha) = 10{,}000 \cdot r_p \cdot N_f \sqrt{1-T_f}$

PARKING NEED
The other part necessary to indicate the parking performance of an area is the parking need generated by the traffic. Part of this is generated by external traffic (visitors, for instance) but most of the need will be generated by homes and work places in the area (except for areas dominated by shopping centres, cultural centres or other large attractors). In other words, the parking need is largely generated by the floor area, which can be expressed in terms of FSI. For housing the required parking can either be related to the number of dwellings or to the amount of floor area. In the last case this is mostly expressed as the number of parking places per 100 m² of floor area. For offices and other work places norms are often used that relate the required parking to floor area.

In its simplest form the parking need of a plan area can be expressed as follows:

⬠   Parking need $= \dfrac{FSI_f \cdot n_p}{100}$

    n_p the number of parking spaces needed
         for every 100 m² of floor area.

In most cases the total programme of a fabric, FSI_f, is composed of different functions (houses, work places, services, etcetera). Different parking norms can be defined for every separate programme and different values can even be defined for different types of housing. In the event of a programmatic spread (functional mix) we can define the needed parking as follows:

❖   Parking need $= \dfrac{FSI_f \cdot (x_q \cdot n_{pa} + \ldots + x_z \cdot n_{pz})}{10{,}000}$

x_a the percentage of programme a;

n_{pa} the number of parking spaces needed for every 100 m² of floor space with programme a.[13]

13
Example of parking norms used by Goudappel-Coffeng for a project in Hoorn in 2008: 1.6 parking spaces per dwelling (including visitors), 4 parking spaces per 100 m² of shop space, 2 parking spaces per 100 m² of office space.

Parking Performance Index

The thresholds where public parking will become problematic or, more importantly, when built parking solutions will be necessary, can be derived from the combination of need and capacity. We can now return to ❖ and compose the Parking Performance Index, PPI, by inserting ❖ and ❖ in ❖:

❖ $PPI = \dfrac{FSI_f \cdot n_p}{100 \cdot r_p \cdot N_f \sqrt{1 - T_f}}$

Values of PPI lower than 1.0 mean that the network can accommodate the generated parking need with the chosen parking solution. If the PPI exceeds 1.0 this means that the capacity of the network is too low or that the required number of parking spaces is too high (too many cars for too few parking lots). The value of the index also gives an idea of how dominant parking will be in the street. For instance, a PPI of 0.6 means that there is an overcapacity and only 60 per cent of the network will be needed for parking in the chosen layout. In the case that the PPI exceeds 1.0 we can choose to either change the norm; create more capacity by adding more network; add parking on the island (surface or underground); choose another parking layout (perpendicular instead of parallel, for instance); or decrease the built programme. A combination of all these measures could also be applied.

The maximum programme that can be realized in an area before built parking will be necessary is:

❖ $FSI_{max} = \dfrac{100 \cdot PPI \cdot r_p \cdot N_f \sqrt{1 - T_f}}{n_p}$

In this case the value of n_p has to be adapted to the theoretical street width, b. The choice for a value for PPI determines the acceptable amount of parked cars in the street space.

An indication of the performance concerning surface parking can be derived through positioning some of the empirical samples in a $FSI(N)$

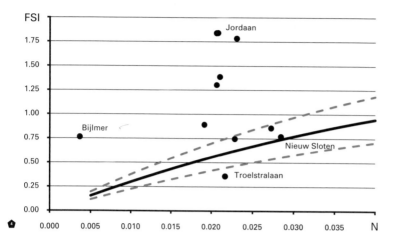

$FSI_f(N_f)$ diagram with varying PPI. r=0.4 parking spaces per metre of network, and n=1.25 car per 100 m² of floor space.

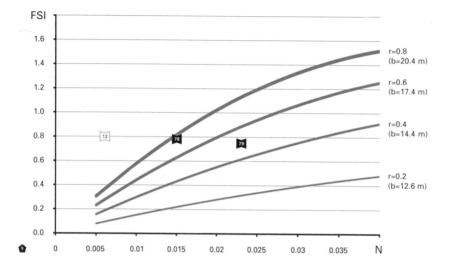

FSI(N) diagram with parking thresholds for different parking layouts and corresponding profile widths (n=1.25; PPI=1.0). Numbers refer to samples in ⬠.

diagram. ⬠ shows a situation where a parking capacity of 0.4 parking spaces per metre of network and 1.25 cars per 100 m² of floor space has been handled to construct thresholds for a specific parking layout ($r_n=0.4$; $n_p=1.25$). Only those samples with a theoretical street width of around 15 m have been used. Samples located under the grey dotted line (PPI=0.75) have little problem solving all the parking along the network. Between this line and the black continuous line (PPI=1), more than 75 per cent of the streets are taken up by parking and the car thus dominates public space. A position above the black line implies that there is too much programme and/or too little network realized to solve the parking in the network. In such cases the excess need can be accommodated by parking on private land (surface or underground), or by accepting a less generous parking norm (a lower value for n_p). However, if the performance is satisfactory, meaning that PPI<1, views can still vary as to whether this is acceptable or not. Some might find it too

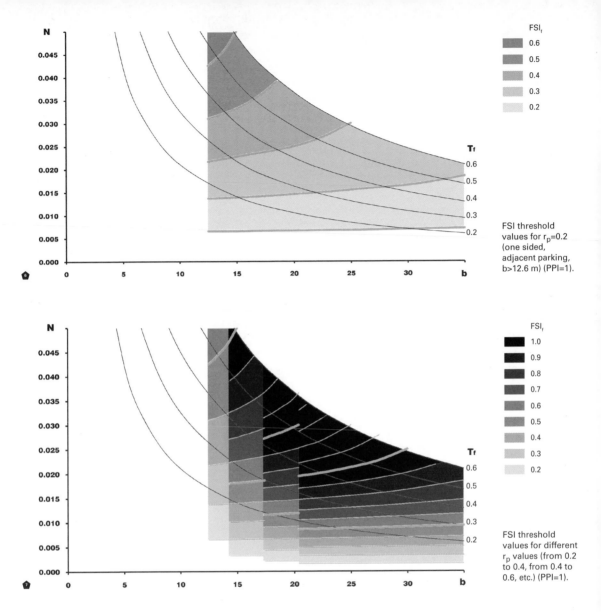

FSI threshold values for $r_p=0.2$ (one sided, adjacent parking, b>12.6 m) (PPI=1).

FSI threshold values for different r_p values (from 0.2 to 0.4, from 0.4 to 0.6, etc.) (PPI=1).

crowded with cars; others could claim that the norm is too low and would prefer at least 2 cars per 100 m² of floor space instead of 1.25.

In the example described above the chosen parking layout was two-sided parallel parking (or one-sided perpendicular) with r_p=0.4. ⬟ shows the maximum FSI for different parking layouts and PPI=1.0. A higher network density, or smaller islands, allows for a higher FSI. The slightly curved lines of the figure are due to an increased number of crossings as the network density increases. The three examples used in the beginning of this paragraph are positioned in the diagram to illustrate the relation between FSI and N, and parking performance. From the graph it is obvious that in the first sample, Zuidwest Kwadrant 3 (⬛ in ⬟), all parking can easily be solved on the streets and that the second, Zuidwest Kwadrant 2 (■ in ●), needs the entire street capacity for parking (two-sided, perpendicular). The last sample, Parksiedlung Spruch (▢ in ●), cannot solve the parking need in the public street, and a large underground parking garage has been constructed to accommodate the cars. The diagram is here used to evaluate three built environments, but could also be used to guide the design process. Based on, for instance, a given programme (FSI_f), street profile, and the goal to accommodate all the required parking space on the streets, the most efficient network density can be derived from the diagram.

THRESHOLDS OF PARKING

The thresholds of surface parking are important, particularly for low-rise developments as built parking solutions are mostly unfeasible here. As shown above, the capacity of the network to accommodate the parking need generated by the dwellings depends on the network density and the width of the street profile that determines the possible parking layout options. There are many variables that are interdependent of each other and that together determine the parking performance. To better understand the relationship between these variables another trend can be gauged with the help of the earlier used N(b)-diagram. In the diagram in ● the gradient is drawn of the maximum FSI that can be realized if the entire capacity of the network is used (PPI=1). The diagram conveys the situation of one-sided parking, adjacent to the street (r_p=0.2 and thus starting at a street width of 12.6 m). The maximum FSI for other parking solutions can be derived using the formula ◆. The diagram in ● shows how the continuously increasing profile width brings with it a sudden jump in capacity when enough measure (street width) allows for a parking layout with larger capacity (r_p increases from 0.2 to 0.4, from 0.4 to 0.6, etcetera).[14]

DAYLIGHT[15]

This section serves to unravel some of the conditional aspects of density on the daylight performance of the urban fabric. In what follows, we will conclude that OSR plays a central role herein. The uncovered correlation between OSR and daylight performance can be seen as rehabilitating this indicator of spaciousness and, with hindsight, credit Hoenig for his aspiration to create a qualitative spatial indicator. The daylight performance, this section will show, can be integrated with the Spacemate, making it possible to gauge this performance in the interior, the exterior and for different floor levels of a section.

Daylight and solar radiation have a great impact on the climate in the city, both in the interior of buildings and in public space. Furthermore, the potential to create high-quality interiors in a dense urban situation is dependent on the amount of daylight that is allowed to penetrate the interiors of the buildings. With enough artificial light, anything goes, but if daylight is considered essential to human well-being and an important ingredient for high spatial qualities and energy saving, the daylight intensity of the exterior and interior of the urban fabric has a strong influence on the limits of density and building types. The basic question posed in this section is to what degree the conditions created

14
Next to the capacity of the streets, the islands can also offer additional parking space within the non-built parts of the island or with built parking garages. The extra parking needed in the case that the PPI for the fabric exceeds 1.0 (= shortage) can be expressed as PPIp=20*(FSIf*np/100–rp*N*root(1–Tf))/(1– Tf), where PPIp = the percentage of the privately available land (*uitgeefbaar*) needed for parking.
15
Parts of this paragraph use results from a research project on which the chairs of Architecture, Urbanism and Building Technology have been cooperating (financed by *Verrijking door Samenwerking* at Delft University of Technology, 2004). The project is described in Haupt, P. and M. van Esch, 'Daylight and Urban Density', in: H. Bekkering et al. (eds.), *The Architectural Annual 2005–2006*, Delft University of Technology (Rotterdam: 010 Publishers, 2007), 86–91.

by the amount of *programme* (FSI) and *primary distribution*–coverage (GSI) and building height (L)–determine the daylight performance in the urban exterior and the architectural interior. If this is substantial, how great is the influence of *secondary distribution*–in this case building depth–compared to these basic conditions? This part of the research employs both deduction and data from DIALux[16] simulations. The focus here is on indirect daylight and not on solar radiation and shading.

Daylight performance is, on the one hand, a result of a series of reductions of daylight access and on the other, an increase of light through reflections. The reduction of daylight in the interior can be described as a situation in which the sky is gradually obstructed by the ceiling, neighbouring buildings, the partitioning walls of the interior, and finally by the façade covering the interior. The daylight performance of the exterior (street, courtyard) is primarily influenced by the street (or courtyard) profile properties, defined as the distance between buildings and the height of those buildings. The loss of daylight can in both cases partly be compensated by reflections through the texture and colour of interior and exterior surfaces (ground, walls and façades).

The most basic situation in the section was examined to illustrate how the daylight performance of the exterior and the interior of buildings differs in situations with varying FSI and GSI. It represents only a partial description of the urban fabric but it does have the advantage of providing a manageable amount of information and variables. The conclusions on the performance of the sections should not be extrapolated into general conclusions on urban fabrics, but they certainly do indicate trends and can be used as a guide for further investigation of urban fabrics in all its dimensions.

ANY LIGHT VERSUS NO LIGHT

In its most simplistic form, the daylight performance can be described as the percentage of the total floor area that is exposed to the sky and thus lit. Daylight performance in general can be described by the Daylight Performance Index, DPI_n. The notation n indicates the value of the Daylight Factor (*daglichtfactor*), DF, which expresses the quotient between the light intensity (lux) at a certain point and the light intensity in a non-obstructed situation in 'the open field'. In an open field, no obstructions are present and DF is 100. In a compact alley DF might decrease to 30, and at a point a couple of metres behind the façade, this value might be reduced to 3. This means that the intensity of the daylight in the alley of this example is 30 per cent of the intensity that we could measure–and experience–in an open, non-obstructed field. In the interior this is further reduced to just 3 per cent of the open-field situation.

DPI_0 describes the daylight performance by comparing areas with a Daylight Factor of any value above zero with all of the available floor area. DPI_0 thus only makes a distinction between areas exposed to daylight (DF>0) and dark (non-exposed) areas (DF=0). A DPI_0 of 100 (or more) means that all of the floor area is exposed to some amount of daylight.

For a section without interior walls and with no reflection (which we can call the urban casco), the consequences for the daylight performance on the ground floor, the floor level with the least daylight, have

16
DIALUX was originally a simulation program for artificial light, but since 2007 daylight simulation has been added (see www.dialux.com).

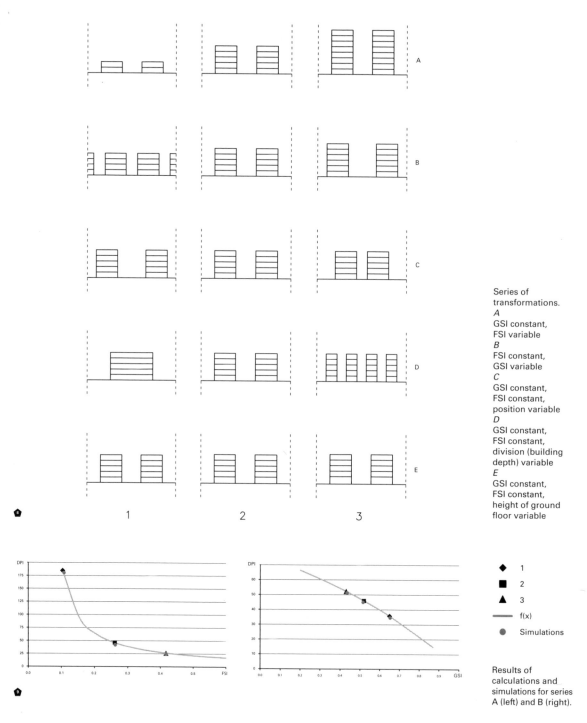

Series of
transformations.
A
GSI constant,
FSI variable
B
FSI constant,
GSI variable
C
GSI constant,
FSI constant,
position variable
D
GSI constant,
FSI constant,
division (building
depth) variable
E
GSI constant,
FSI constant,
height of ground
floor variable

◆ 1

■ 2

▲ 3

—— f(x)

● Simulations

Results of
calculations and
simulations for series
A (left) and B (right).

been examined using a series of variations. ⬠ In the first series (A), the amount of programme is changed while the ground coverage remains constant. This means that the GSI has been kept constant as FSI and L vary. The second series (B) describes different primary distributions. In this case, the amount of programme, or FSI, remains the same, and the ground coverage and height differ.

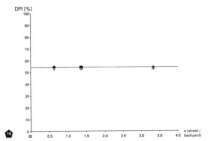
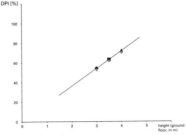

The results for the different scenarios have been arrived at through simulations with DIALux and with calculations. ⬟ shows that the performance is proportionally inverted to the FSI, or the amount of programme. More programme means less daylight on the ground floor. This conclusion could in most cases be made based on individual experience, but the non-linear character of the trend is difficult to unravel purely by intuition and practical experience. The rate of decrease is high when the FSI is low and slows down when the FSI becomes higher.

This demonstrates the relationship of daylight performance to the amount of programme, but how does the primary distribution of this programme influence the daylight performance? If a comparison is made between situations with the same FSI (amount of programme), but with differing GSI (coverage), the trend is also one of decline. A distribution with high buildings and low GSI has a better performance than low buildings with less distance between each building, and thus a high GSI, although they both accommodate the same amount of programme (FSI).

The formula for the geometry of the section that combines these trends can be expressed as follows:[17]

$$\text{DPI}_0 = \frac{200(1-\text{GSI})}{\text{FSI}-\text{GSI}}$$

This formula shows that for the section, the percentage of floor surface exposed to *any* daylight (DPI_0) can be described purely with density variables. The diagrams in ⬟ show the correlation between theory ◆ and computer simulations with DIALux.

Two other series of transformation, regarding the distribution of building mass with a constant Spacemate density, have been studied to understand the influence of the secondary distribution on daylight performance. If a situation with a constant distance between buildings is compared to a situation where the street width differs from the size of the courtyards, it appears that the daylight performance remains constant. (Series C ⬟ and left ⬟) Also when deep buildings, placed at great distance from each other, are compared to slender buildings close to each other, no difference in performance occurs. (Series D ⬟) This further confirms the conclusion that daylight performance to a large extent is conditioned by density, that is, FSI and GSI.

17
For an extensive
argumentation of the
construction of the
functions, see ◆.

215

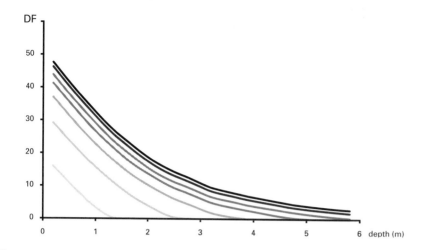

5 m
10 m
15 m
20 m
25 m
35 m
50 m

Simulations of the different intensities at the interior with different degrees of obstruction (street width).

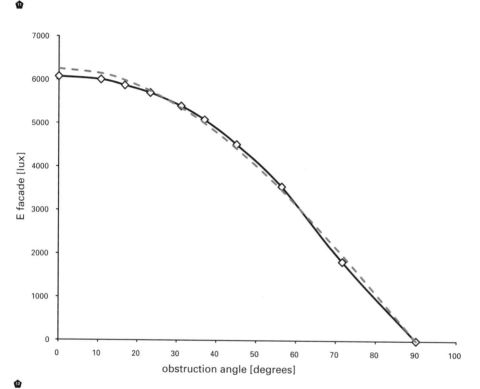

Simulation

Cosinus

The trend at the façade can quite accurately be described by a cosine function.

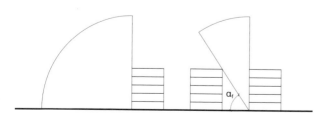

Contribution of the sky to the intensity at the façade without (left) and with (right) external obstruction.

Finally, the influence of the floor height has been investigated. The above ✦ can be transformed into:

$$✦ \quad DPI_0 = \frac{200 \cdot h_n \left(\dfrac{1}{GSI} - 1 \right)}{H}$$

h_n the floor height on the nth floor (m);
H the remaining building height above the nth floor (m).

Here we can see that the daylight performance is directly proportional to the height of the floor considered. This is also confirmed by DIALux simulations. (Series E ⬠, and right diagram ◉)

REAL LEVELS OF DAYLIGHT

Up to now the position of zero lux (or DF=0) in the interior has been used to trace density trends. This, of course, is not very relevant to the real situation where sufficient levels of daylight for different activities are used. For instance, DF=0.5 can at the latitude of the Netherlands be considered enough for a human being to be able to orientate in a room, DF=2.5 is required to read and do paperwork, and, if this is done during the whole day, DF=5 is preferable.[18] It should be noted, however, that the absolute values of the intensity greatly varies during the day, and are dependent on the season and geographical position. A Daylight Factor of 60 at a specific position, on the other hand, means that the daylight intensity at this position will always be 60 per cent of the open field intensity: 60 per cent of the low intensity on a clouded and grey afternoon, but likewise 60 per cent of the intensity on a clear summer noon. The Daylight Factor thus describes a property of a building and its environment itself, no matter if it is the sun or the moon that is shining (or not).

Besides these objections with respect to the performance of the interior, the intensity in the exterior (streets and courtyards) also needs to be scrutinized based on real values and levels of acceptance. An exterior with no light, DF=0, does not exist (otherwise it would by definition not be an exterior), but still, there are of course variations in the intensity of the daylight at the exterior.

To expand the discussion to real levels of daylight, we start by looking at the distribution of daylight in the interior. ◉ shows the different intensities in the interior with different degrees of obstruction. In the diagram, the distance of an obstructing object varies between 5 and 80 m. If the different intensities at the façade are related to the angle of obstruction, a diagram as shown in ◉ can be constructed. This shows a trend that quite accurately can be described by a cosine function. At the façade, with no external obstruction, the intensity is half of the intensity in the open field, or, DF=50. ◉ This means that the intensity at the façade as a function of the angle of obstruction, $DF_f(a_f)$, can be described as follows:

$$✦ \quad DF_f = 50 \cdot \cos a_f$$

DF_f Daylight Factor at the façade;
a_f the angle of obstruction at the façade.

18
NEN 12464–1:2002 Light and lighting – Lighting of work places – Part 1: Indoor work places (NEN 2003). For office work 500 lux is recommended and for most home activities between 200 and 300 lux is recommended. The DF thresholds are based on a conservative estimation of an intensity of 10.000 lux in the open field through which we arrive at a Daylight Factor of 5 for office work and 2.5 for home activities.

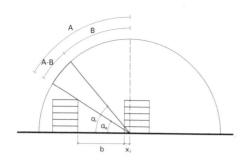 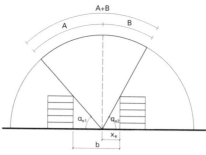

Contribution of the sky to the intensity in the interior, A–B (left); and exterior, A+B (right).

To be able to describe the intensity at any other position than the façade, we must take into account both the *internal angle of obstruction* (a_i) and the *external angle of obstruction* (a_e). The gap between these two, the *daylight angle*, determines the intensity at a random point in the interior.

It can be shown, by using ◆ that the Daylight Factor, DF_i, at a point in the interior of the building at a distance x_i from the façade can be determined by $DF_i = 50 \cdot (\cos a_e - \cos a_i)$, where a_e is the external angle, and a_i the internal angle of obstruction. For the exterior, the formula changes into $DF_e = 50 \cdot (\cos a_{e1} + \cos a_{e2})$, where a_{e1} and a_{e2} are the two exterior angles of obstruction.

The daylight factor at the distance x from the façade for interior (DF_i) and exterior (DF_e) thus becomes:

◆ $DF_f = 50 (\cos a_e - \cos a_i)$

◆ $DF_e = 50 (\cos a_{e1} + \cos a_{e2})$

The different angles can be derived through the geometry of the section ♟:

$$\tan a_e = \frac{L \cdot h}{(b + x_i)}$$

$$\tan a_i = \frac{h}{x_i}$$

$$\tan a_{e1} = \frac{L \cdot h}{(b - x_e)}$$

$$\tan a_{e2} = \frac{L \cdot h}{x_e}$$

L   number of floors;
h   average floor height (m);
b   profile width (m);
x_i distance from façade, interior (m);
x_e distance from façade, exterior (m).

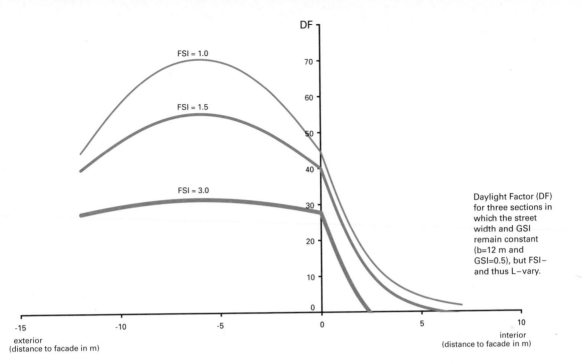

DF

FSI = 1.0

FSI = 1.5

FSI = 3.0

70

60

50

40

30

20

10

0

Daylight Factor (DF)
for three sections in
which the street
width and GSI
remain constant
(b=12 m and
GSI=0.5), but FSI–
and thus L–vary.

-15   -10   -5   0   5   10

exterior
(distance to facade in m)

interior
(distance to facade in m)

It now becomes possible to continuously describe the daylight factor at every position through the section:

$$DF_i = 50\left(\cos\left(\arctan\left(\frac{L \cdot h}{b + x_i}\right)\right) - \cos\left(\arctan\left(\frac{h}{x_i}\right)\right)\right)$$

$$DF_e = 50\left(\cos\left(\arctan\left(\frac{L \cdot h}{b - x_e}\right)\right) + \cos\left(\arctan\left(\frac{L \cdot h}{x_e}\right)\right)\right)$$

Based on these formulae the Daylight Factor has been calculated for three sections in which the street width and GSI remain constant (b=12 m, and GSI=0.5), but the programme – and thus building height – vary: FSI=1.0 and L=2; FSI=1.5 and L=3; and FSI=3.0 and L=6. The Daylight Factor through the section is represented in ◉.

For the series A to D that were described earlier, the trends for real values can now be studied, both for the interior and the exterior. Diagrams in ◉ show that the decrease of the Daylight Factor on the *exterior* follows the same trend as the interior, both in its dependency on the FSI and the GSI. In addition to this, the real values for the *interior* can be compared to the simulated and theoretical result for DPI_0 that were shown in ◉. They are, as could be expected, lower, but follow the same trends. ◉

This continuous description of the light intensity for the exterior and the interior shows how daylight performances of built space can be described. Depending on the programmatic requirements one can for an interior define (1) the required minimum Daylight Factor for an activity

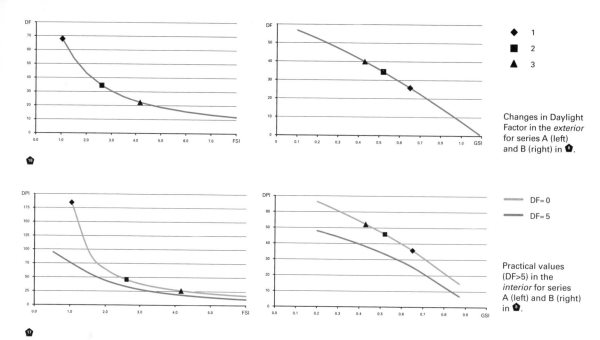

Changes in Daylight Factor in the *exterior* for series A (left) and B (right) in 🖬.

♦ 1
■ 2
▲ 3

DF= 0
DF= 5

Practical values (DF>5) in the *interior* for series A (left) and B (right) in 🖬.

or programme, and (2) the desired amount of surface with that minimum Daylight Factor in relation to all built surface. In housing, for example, one could define the required Daylight Factor for served areas (*verblijfsgebied*) as at least 2.5, and attempt to have a minimum of 60 per cent of the floor area at such levels. This means that $DPI_{2.5}$ should be larger than 60. The remaining 40 per cent would then be suitable for circulation, service spaces, storage, and so forth.

With the use of practical levels of daylight intensity the building depth becomes essential to the practical performance of the interior, whereas this is of no relevance to the theoretical approach of zero lux (DPI_0). In an unobstructed situation the theoretical DPI_0 will always be 100 per cent, whatever depth the building might have. However, when we gauge practical values, such as DF>5, there are limitations. This can be explained by the above formula ◆ and is also easy to confirm with simulations. For a floor height of 3 m this means that a Daylight Factor larger than 5 can never be reached at a distance greater than 6 m from the façade, even with no external obstruction whatsoever. 🖬 This applies, as in previous examples, to situations with an open façade, no partition walls and zero reflection.

In the earlier series D, where the building depth varied with constant FSI and GSI 🖬, the daylight performance (DPI_0) was constant, independent of the building depth. When the series is studied for real values, however, the values are not only lower, but also vary. 🖬 Here one can identify a clear optimum for the performance at a certain building depth. In the case of series D (FSI=2.6; GSI=0.5), the maximum performance of the interior takes place in buildings with a depth of approximately 10 m.

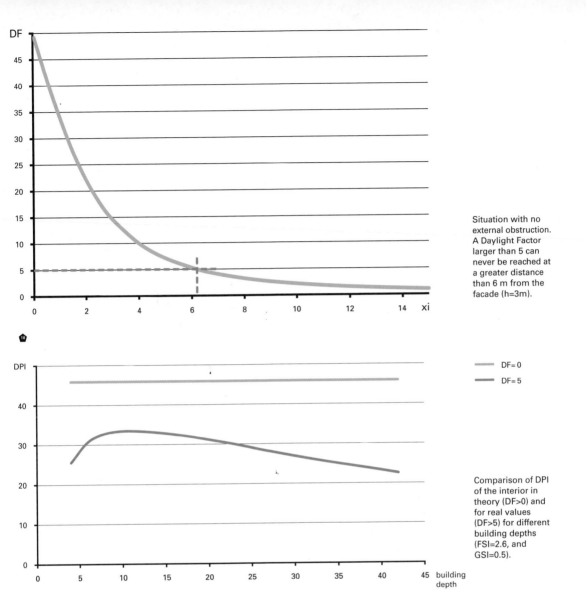

Situation with no external obstruction. A Daylight Factor larger than 5 can never be reached at a greater distance than 6 m from the facade (h=3m).

DF=0

DF=5

Comparison of DPI of the interior in theory (DF>0) and for real values (DF>5) for different building depths (FSI=2.6, and GSI=0.5).

For other densities, the peak performance takes place at different building depths. A lower density has its optimum with less deep buildings, in this case 7 m, and for a higher density the maximum performance is achieved with rather deep buildings of around 15 m.

When it comes to the trade-offs between building depth and the width of the open space (courtyards and streets), one can conclude that with one and the same density the daylight performance of the *exterior* increases when building mass is concentrated: thicker buildings mean wider open space, and thus a smaller angle of obstruction and more daylight in the exterior (GSI and FSI constant). At the same time, increasing the building depth beyond the peak, as shown in ☻, results in a reduced performance of the *interior*.

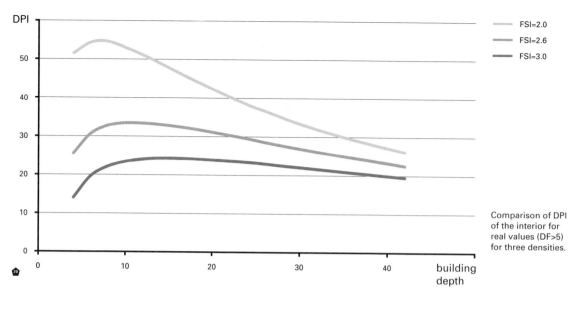

DPI

— FSI=2.0
— FSI=2.6
— FSI=3.0

building depth

Comparison of DPI of the interior for real values (DF>5) for three densities.

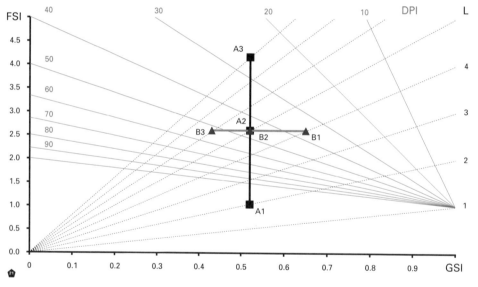

DPI in the interior as gradients in Spacemate (series A and B: see).

DAYLIGHT PERFORMANCE INDEX AND SPACEMATE

So far we have investigated the dependence of the daylight performance (in interior and exterior) on the different density indicators. As those indicators (GSI, FSI) are the same ones that constitute the core of the Spacematrix method, it could be revealing to represent the daylight trends in one of its projections, the Spacemate. The series of transformation that were described earlier (A1 to A3, and B1 to B3) can be positioned in the Spacemate diagram. By using the formula , $DPI_0 = 200(1-GSI)/(FSI-GSI)$, gradients can be added which describe the daylight performance of the interior for each specific density condition.

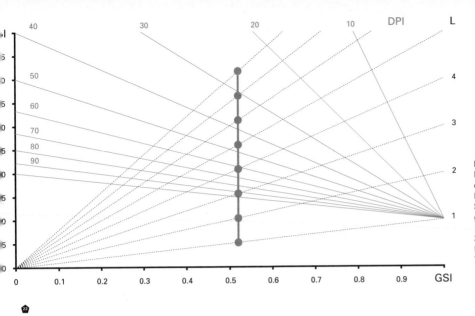

Example of the way DPI for each storey can be gauged based on a given Spacemate position; ground floor [26]; 1st [31]; 2nd [37]; 3rd [46]; 4th [62]; 5th [92]; 6th [100]; 7th [100].

The DPI_0 gradients are comparable to the Open Space Ratio gradients as can be seen when comparing the above formula to formula ◆, OSR= (1–GSI)/FSI, derived in Chapter 3. The only difference between OSR and DPI_0 is that for calculating the daylight performance, the floor area on the ground level is subtracted from the total amount of building bulk. This means that daylight performance on the ground floor can be described as the OSR of the floors above.

So far, only the daylight performance on the ground floor has been examined. By using the Spacemate diagram the daylight performance of all floors above the ground floor can easily be assessed. ⬠ shows the position of section A3 ⬠ in the Spacemate. For the ground floor the daylight performance can be read directly from the diagram (DPI_0=26). For each storey above the ground floor the performance can be reached by subtracting the lower storeys. In the diagram this means to move down step by step, from layer to layer, until the last gradient of one storey is reached. In the example the daylight performance of the top two floors, the seventh and eighth floors, are more than 100 per cent.

⬠ ⬠ show the gradients for the DPI using the zero lux (or DF>0) demarcation of 'dark' and 'light' areas. To describe the performance for *real* values in the section that has been investigated in this paragraph, two more factors that complicate the performance of the exterior and interior must be taken into account. These are the Daylight Factor values and the depth of the buildings. However, even when these factors are taken into consideration, the trend of the gradient does not change. ⬠ The spread of its absolute values change only when a different daylight factor is used as a standard or another building depth is applied.

Finally, the performance of the *exterior* in relation to density can be represented with the use of Spacemate. In the middle of a street or courtyard, the two angles in ◆ have the same value. This means that the

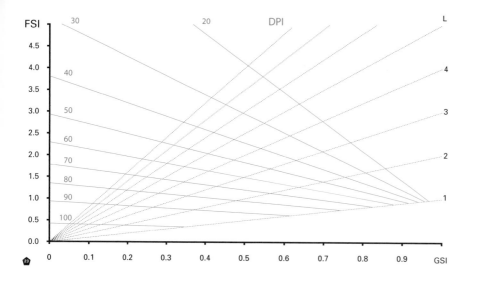

Spacemate with gradients DPI in the *interior* (DF>5; d=12 m, h=3 m).

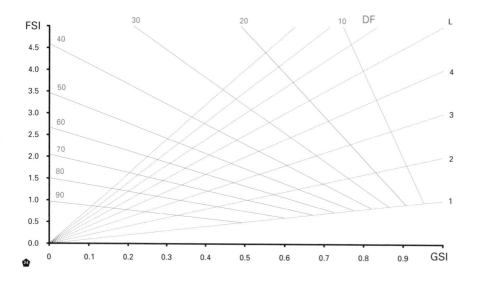

Spacemate with gradients of daylight factor (DF) in the *exterior*, in the middle of the open space (d=12 m, h=3 m).

formula for the performance *in the middle* of the open space, can be described as:

◆ $DF_e = 100 \cdot \cos \alpha_e$

The external obstruction angle in the middle of the open space can be arrived at through:

◆ $\tan \alpha_e = \dfrac{2 \cdot h}{d \cdot OSR}$

    h   floor height;
    d   building depth

◆ then becomes:

$$\text{DF}_e = 100 \cdot \cos\left(\arctan\left(\frac{2 \cdot h}{d \cdot \text{OSR}}\right)\right)$$

The formula shows that for a constant floor height and building depth, the performance of the exterior space depends only on the OSR. This means that also for the exterior, a performance gradient can be constructed in Spacemate. ◆ shows such a gradient for buildings with a depth of 12 m and a floor height of 3 m.

DAYLIGHT AND SPACIOUSNESS

The above investigation shows a basic relation between density and daylight performance of the section. This is the case both for the interior and the exterior. However, the trends only become comprehensible if a multivariable model of density is applied. Sure, intuition, experience and even calculations lead us to conclude that more programme means less daylight, high buildings obstruct more than low ones, and that more compact layouts are less daylight intense than spacious ones. But only when these are combined do the general trends become visible. The analyses and representations in Spacemate show an intimate relation between daylight performance and OSR. This might in retrospective shed some light on the centrality of the concept of spaciousness (*Weitraumigkeit*) introduced by Hoenig in the 1920s and restore some of its aspirations as an indicator of quality of the urban fabric.

The gradients of daylight performance in Spacemate also demonstrate that for one and the same amount of programme (FSI), a high and spacious layout will perform better than a lower and more compact one, both in the interior and the exterior. Thus if the performance of daylight in the built interior and exterior is seen as an important part of the overall quality of the built environment (biological and psychological well-being, energy saving, etcetera), and if we regard intensive land use as a necessity in a world of limited space and resources, then we have to conclude that high and spacious fabrics score better than low and compact ones. On the other hand, high-rise developments are often critiqued for a lack of human scale of buildings and open spaces. Some might therefore end up promoting the compact historical city of the nineteenth and beginning of the twentieth centuries as an attractive alternative to the spacious post-war urban expansions that are too high and the compact suburban developments of more recent years that are too low. This does not change the fact that even such a familiar city form should be scrutinized and constantly investigated to be further understood, optimized and judged. Not least in matters concerning daylight performance.

'URBANITY'

Since the 1980s, 'urbanity' has achieved a central position in discussions on the city, mostly as a concept with rather positive connotations. 'Overcrowding' and 'urbanity' might be regarded as two different interpretations of similarly intense situations, the choice between the two terms depending on how the quality of life taking place in an area is judged: *overcrowding* can be used to describe collectives of people in the ghettos a century ago or the cramped settlements in developing countries today, whereas *urbanity* might be more suitable to large gatherings of people, composed of emancipated individuals, consuming and interacting on terraces, around museums and along shopping streets. Urbanity has in its present use a positive connotation while overcrowding is mostly associated with the negative value of combining physical concentration and social misery.

Eduardo Lozano describes urbanity as the potential for inhabitants and institutions in a town or city to interact.[19] This potential is partly created by density and, in turn, encourages higher density, according to Lozano. Diversity, complexity, identity and flexibility are terms that are often associated with urbanity. The concept is frequently used to describe a human condition of plurality, difference, interaction and communication.[20] Although all kinds of social and spatial factors are involved in producing diversity, a dense concentration of people is, according to both Jane Jacobs and Lozano, one of the prerequisites for a flourishing and diverse city: 'The other factors that influence how much diversity is generated, and where, will have nothing much to influence if enough people are not there.'[21]

The term 'urbane' has its origin in the Latin dichotomy of *urbanus* versus *ruralis*.[22] To be urbane is to be equipped with courtesy, refinement, politeness and civility. *Urbanus* was the domain of the civilized citizen of the Roman city, in contrast to *ruralis*, the uncontrolled areas of the barbarian and uncivilized rural masses, alternatively the tranquil backwardness of the countryside. In many ways urbanity still has connotations of a smooth and literate style, free of barbarism and other inappropriate behaviour. Richard Sommer remarks that a concept such as urbanity also often works as an attractive front, shielding much of the blunt commercial and exclusive character of urban developments.[23] A high concentration of purchasing power thus seems to be stimulating to urbanity, while a high concentration of poverty tends to be deemed as dull, overcrowded and a suitable opportunity for regeneration. The urbanity that is striven for in present policies can from such a perspective be criticized for being largely covert gentrification, revitalizing not so much the chances of ordinary citizens, but describing a win-win situation for the city elites (developers, politicians and the creative and middle and upper classes):

> The good city is primarily associated with the ability of its physical spaces to support a rich and intricate visuality that promotes what is, in practice, the pleasures of the yuppie lifestyle and its programme of shopping and dining, of fitness, of stylishness and mobility, and of a certain level of associative urban connoisseurship.[24]

Present enthusiasm for urbanity and the dynamics and vitality of city life is not a neutral phenomenon, but carries ideological bias. Next to the affirmative stance towards the accelerating intensity of urban life, there exists also a critical and sometimes dystopian intellectual tradition. To the first, the modern urban condition equals opportunity and expansion, to the second it leads to alienation and loss of personal and

19
Lozano, 'Density in Communities', op. cit. (note 6).
20
Hajer, M., *De stad als publiek domein* (Amsterdam: Wiardi Beckman Stichting, 1989); Heeling, J., H. Meyer and J. Westrik, *Het ontwerp van de stadsplattegrond* (Amsterdam: SUN, 2002); Jacobs, J., *The Death and Life of Great American Cities* (New York: Random House, 1992), originally published in 1961; Meyer, H., F. de Josselin de Jong and M.J. Hoekstra (eds.), *Het ontwerp van de openbare ruimte* (Amsterdam: SUN, 2006), 9–30; Urhahn, G.B. and M. Bobic, *Strategie voor stedelijkheid* (Bussum: Uitgeverij THOTH, 1996); Wouden, R. van der (ed.) *De stad op straat: De openbare ruimte in perspectief* (The Hague: Sociaal en Cultureel Planbureau, 1999); Zijderveld, A.C., *Steden zonder stedelijkheid: Cultuurhistorische verkenning van een beleidsprobleem* (Deventer: van Loghum Slaterus, 1983).
21
Jacobs, J., *The Death and Life*, op. cit. (note 20), 205.
22
Thesaurus: urbane; 'The sophisticated manners of a true cosmopolite.' Refinement, assurance, wide social experience, charm, good taste, tact and propriety, etcetera.
23
Sommer, R.M., 'Beyond Centers, "fabrics," and the Culture of Congestion: Urban Design as a Metropolitan Enterprise', *Harvard Design Magazine* fall 2006/winter 2007, 50–59, 50.
24
Sorkin, M., 'The End(s) of Urban Design', *Harvard Design Magazine* fall 2006/winter 2007, 5–18, 12.

cultural identity. Terms such as alienation, loss of the Self, and chaos are associated with this line of thought on the effect of the modern city on human experience. Writers such as Charles Baudelaire, Walter Benjamin and Knut Hamsun point to the destabilizing effects on humans of the dynamics and speed of the rapidly modernizing city.

José Lluís Sert and Lewis Mumford and, more recently Mike Davis and Michael Sorkin, are examples of intellectuals that have all taken a critical stance on (aspects of) modernity, capitalism and the impact of the city on human life. Mumford favours a decentralized regionalism against the 'The Myth of Megalopolis'.[25] In a spirit resembling the scepticism towards industrialization and mass production of William Morris and the Arts and Crafts movement in England – but perhaps more misanthropic and less romantic – Mumford grieves the loss of humanism through modern history. He views urban history through the 'oft-repeated urban cycle of growth, expansion, and disintegration', and warns that the modern megalopolises face the same destiny as antique Rome. Davis's recent neo-Marxist criticism of the urban condition attacks the 'dynamic, ever-growing social inequality, [which] is the very engine of the contemporary [neoliberal] economy'. In the book with the apocalyptic title *Evil Paradises: Dreamworlds of Neoliberalism*, Davis describes how 'the spatial logic of neoliberalism (cum plutonomy) revives the most extreme colonial patterns of residential segregation and zoned consumption'.[26] In a global perspective, 'the bright archipelagos of utopian luxury and "supreme lifestyles" are mere parasites on a "planet of slums"'. This reads like a twenty-first-century global version of Engels' book on Manchester: *The Conditions of the Working Class in England in 1844*.

In contrast to these sceptics, Jacobs can be seen as central to the rehabilitation of the city and its dynamic potential against both modernists (Le Corbusier, et al.) and regionalists such as Mumford. Present day examples of affirmative attitudes to urban economic and psychosocial dynamics can be found in Richard Florida's emphasis on the relationship between the urban, a creative class and economic competitiveness, and Peter Hall's book *Cities in Civilization* in which the golden ages of civilization through history are recorded and related to the culturally and economically innovative and productive climate of interactive city life.[27]

The wide range of analyses and judgements on the urban condition and its positive and negative connotations, where in the examples mentioned here 'modernity is either embraced with blind and uncritical enthusiasm or otherwise condemned with a neo-Olympian remoteness and contempt',[28] shows that it is not easy to distil a consensus from the existing views of what can be understood by 'urbanity'. Furthermore, even the intrinsic relationships to physical conditions have at times also been questioned. Melvin Webber describes urbanity as mainly being dependent on openness and accessibility.[29] These are aspects that do not necessarily have to be conditioned by the physical givens of the built environment. With modern communication technologies, an urbanity defined in this way can be sustained that is not dependent on the physical contacts between people, according to Webber. The research group OSA (*Onderzoeksgroep Stedenbouw en Architectuur*) at the University of

25
Mumford, L., *The City in History: Its Origins, Its Transformations, and Its Prospects* (New York: Harcourt, Brace and World, 1961).

26
Davis, M. and D.B. Monk (eds.), *Evil Paradises: Dreamworlds of Neoliberalism* (New York: The New Press, 2007).

27
Florida, R., *Cities and the Creative Class* (New York: Routledge, 2005); Hall, P., *Cities in Civilization* (London: Phoenix, 1999).
28
Berman, M., *All That Is Solid Melts into Air: The Experience of Modernity* (New York: Penguin Books, 1988, first published in the USA by Simon & Schuster in 1982), 24.
29
Webber, M., 'The Urban Place and the Non-Place Urban Realm', in: Webber, M., et al., *Explorations in Urban Structure* (Philadelphia: University of Pennsylvania, 1964).

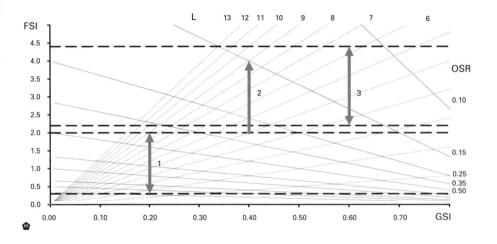

Spacemate with
thresholds for
urbanity as
expressed by Lozano
and Jacobs (scale:
fabric).
1
thresholds for
community fascilities
(Lozano 1990)
2
thresholds for a wide
variety of activities
(Lozano 1990)
3
thresholds for
urbanity and diversity
(Jacobs 1961)

Leuven in Belgium adds 'network urbanity' to the discussion. This is an urbanity which has no relationship to the old, dense city and develops on the urban fringe.[30]

It can be concluded from this that the notion of urbanity is a very elastic one. We do not here want to take a stance on any correct definition or suggest a new one, but prefer to delineate the notion of urbanity into separate sub-properties, focusing on the physical-spatial properties of the built environment. We suggest that physical factors such as interface (the relationship between buildings and network), building surface (coverage), grain (or block) size, profile width and tare space (proportion of private and public space) can be viewed as elements contributing to a description and understanding of the concept of urbanity. In this paragraph we will, therefore, discuss the performance of some of these properties in relation to density. If such properties are seen as being central to the definition of urbanity, then the outcome might help to judge the degree of urbanity in an area. If this is not the case, if for example the more traditional definition of urbanity as physically conditioned is deemed irrelevant, then these performances can still convey specific characteristics of the built landscape without explicitly being labelled conditions for urbanity. Depending on the view taken on urbanity, one is free to incorporate the performances of the sub-properties as a description of a situation as being more or less urbane, or just leave them as descriptions among others, but not necessarily essential to the chosen notion of urbanity. Below we will discuss the sub-properties *user intensity, catchment* and *network and connectivity ratio*. This series of sub-properties is certainly not exhaustive, and, as was the case for parking and daylight access, the analyses constitute starting points for further investigation rather than presenting absolute values of performances.

USER INTENSITY

Lozano describes the relationship between density, user intensity and urbanity in North American cities as based on the concept of viable thresholds:

30
Mulder, B. de, 'Old
Dispersions and Scenes for
the Production of Public
Space. The Constructive
Margins of Secondarity',
Architectural Design 78 (1)
2008, 28–33.

At certain densities (thresholds), the number of people within a given area is sufficient to generate the interactions needed to make certain urban functions or activities viable. Clearly, the greater the number and variety of urban activities, the richer the life of a community; thus, urbanity is based on density.[31]

31
Lozano, 'Density in Communities', op. cit. (note 6), 316.

Following this line of thought, Amsterdam in 1880 can be described as being much more urbane than it is today. In 1880 the average population density in Amsterdam was almost 600 inhabitants per hectare. Today, the city is nine times less intensely inhabited; the population density was 64 inhabitants per hectare in 2000.

Lozano describes a series of density thresholds as being critical to different levels of urbanity (or lack of it). The distinctions made are based on housing density[32] and are very much related to development types commonly found in the USA. According to Lozano, the first threshold can be found at 20 dwellings per hectare (40 inhabitants per hectare) 'since below that level it is difficult to provide community facilities in close proximity to the dwellings'.[33] The urban fabrics are dominated by detached houses and semi-detached two-family houses and can be positioned in Spacemate (FSI_f=0.3; GSI_f=0.15).[34] ● The next threshold is found starting at 130 dwellings per hectare (260 inhabitants per hectare or FSI_f=2.0). Above this level, according to Lozano, 'there can be a wide variety of facilities and activities easily accessible to each dwelling'.[35] Jacobs argues that an even higher density is necessary if we are to speak of urbanity.[36] The bandwidth described by Jacobs starts at 175 dwellings per hectare (350 inhabitants per hectare or FSI_f=2.2) and has a maximum of 350 dwellings per hectare (700 inhabitants per hectare or FSI_f=4.4). Higher intensities, according to Jacobs, lead to standardization and, therefore, to an absence of diversity. Lozano, in a similar way, highlights different complications and less positive performances when densities become very high. Urbanity is certainly present, but in Lozano's opinion issues such as parking, congestion, lack of open space and privacy make it a very unattractive form of urbanity.

32
Lozano uses dwelling units per acre (1 acre = 0.404 hectare).

33
Lozano, 'Density in Communities', op. cit. (note 6), 317.
34
Based on the following assumptions: an occupancy rate of 2.0 (similar to the situation in Amsterdam in 2000); the gross floor area of a dwelling is 150 m²; and the network tare space is 30 per cent.
35
Lozano, 'Density in Communities', op. cit. (note 6), 317.
36
Jacobs, J., The Death and Life, op. cit. (note 20).

Discussing user intensity, one also needs to take into account the split between residential and non-residential users, as well as the composition of the latter. Workplaces, tourists and visitors of different kinds of amenities; all contribute differently to the user intensity of network and other public spaces. A one-sided focus on residential users overlooks a great deal of important activity that further increases user intensity.

Potential user intensity is dependent on internal and external factors. One internal factor is the one sketched so far; the potential for a presence of plenty of people in an area, generated by the floor space present in that area. The second, the external factor, depends on the modes of transport and the accessibility for those different modes in an area. Inner-city shops do not only rely on clients who live within walking distance. Even if an area has a relative high density, it will probably not generate enough consumers locally to support a large and diverse mix of retail outlets. A large portion of consumers come to those shops over long distances, all using different modes of transport. Therefore, the potential in this case consists of an internal component generated by the

Three modalities compared in terms of space consumption.

area itself and an external component. In many cases amenities rely almost entirely on external users. Malls and hospitals on the fringe, and a restaurant with a good reputation in an 'off' location are examples of attractors that have virtually no local user component. Necessity and choice, in combination with good transport (private car or public transport), draw visitors from a large catchment area. Matters such as centrality, transportation techniques, real estate economics, historically grown concentrations, transport pricing, and so forth all affect this external component. This complex matter is beyond the scope of this research, but certainly has a great impact on the viability of amenities and associated urbanity. Depending on the character of the amenity the proportion of internal and external components differs. In what follows we explore the relationship between density, transport modalities and the catchment area.

TRANSPORT, ENERGY AND DENSITY

Preindustrial, dense city settlements provided (and still do) a relatively large catchment area, even when most movements were made on foot. Much of the general decline in density discussed in Chapter 2 has been possible because of developments in transport techniques. The sprawling suburbs of North America are impossible to imagine without the private car. But in relation to density and catchment area, what do these historical changes look like?

A half-hour trip by foot, bike or by car approximately covers an area of 20, 175 and 700 km² respectively.[37] For equal densities one could roughly state that the car has increased the potential for employment, commercial spending and social contact by more than 35 times compared to the most ancient transport method and four times compared to the bike. However, if a high-density city layout (the inner city of Amsterdam, for instance, with an FSI_f of 2.0) with walking and biking as dominant modalities is compared to a layout with low densities relying mainly on transport by car (for instance Phoenix, Arizona, FSI_f 0.1), and the catchment is expressed in floor area and not in ground surface only, then the advantage of potential interaction for the car decreases to a factor of al-

37
Based on a half-hour trip with an average walking speed of 5 km/h, biking speed of 15 km/h, and driving speed of 30 km/h.

most two compared to walking. In such a comparison the bike in Amsterdam performs better than the car in Phoenix: five times as much floor space is within the reach of the biker compared to the motorist. If the sizes of dwellings are considered – larger suburban villa's in Phoenix (175 m²) versus smaller apartments in Amsterdam (75 m²) – the walker in Amsterdam performs slightly better than the motorist in Phoenix (1.3 times more dwellings can be reached on foot). By bike, almost 12 times more addresses can be reached than by car in this example.

If public transport options such as tram, bus and metro are considered, the car's reach remains larger. Public transport covers areas between 150 and 400 km², compared to 700 km² for the car.[38] If a comparison is made between the two city layouts used above (FSI$_f$ 2.0 based on public transport and FSI$_f$ 0.1 relying on the car), however, then the picture looks different. In terms of potential floor area that can be reached, public transport scores between four (tram and bus) and twelve (metro) times better than the private car.

As ✿ on page 72 illustrated, there seems to be an inverted relation between transport energy consumption and built density. Focusing on another aspect of transport, CO_2 emission, we find even larger differences between the sprawl and more dense settlements. The half-hour journey by car produces between 1.8 to 3.8 kg of CO_2, depending on the type of car. The comparable journey by public transport produces between 0.3 and 0.5 kg of CO_2. If these two factors are combined – absolute CO_2 production and the amount of floor area that potentially can be reached in the two examples – the efficiency can be calculated. The car can potentially reach 20 to 40 m² of floor area for every mg of CO_2 that is produced, while public transport brings an individual the choice of 800 to 1,600 m² of floor area for the same mg of CO_2. In a situation with better filled busses than the present averages, the difference becomes even more remarkable: 20 to 40 m² of floor area compared to 3,400 m² of floor area per mg of CO_2 (factor 85 to 170).

Low-density, car-dependent layouts provide less choice (less potential floor area, or activity, to interact with), while consuming more energy and producing more CO_2 compared to higher densities with public transport. In addition to the larger efficiency in interaction for public transport in dense settlements, the space consumption of the transportation modalities themselves differ significantly, as ✿ illustrates.

NETWORK AND CONNECTIVITY RATIO
Besides user intensity in general terms, the number of people and vehicles moving and staying in the public streets can also be viewed as elementary to urbanity. This intensity can roughly be captured by the indicator GSI (coverage), as a high coverage within the islands, and thus little open (private) space, forces people into the public streets. The coverage mentioned by Jacobs as successful for generating urbanity range from 60 to 80 per cent of the lots (or islands), leaving the other 20 to 40 per cent non-built as courtyards. This high coverage on the scale of the island, combined with high built intensity (FSI) and little network (tare) space, should then generate a high intensity of movements and interaction between people in the streets.

38
Again, based on a half-hour trip with an average speed for bus and tram of 20 km/h, metro 35 km/h and car 30 km/h. Although the speed of tram, bus and metro is similar to the car, the catchment for public transport is lower due to the fact that a part of the travel time is spent walking to and from the stops, 12 minutes walking (1 km) in this example. For both car and public transport (tram and bus), the average speed is generally limited by higher densities due to congestion. This is not taken into account here.

The basic definition of OSR describes the relationship between gross floor area and all non-built space of the fabric. Often, however, it is of interest to assess the relation between gross floor area and the public portion of the non-built space (in this case the network area). This network ratio, ΔOSR, can be calculated as the difference between the OSR values of the fabric and island:

❖ $\Delta OSR = OSR_f - OSR_i$

Examples with a very low network ratio (ΔOSR) and thus a high pressure on the public network are the medieval parts of Barcelona (Gotic, Raval). In these compact areas with narrow alleys, a combination of a high coverage within the islands (90 per cent), little network tare space (less than 20 per cent), and high built intensities (FSI_f of almost 4.0) contribute to a very low network ratio. The lowest network ratio in Amsterdam can be found in the city centre (Jordaan, De Pijp, Grachtengordel), but also areas of more recent date such as Java and KNSM have low rates.

This is one way to indicate the pressure or intensity in the public network generated by the floor area. However, its value is very much dependent on the surface area of the network. Two areas with the same network ratio, such as the Grachtengordel and De Pijp, can have different network densities. The amount of floor area in relation to network length thus differs. This relation, FSI/N, translates into the possibility for public and/or commercial functions to interact with potential users in the street. The number of potential passers-by increases with an increase in programme and a decrease in network density.

If these two indicators are considered in isolation, more programme on larger islands increases the 'pressure' on the public network. However, the exposure or accessibility of the islands contradicts these findings. The potential exposure of private space (islands) in relation to public (network) space depends on the measurements of the islands alone. Large islands have relatively little exposure (or accessibility) as the façade length is limited. This exposure ratio can be formulated as the potential façade length to island area in which the potential façade length is equivalent to the length of the perimeter of the island.

The number of intersections as an indicator for circulation convenience is considered to be another important factor in relation to urbanity.[39] The (internal) connectivity of a fabric can be said to be conditioned by this factor.[40] In fabrics with more streets and intersections (and thus smaller islands), people have a larger variety of routes to choose from. This stimulates interaction which, as discussed earlier, is seen as one defining characteristic of urbanity. Both island size and the numbers of crossings are related to network density (N). The connectivity ratio, or the amount of crossings per hectare, increases proportionally to the square of the network density:

❖   Connectivity Ratio $= \dfrac{N^2}{4}$

An interesting observation that can be made from the above analysis of the basic geometry of the fabric (and its relation to properties that are often considered to be central to urbanity), is the conflicting nature of the pressure on public space (network ratio), the exposure and the (internal)

39
Jacobs, J., *The Death and Life*, op. cit. (note 20);
Siksna, A., 'The Effects of Block Size and Form in North American and Australian City Centres', *Urban Morphology* 1 (1997), 19–33.
40
Marshall, S., *Streets & Patterns* (Oxon: Spon Press, 2005).

connectivity depending on the amount of crossings. All are regarded as important to urbanity. Intensity is (internally) generated not only by the amount of programme and its primary distribution, but also by the amount of network that has to accommodate the generated movements. Less network, and thus larger islands, concentrates the movements and thus increases the intensity within the network in terms of network ratio. However, this increase of scale – more programme on larger islands and thus more intensity within the public network – conflict with and are tempered by the architectural organization of the island. The exposure and accessibility of the island and the human scale of a walkable urban fabric put a limit on the simplistic endeavour for more intensity, which to some is supposed to equal urbanity. The tension between these performances produces an outcome that is a compromise, neither too large nor too small.

EVALUATION OF FOUR SAMPLES

To make the above-sketched sub-performances of urbanity more comprehensible, four samples will be discussed. ◑ These are De Pijp and Zuidwest Kwadrant in Amsterdam, Goedereede (a small village south of Rotterdam), and Märkisches Viertel in Berlin. Both De Pijp and Märkisches Viertel have a high built intensity (FSI_f 1.78 and 1.81 respectively) and a relatively high network ratio, but the latter is probably not considered as being very urbane. The differences in the other properties described above, exposure ratio and connectivity ratio, point to defining the first as urbane and the second as not. De Pijp has a relative high coverage (GSI_f 0.47) in comparison to Märkisches Viertel (GSI_f 0.13). Both have street profiles of approximately 20 m, but the grain size in De Pijp (90 m) is four times smaller than in Märkisches Viertel (400 m). The exposure and Connectivity Ratio is therefore much higher in De Pijp. Goedereede has the same amount of programme as Zuidwest Kwadrant, FSI_f 0.86 and 0.78 respectively, but the buildings are only half the height. Still it could be regarded as more urbane due to the same reasons as mentioned earlier. In Goedereede, the network ratio is more than two times lower than in Zuidwest Kwadrant and the streets are thus (potentially) more intensely used. Besides, the grain of the urban fabric is smaller in Goedereede, 60 m compared to 135 m, which results in a high exposure ratio.

No simple formula exists for urbanity, only different solutions that can be critically judged based on sub-properties that can all contribute to conditions favourable to urbanity.

PERFORMANCE BASED DESIGN

Every performance can be viewed as a descriptive layer that, when combined with others, can be used to clarify different consequences for the quality of urban environments. It is important to emphasize that the performances that have been discussed above define a – mostly maximal – potential. The conditions that are set by density in these cases are primary conditions that limit the performance of a fabric. This in no way indicates that a particular concrete form designed under those conditions automatically performs accordingly. The potential and limits are defined, but in every particular instance this potential can be (more or less) fully actualized or (more or less) 'sabotaged'. However, being a con-

De Pijp

Zuidwest Kwadrant 2

Goedereede

Märkisches Viertel

Performance of urbanity of four samples.

dition does indicate that limits are set on that which is possible. For example, in the case of daylight access, an open façade makes maximum use of the daylight potential, a glass curtain wall will decrease the performance a little due to pragmatic reasons, while a totally closed façade can be said to 'sabotage' the existing potential.

As discussed earlier, performance can be defined as a combination of objective properties defined by density and contextual standards. In the case of daylight access the standards will differ due to, for instance, geographical location. In Sweden the urge to maximize daylight access (light and passive solar energy) is larger than in Spain (heat). For parking, the standards are very dependent on political restrictions and market demands.

Urban form can be considered as one of the performances. Here we have added parking, daylight and 'urbanity', the last redefined as a composite concept, as descriptive layers that can serve in evaluating density. In an urban design in which urbanity is thrived for, this approach could help to first define urbanity more adequately in terms of FSI, network ratio, exposure ratio and connectivity ratio. Secondly, the effects of these performances on others, such as urban form, parking and daylight, can be monitored. As such all performances become negotiable and can be used to identify conflicting programmes and necessary trade-offs. And by so doing the design task can be formulated with greater precision. Difficulties or inconsistencies can be spotted at an early stage in the design process. Designers who engage with the built environment on this basis would have more space and time for a more detached analysis of the properties of density, instead of making instant quick leaps to normative judgments that rely on intuitive conclusions and personal experience. Sometimes quick judgements can get in the way of experimentation and innovation. A suspension of judgement can be achieved by engaging with density and performance in an iterative fashion.

To work with performances in this way could strengthen the role of the urban professionals earlier in the design process and in relation to other disciplines such as engineers, economists and planners. As described in Chapters 1 and 2, this becomes more important in the process of negotiation between private and public actors engaged in the earliest phases of designing and planning the city. Urban density and performance could help urban professionals to reclaim technical, economic and demographic issues that have fallen, or are in danger of falling, outside the urban discipline.

The performances that have been discussed above have all been defined by the use of properties that to a large extent are conditioned by density. Although the core of the density model that is used is pretty straightforward – GSI, FSI and N – the derived indicators and the trends in performance quickly become complex. We are convinced that the fusion of computerized data management and analysis can enhance the analytical and predictive power of not only single performances, such as the ones sketched above, but of the simultaneous compound of many different sub-performances on different levels of scale. This simultaneous grasping of many strata or layers of performance – which are often incompatible with each other – can both be useful to the morphological and historical interpretation of existing built environments as well as demystifying some of the trade-offs taking place in the designing and planning of new urban landscapes.

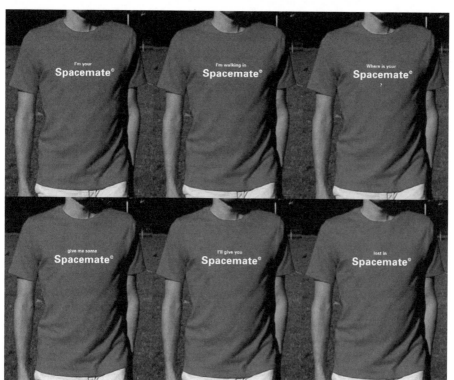

A Spacemate team.

6
PROJECTS FROM PRACTICE

As discussed in Chapter 2, urban density has been used for a long time, first to describe and later to also prescribe aspects of the built environment. Despite the fact that the relevance of density has often been questioned, it will continue to be used. The definitions proposed in Chapter 3 can be used to improve its effectiveness. As presented in Chapters 4 and 5, the knowledge gained by using the Spacematrix method can inform reasoned decisions concerning the distribution of building mass and open space, potential urban form, and performances of the urban fabric.

This chapter describes some applications of one projection of the Spacematrix, the Spacemate, in the urban planning and design process carried out by Permeta architecten[1] between 2001 and 2007. It is important to emphasize that these projects should not be regarded as test cases to posteriorly demonstrate the effectiveness of the method, but merely as cases central to its development. The project in the Western Garden Cities, executed in 2001, was the trigger for the research and development of the Spacematrix method. This and other projects helped us to construct the method and define the most effective moment of its implementation into the design and planning process. It has also made us aware of the shortcomings and pitfalls of the method due to its complexity and a certain discomfort felt by professionals to use a quantitative method to discuss spatial qualities.

The fact that we have applied the Spacemate method in many commissions since 2001 demonstrates its value to commissioners and an actual presence of the method in the design and planning practice. Besides this, the recognition of the method by urban designers and related professionals shows through the amount of publications in which it figures. It is used in reference catalogues of different municipalities such as *De Rotterdamse woonmilieuprofielen-atlas*, and *Haagse referentieprojecten*;[2] in publications discussing different methods used in urban planning and design, such as *Urban Jazz, pleidooi voor de zelfgebouwde stad*, *Ruimtegebruik in de Stedebouw*, and *DBOOK: Density, Data, Diagrams, Dwellings*.[3] The method has also been applied in actual plans, such as the *Uitwerkingsplan Kerngebied Reimerswaalbuurt* in Amsterdam, Prinshavengebied in Tilburg, *Studie Hoogbouw in Amsterdam-Noord*, and currently the method is being used in the new structural vision (*structurvisie*) for 2040 in Amsterdam.[4] Spacemate has further played a role in different educational programmes at, for instance, Delft University of Technology and Breda University of Applied Sciences.[5] In addition to these examples, the use of the open source database on www.spacecalculator.nl – launched by us in June 2004 – demonstrates that a large number of professionals, researchers and students are familiar with the method. At this moment, the Spacecalculator has more than 500 registered users, and the site has had almost 9.000 visitors; 80 per cent of which come from the Netherlands.[6]

There is clearly a growing need for ways to understand density better and relate programme to spatial goals. The municipalities of Amsterdam and Rotterdam have begun to develop projects using the concept *Rekenen en Tekenen* (measuring and designing)[7] in order to relate spatial

1
PERMETA architecten was founded in 1998 by the authors of this thesis, Meta Berghauser Pont and Per Haupt. The office is located in Amsterdam. Some of the recent projects mentioned in this research have been executed in close cooperation with Delft University of Technology.
2
Municipality of Rotterdam, *Stadsvisie Rotterdam: Spatial Development Strategy 2030* (Rotterdam: dS+V, 2007); Municipality of The Hague, *Haagse referentie projecten: Achtergronddocument: Uitwerking structuurvisie den Haag 2020* (The Hague: DSO-ROMZ, 2006).
3
Kuenzli, P. and A. Lengkeek, *Urban jazz: Pleidooi voor de zelfgebouwde stad* (Rotterdam: 010 Publishers, 2004); Zimmerman, A.L., *Ruimtegebruik in de stedebouw* (Amsterdam: Woningstichting Eigen Haard, 2007); Fernandez Per, A., and J. Mozas, *DBOOK: Density, Data, Diagrams, Dwellings* (Vitoria-Gasteiz: a+t ediciones, 2007).
4
Municipality of Amsterdam, *Uitwerkingsplan kerngebied Reimerswaalbuurt* (Amsterdam: Neighbourhood Council Osdorp/Ymere, 2005); Municipality of Tilburg, *Ontwikkelingsvisie Piushavengebied* (Tilburg, 2002); Municipality of Amsterdam, *Studie hoogbouw in Amsterdam-Noord* (Amsterdam: Neighbourhood Council Amsterdam-Noord, R&EB, 2003).
5
Spacemate was used in the Urban Studies Programme 2007/2008.
6
Followed by Germany (4 per cent), Belgium (3 per cent), Spain (1 per cent), the USA (1 per cent), the UK (1 per cent). Source: Motigo webstats (1 April 2009).

ambitions and designs to programmatic and financial conditions and objectives. Adri Duivesteijn[8] argues in the *Notie van Ruimte* report that, judged by the guidelines of The Fourth National Policy Document on Spatial Planning Extra (Vinex), the quantitative goals of the Vinex operation have been met, but the quality of the result could have been much better.[9] Further exploration into the relationship between programming, urban form and performance would have given more weight to the qualitative aspects of space consumption. We argue that, contrary to what Maarten Hajer claims in his article 'Rekenen of tekenen?', it is not too many calculations that have caused a decline in spatial qualities, rather the opposite is true.[10] The calculations that *have* taken place are mainly for programming purposes and to secure financial feasibility and optimization. What is lacking are, in fact, calculations that support the analysis of the relation between these programmatic and financial objectives and their spatial implications. The Spacematrix method could be effective in relating them.

For the projects discussed in this chapter, we make the distinction between prescribing and describing density as used in previous chapters. Using density to prescribe, or being 'forced' to design under certain density conditions, implies that the density standard is first applied and then form emerges. The introduction to the essays published in the *Harvard Design Magazine* reader *Urban Planning Today* sketches such a conditional approach to planning when it defines the future role of governments as establishing intelligent and flexible guidelines, or incentives.[11] These guidelines should not prescribe solutions or particular built forms, but should define principles or performance criteria that leave the designer free to be creative in solving design problems.[12] In this chapter we attempt to demonstrate that Spacematrix can aid in achieving this.

The discussion about density as a prescriptive concept raises questions about top-down versus bottom-up control, and regulated versus unregulated design. Although the use of guidelines in planning is often considered as a top-down approach, we argue that there is also a need to agree on certain spatial qualities and programmatic goals in less regulated or more bottom-up approaches. Jonathan Barnett describes, in the article 'Omaha by Design – All of It: New Prospects', a public hearing in which the architect of a new Wal-Mart shopping mall is asked why his building looked less appealing than a Wal-Mart in another city (Fort Collins). His reply was: 'Fort Collins had design guidelines, and you don't.'[13] Formulating guidelines can and should be part of any urban design process. General considerations, often at a higher scale than the actual design, should guide the process. We will not delve further into this subject, but find it important to point out that guidance, a bottom-up approach and flexibility do not have to be mutually exclusive.

In the second case, when using density to *describe* a specific part of the urban landscape, form already exists and density is a descriptive outcome. Describing urban environments with Spacematrix can be helpful when analysing built environments and comparing them with others. The method can also be used to monitor new developments or transformations, explore spatial and programmatic options, and optimize the relationship between urban density, form and performance.

7
Urhahn Urban Design worked on a project in Almere Hout entitled *Rekenen en Tekenen* (2005); Inbo advisors advertises with the slogan 'Rekenen en Tekenen' (2008).
8
Adri Duivesteijn was chairman of the commission responsible for the report *Notie van Ruimte* (*Notion of Space*).
9
Duivesteijn, A., *Notie van ruimte: Op weg naar de vijfde nota ruimtelijke ordening*, Parlementaire werkgroep vijfde nota ruimtelijke ordening (The Hague: Sdu uitgevers, 2000)
10
Hajer, M., 'Rekenen of tekenen?', *Staatscourant*, 11 October 2000, 3.
11
Saunders, W.S., 'Cappuccino Urbanism, and Beyond', *Harvard Design Magazine* fall 2006/winter 2007, 3.
12
Punter, J., 'Design Guidelines in American Cities: Conclusions', in: M. Larice and E. Macdonald (eds.), *The Urban Design Reader* (Oxon: Routledge, 2007), 500–516.

13
Barnett, J., 'Omaha by Design – All of It: New Prospects in Urban Planning and Design', *Harvard Design Magazine* Spring/Summer 2005, 44–49.

The Western Garden Cities in Amsterdam.

1,000 m

In the following pages we distinguish three areas of application:
— Prescriptive: guiding the urban design process;
— Descriptive: analysing and comparing urban environments and monitoring spatial developments;
— Explorative: optimizing the relationship between urban density, form and performance.

PRESCRIPTIVE USE OF SPACEMATE

Using Spacemate to prescribe densities and related spatial qualities has been tested in the urban renewal project *ParkStad* for the Western Garden Cities (*Westelijke Tuinsteden*) in Amsterdam.[14] The Western Garden Cities ❷ are part of the General Extension Plan Amsterdam (AUP), developed by Cornelis van Eesteren and Th. K. van Lohuizen in 1934.

RENEWAL PLAN PARKSTAD

In 2000 the municipality of Amsterdam presented a vision for the transformation of this area. At that moment the area contained 54,000 dwellings, of which almost 80 per cent consisted of social housing.[15] The goal was to create more diversity in dwelling typologies, in types of ownership (less social housing), price (to attract more middle-class incomes) and size (bigger dwellings). In 2001, Bureau Parkstad,[16] the organization responsible for the coordination of the transformation of the area, published a renewal plan (*ontwikkelingsplan*) in which, apart from the social and economical revitalization, an additional 11,000 dwellings were foreseen to keep pace with the decreasing number of inhabitants per dwelling.[17] This increase in the number of dwellings would amount to 20 per cent intensification. Nobody mentioned that, due to the larger size

14
Permeta architecten, *FSI-GSI-OSR als instrumentarium voor verdichting en verdunning: Case study Nieuw West*, commissioned by Bureau Parkstad (Amsterdam, 2000); Bureau Parkstad, *Richting ParkStad 2015: Ontwikkelingsplan voor de vernieuwing. Samenvatting*, Concept (Amsterdam, February 2001).
15
Municipality of Amsterdam, *Midwest: Differentiatie en intensivering in de Westelijke Tuinsteden* (Amsterdam: dRO, 1999); Bureau Parkstad, *Richting ParkStad 2015*.
16
The board of Bureau Parkstad consisted of members of the different municipal districts (Osdorp, Bos en Lommer, Geuzenveld-Slotermeer and Slotervaart-Overtooms Veld) and the central municipality of Amsterdam.
17
Demolition of 13,300 dwellings (social housing), construction of 24,300 new dwellings. See Bureau Parkstad, *Richting ParkStad 2015*, op. cit. (note 14).

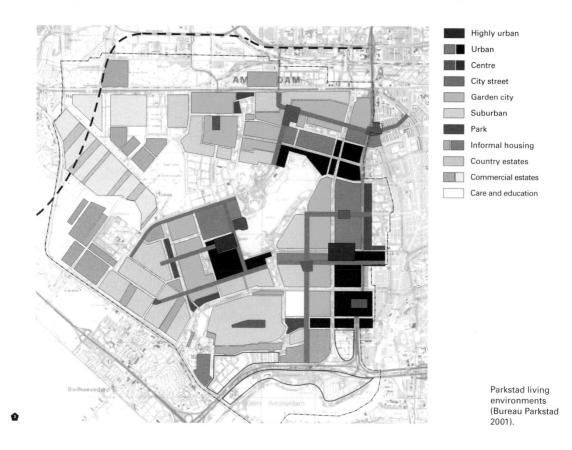

■	Highly urban
■	Urban
■	Centre
■	City street
■	Garden city
■	Suburban
■	Park
■	Informal housing
■	Country estates
■	Commercial estates
□	Care and education

Parkstad living
environments
(Bureau Parkstad
2001).

of these dwellings, the intensification in terms of FSI amounted to 30 per cent.[18] And in addition, when the floor area committed to economic functions was taken into account as well (475,000 m² of offices and shops[19]), the FSI increased by more than 40 per cent.

To achieve more density and diversity, ten different living environments were defined and mapped ⬟, characterized by lifestyles,[20] functions (social and economic) and physical properties (functional mix, connectivity, parking, public space and density). The living environments were categorized as *highly urban, urban* (including *centre* and *city street*), *garden city, park, suburban, country estates, deregulated housing constructions* and *commercial estates*.[21] The category *urban* was characterized as an environment with a mix of functions, with good connectivity and collective open spaces within the building blocks. The category *suburban*, on the other hand, was characterized as an environment consisting of mainly (attached) single-family houses, private gardens and employment opportunities within the residences. Permeta architecten was asked to use Spacemate to improve on the specification of these ten different living environments so that the distribution of the programmatic ambition (intensification of 40 per cent) within the whole area could be monitored and designs for local urban plans could be assessed at a later time during the process.[22]

18
The average dwelling size in the areas Osdorp, Bos en Lommer, Geuzenveld-Slotermeer and Slotervaart-Overtooms Veld is 72 m² of usable floor area (*gemiddeld gebruiksoppervlak, gbo*) (www.os.amsterdam.nl) and the average size of the new dwellings will be 90 m² of usable floor area (*gbo*) in 2015, see: Bureau Parkstad, *Leefmilieus Park-Stad: Bijlage 5 – Richting Parkstad 2015*, Concept (Amsterdam, February 2001).
19
Ibid.
20
Based on the categories described in Urhahn Urban Design, *De woonwijk van de toekomst*, Idea book for the Bouwfonds Award, organized by the NIROV, 2000.
21
Bureau Parkstad, *Leefmilieus*, op. cit. (note 18).

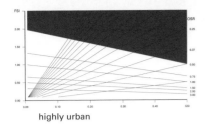

FSI
2.00
1.50
1.00
0.50
0.00

OSR
0.25
0.37
0.50
0.75
1.00
1.50
2.00
3.00

0.00 0.10 0.20 0.30 0.40 GSI

highly urban

FSI
2.00
1.50
1.00
0.50
0.00

OSR
0.25
0.37
0.50
0.75
1.00
1.50
2.00
3.00

0.00 0.10 0.20 0.30 0.40 GSI

urban

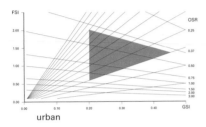

FSI
2.00
1.50
1.00
0.50
0.00

OSR
0.25
0.37
0.50
0.75
1.00
1.50
2.00
3.00

0.00 0.10 0.20 0.30 0.40 GSI

garden city

FSI
2.00
1.50
1.00
0.50
0.00

OSR
0.25
0.37
0.50
0.75
1.00
1.50
2.00
3.00

0.00 0.10 0.20 0.30 0.40 GSI

suburban

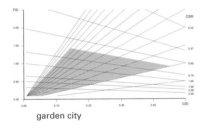

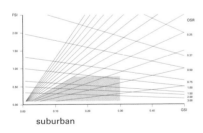

FSI
2.00
1.50
1.00
0.50
0.00

OSR
0.25
0.37
0.50
0.75
1.00
1.50
2.00
3.00

0.00 0.10 0.20 0.30 0.40 GSI

park

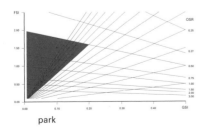

Parkstad living environments as a zone in the Spacemate diagram. On the right reference areas that fulfil these density criteria (Permeta architecten 2001).

We organized three workshops for all of the major actors in the renewal process and worked together to define these living environments with Spacemate.[23] Those attending discussed the spatial characteristics of the different environments; these included building type, the amount and type of open space and functional mix. Reference areas were used to guide the discussions. After three workshops, we presented a set of density characteristics for each living environment defined as a zone within the Spacemate graph. This zone, combined with the scale of assessment and some other factors (mix of functions and parking guidelines), ended up describing the bandwidth of design options. ♦ For the highly urban environment, for instance, a maximum OSR was defined to guarantee enough intensity (in public space). The OSR limit proposed here is actually the inverse of the minimum standard defined by Anton Hoenig in 1928 to guarantee enough green open space for the inhabitants (OSR>1.0). The suburban environments were bounded by height, FSI and GSI to guard a certain spaciousness and at the same time exclude building types that were too high and too compact.

EVALUATION OF THE DENSITY GUIDELINES

In the evaluation five years later, in 2005, the diversity in the living environments desired turned out to be less manifest than expected. The realizations of the *urban* type were seen as not 'urban' enough, the *garden city* type as too dense, and the *suburban* type as too compact.[24] We were asked to analyse some of the urban designs and concluded that not only did the plans have few formal differences, their Spacemate values were also very similar. In other words, the plans did not meet the density requirements of Parkstad. The Van Tijenbuurt in the northern part of the Western Garden Cities, for example, should have been realized within the category suburban, but when evaluating the design, it proved to be urban. Besides rows of low-rise dwellings, it included several apartment buildings of up to 10 storeys high. The plan for Delflandplein, an area near the ring road of Amsterdam, consisted of three perimeter building blocks with building heights varying from three to 12 storeys. This design fulfilled the requirements of the renewal plan. For the Reimerswaalbuurt in Osdorp, one of the sub-municipalities within the Western Garden Cities, the prescribed environment was *garden city*. As was the case in the Van Tijenbuurt, the design was less spacious and more urban than prescribed. The building blocks were practically closed and had heights ranging from three to seven storeys. In ♦ we can observe that for all three designs the dominant building type is the closed perimeter building block. In the Spacemate graphs we can see that in all three cases the OSR is halved due to the more compact urban layouts (higher GSI). We suspect that, as was noted in the evaluation report, the attempt to optimize economic feasibility for each individual project resulted in these 'mediocre solutions'. The application of the Spacemate method as such was not questioned in the report, but the implementation in the process of city development was deemed ineffective, especially the assessment of the urban designs failed.

When developing individual buildings, professionals in the Netherlands are accustomed to working with a clear set of regulations, laid out in the *Building Decree* (*Bouwbesluit*). These regulations are non-nego-

22
Parts of the Spacemate method were developed for this commission and later further explored during the research at Delft University of Technology. The density indicators used in Parkstad are FSI, GSI, OSR and L.
23
The workshops took place in 2001. Participants were the city of Amsterdam and the municipal districts Osdorp, Slotervaart-Overtoomse Veld, Bos en Lommer, Geuzenveld-Slotermeer (participating in Bureau Parkstad) and the three consortia of housing corporations (Far West, Prospect Amsterdam, Westwaarts).

24
Bureau Parkstad, *Een blik vooruit: Vijf jaar vernieuwingsoperaties in Amsterdam Nieuw West: evaluatie en keuzerichtingen* (Amsterdam, 2005).

Van Tijenbuurt old situation

Van Tijenbuurt new situation

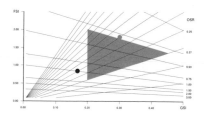

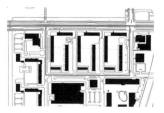

Delflandplein old situation

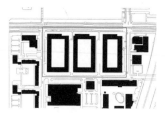

Delflandplein new situation

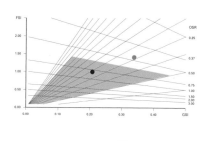

Reimerswaalbuurt old situation

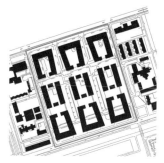

Reimerswaalbuurt new situation

● Old situation

● New situation

tiable and must be met before obtaining a permit. In city development, in contrast, negotiations about regulations and/or project goals are quite common. A legal procedure, the so-called 'Article 19', allows for the approval of a project that diverges from the regulations set out in the zoning plan and is widely used in the Netherlands.[25] In addition, when a supervisor (or quality coordinator) plays an important role in the development of a plan, negotiable planning is widespread. This implies that the actors involved in the city development process are not used to strict, non-negotiable guidelines. Because every specific, urban design in the Western Garden City was negotiable, the large-scale renewal scheme became merely a result of these local initiatives. Looking at the large downtown urban redevelopment project in Vancouver of the 1980s it is clear that providing direction in predefined urban guidelines can be very successful if we dare to say *No* now and then. Vancouver's planners managed to attract people to the city centre by creating vibrant, mixed-use, high density, high-rise residential neighbourhoods.[26] To do this they had to fight the prevailing 'suburban ideal' of the time. Larry Beasly, the

Evaluated projects: Van Tijenbuurt, Delflandplein, Reimerswaalbuurt (Permeta architecten 2002).

25
Maarse, A., 'Wetten en regels', *Rooilijn* 41 (3) 2008, 155.

26
Sandercock, L., 'Anatomy of Civic Ambition in Vancouver: Toward Humane Density', in: W.S. Saunders (ed.), *Urban Planning Today* (Minneapolis: University of Minnesota Press, 2006), 48–62.

former co-director of planning in Vancouver, explained that the success of this long-term project was partly due to the attitude of the city council. He stated:

> We have an unusual attitude about development here. Our attitude is 'If you don't measure up, we're not afraid to say No in this city.' Many cities are so afraid to say No to any developer and so they get what they deserve. But for those cities it may be above all important to promote business growth. We want quality of life first.[27]

With this example we underline the fact that predefined guidelines that have been agreed upon by all involved parties in the very first steps of the planning process, and consequently abided to, are necessary to achieve planning goals. In the Parkstad case, the Quality Team[28] was responsible for the evaluation of the different local plans and their qualitative consistency. The team was, however, not familiar with the Spacemate method and most probably felt a certain discomfort with a method that attempts to quantify spatial qualities. In addition, the different living environments were defined in Spacemate with bandwidths that overlapped one another. This was done deliberately as the workshops demonstrated that some references were difficult to characterize as one type or another. The decision was therefore to characterize them as both. Further, certain inconsistencies were related to the lack of clear agreements on how to define the scale at which the Spacemate guidelines were to be assessed and the precise demarcation of the plan area to which the guidelines were to be applied.

REVISED RENEWAL PLAN

Two steps were taken after the publication of the evaluation report. First, the living environments were redefined and the number of categories reduced from ten to three. ❂ This decision was practical and would make using them simpler, at least such was the hope. The types were as follows: a *suburban* category with low-rise dwellings, an *urban* category with apartment buildings of medium height, and a *garden city* type, characterized by higher buildings and more open space. New zones in the Spacemate were defined for these three types, without overlap in terms of density, making the distinctions between them more specific. Secondly, the definitions of scale and base land area were defined more precisely. For the urban and suburban categories, the zones defined within the Spacemate graph needed to be set at the scale of the fabric as a whole, as well as at the scale of the sub-areas within the fabric, allowing for a more uniform urban pattern. For the garden city category, the variation in density within the fabric was again left deliberately open, just as long as the overall numbers fit within the defined zone in Spacemate. After a year of working with these new definitions, the areas of the garden city type demonstrated a substantial variation in fabric type. Both the municipality and developers made use of the flexibility by introducing as many low-rise dwellings as allowable, as this building type was quite in demand in a period with a booming housing market. The large amount of this type was compensated for by other building types so that the combined result met the Spacemate guidelines.

27
Ibid., 58.

28
The Quality Team was responsible for the qualitative cohesion and the evaluation of the different plans. It consisted of independent advisors and a representative of the *Welstand* (aesthetic value committee).

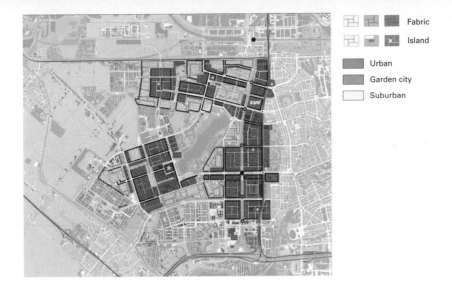

Fabric

Island

Urban

Garden city

Suburban

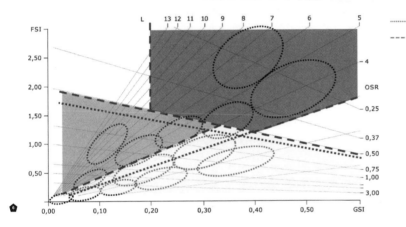

Discussed thresholds

Fixed thresholds

Revised Parkstad living environments, zones in Spacemate and scale level of assessment (Bureau Parkstad 2005).

Such compensation strategies are used regularly, especially in cases where high density numbers play an important role. Borneo Sporenburg in the centre of Amsterdam is a well-known example of an attempt to create a high-density, low-rise environment of 100 dwellings per hectare.[29] However, when measuring those fabrics with only low-rise dwellings, the density is 80 dwellings per hectare.[30] This is compensated for by apartment blocks with a density of up to 180 dwellings per hectare.

DEVELOPMENT PERMITS

We can conclude that the process of negotiation and economic optimization that commonly occurs reduced the effectiveness of the method in the described case. Still, it is possible to guide the design process using Spacemate, but only if a clear set of definitions has been agreed upon. In addition, the plans must be assessed with precision and those designs that do not fit within the defined Spacemate bandwidth should

29
Borneo Sporenburg is an area in Amsterdam developed at the end of the 1990s based on an urban scheme designed by Adriaan Geuze.
30
Based on dwelling numbers of O+S Amsterdam (www.os.amsterdam.nl) for the area G33e and G33f combined with the map and numbers from Fernandez Per and Mozas, *DBOOK*, op. cit. (note 3).

1,000 m

The ZuidoostLob
area in Amsterdam.

not be issued a permit. Saying No to developments that don't measure up should become the attitude. Furthermore, the living environments would have been better defined had network density been included in the guidelines. The performance layers discussed in Chapter 5 had not yet been developed at the start of this project. Both elements would have enriched the characterization of the different living environments.

DESCRIPTIVE USE OF SPACEMATE

Since the 1980s, a number of studies have been published that analyse and compare different built landscapes. These include *DBOOK: Density, Data, Diagrams, Dwellings*; the Lincoln Institute's*Visualizing Density*; *Densité & Formes urbaines dans la métropole Marseillaise*; *De Rotterdamse woonmilieuprofielenatlas*; *Meten met twee maten, referentieplannen bebouwingsintensiteit*; *A Pattern Image*; and *Analyse de 50 périmètres batis situés sur le canton de Genève.*[31] As discussed in Chapter 1, these publications can primarily be characterized as reference catalogues. The Spacemate method can be used in this way as well. In addition, through Spacemate's interpretative framework and the clustering of types, recommendations for spatial and programmatic changes can be made. This section discusses the project ZuidoostLob in which existing urban areas, dominated by industry, enterprises, large-scale shopping malls and offices were analysed and the options for transforming these areas into mixed urban areas were explored.[32]

The ZuidoostLob ⬠ is an area in the south-eastern section of Amsterdam, bounded by the A2 highway that runs from Amsterdam to Utrecht in the west, the railway connecting Amsterdam and Utrecht in the east, the Amstel in the north, and the Academic Medical Center (AMC) in the south. Approximately 38,000 people work in the area, divided over some

31
Ibid.; Campoli, J. and A.S. MacLean, *Visualizing Density* (Cambridge, MA: Lincoln Institute of Land Policy, 2007); Brunner, C., *Densité & forms urbaines dans la métropole marseillaise* (Marseilles: Edition Imbernon, 2005); Municipality of Rotterdam, *De Rotterdamse woonmilieuprofielenatlas* (Rotterdam: dS+V, afdeling Wonen, 2003); Municipality of Amsterdam, *Meten met twee maten: Referentieplannen bebouwingsintensiteit* (Amsterdam: dRO, coördinatieteam Optimalisering Grondgebruik, 2001); Urhahn, G.B. and M. Bobic, *A Pattern Image* (Bussum: Uitgeverij THOTH, 1994); CETAT, *Indicateurs morphologiques pour l'amenagement: Analyse de 50 périmetres batis situes sur le canton de Geneve* (Geneva: Departement des traveaux publics, 1986).
32
Permeta architecten, *Spacemate – Zuidoostlob: Kwantitatieve analyse van dichtheden en transformaties*, in cooperation with Delft University of Technology, commissioned by dRO (Amsterdam, 2004). The mix was defined as the relation between people working and living in the area.

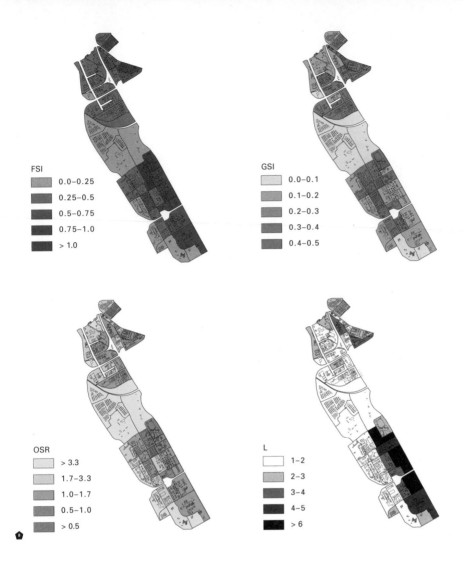

FSI
- ☐ 0.0–0.25
- ☐ 0.25–0.5
- ☐ 0.5–0.75
- ☐ 0.75–1.0
- ■ > 1.0

GSI
- ☐ 0.0–0.1
- ☐ 0.1–0.2
- ☐ 0.2–0.3
- ☐ 0.3–0.4
- ■ 0.4–0.5

OSR
- ☐ > 3.3
- ☐ 1.7–3.3
- ☐ 1.0–1.7
- ☐ 0.5–1.0
- ■ > 0.5

L
- ☐ 1–2
- ☐ 2–3
- ☐ 3–4
- ☐ 4–5
- ■ > 6

Four maps of Zuid-oostlob representing respectively FSI, GSI, OSR and L. (Permeta architecten 2004).

1,300 firms.[33] The aim of the study was to identify the different urban types present in the area and explore their potential to be transformed into mixed urban areas. In the *Structuurplan Amsterdam: Kiezen voor stedelijkheid*, the municipality of Amsterdam planned to transform the areas along the railway tracks into a mixed use, metropolitan area (*groot-stedelijk wonen-werken*).[34] The city was also striving to change the areas adjacent to the highway into a denser, monofunctional working area. We were asked to evaluate these ambitions based on the intrinsic physical conditions of the ZuidoostLob.

ANALYSIS ZUIDOOSTLOB

In a first step, the built densities of the different areas were analysed. To communicate the different density variables, four separate maps were constructed, showing FSI, GSI, L and OSR. ⬠ It is interesting to note that

33
O+S Amsterdam, Statistics available on www.os.amsterdam.nl (2007).
34
Municipality of Amsterdam, *Structuurplan Amsterdam: Kiezen voor stedelijkheid* (Amsterdam: dRO, 2003).

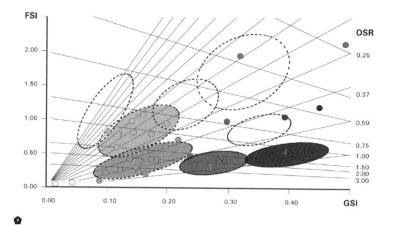

Clusters in the
Spacemate diagram
(Permeta architecten
2004).
1
mid-rise office
towers
2
low-rise small-scale
firms
3
low-rise industry
4
low-rise compact
industry

areas with high intensities (FSI) perform differently in terms of coverage (GSI). The older office areas often combine relatively high FSI values with low GSI values, while the newest office developments have both high FSI and GSI values, due to different building types and built parking solutions. This combination results in a low OSR, or, in other words, in higher pressure on the non-built space in the more recently developed parts. When the map with building heights is compared to the FSI map, it becomes clear that higher buildings do not always result in higher intensities.

By combining these variables, four clusters could be defined in the Spacemate at the scale of the fabric. ✿ These correspond roughly to the residential building types discussed in Chapter 4. Areas with a mix of small-scale firms and offices correspond to the low-rise strip type, areas dominated by mid-rise office towers to the mid-rise strip type, and areas dominated by industrial sheds to the low-rise block type (however, with a lower L). Although different building types could be seen forming clusters in the Spacemate, it became obvious that areas dominated by employment or living cannot be distinguished using only density indicators.

After completing this project, and while writing this book, we analysed the network density for three areas within the ZuidoostLob. ✿ Three samples were selected, representing three different working environments dominated respectively by mid-rise office towers (cluster 1 in ✿), low-rise small-scale firms (cluster 2), and low-rise compact industry (cluster 4).[35] The areas with small-scale firms and office towers have a network density of 0.010 and 0.011 m/m², respectively. This corresponds roughly to an urban pattern mesh size of 200 m. Residential areas of the same FSI and GSI have network densities ranging from 0.015 to 0.027 m/m². These correspond to a mesh size of 75 to 130 m, and are thus clearly smaller in size. We found the same difference in the areas dominated by compact industry. The network density is 0.016 m/m² (mesh size 150 m) for this category, while in an area dominated by housing (Borneo Sporenburg) it is 0.035 m/m² (with a mesh size of 75 m). Based on these three cases, one cannot conclude that working areas in general have lower network densities, or larger islands, than living areas, but

35
This was not part of the 2004 commission. For this research the network density of three typical examples in the Zuidoostlob was calculated.

248

Three samples representing three different urban layouts within the Zuidoostlob area and three clusters in the Spacemate diagram (see ⬠).

[cluster 1] mid-rise office towers		[cluster 2] low-rise small-scale firms		[cluster 4] low-rise compact industry	
FSI	0.81	FSI	0.23	FSI	0.52
GSI	0.14	GSI	0.15	GSI	0.44
OSR	1.05	OSR	3.66	OSR	1.07
L	5.8	L	1.5	L	1.2
N	0.011	N	0.010	N	0.016

one could argue that it becomes possible to differentiate between working and living areas through the use of network density. This is difficult when using only FSI and GSI. Further research should be performed to arrive at more robust conclusions.

TRANSFORMATION STRATEGIES

After completing the first analysis, we critically examined the ambition of the municipality of Amsterdam to transform the areas along the railway tracks into mixed-use urban areas. The mix is defined as 'optimal' when the relation between people living and working in the area is 1:1.[36] We used the same three samples of 10 hectares as discussed earlier, and formulated three transformation strategies for these samples:

1 Addition of dwellings;
2 Replacement of existing buildings with housing;
3 Reuse of the existing buildings.

For the first strategy, the possible increase in terms of coverage (GSI) was estimated. The small-scale industrial environment and the mid-rise office environment have at present a relatively low GSI (app. 0.15). We estimated the potential increase in GSI to be 100 per cent. The GSI of the low rise compact industrial environment is already high with almost 0.45, and here the additional buildings would have to be positioned on top of the existing industrial sheds. Combined with the building height, we arrived at a maximum intensification and could calculate the resulting mix (all new constructions are for housing). When adding buildings with an average building height of four storeys, the low rise small-scale industrial environment would arrive at a mix of 1:0.5 (or two inhabitants per employee), the low rise compact industrial environment at a mix of 1:1, and the mid-rise office environment at a mix of 1:3.7. The good mix was thus easiest to achieve in the first sample and most difficult in the last. And although the second sample seems to arrive at an optimal mix by adding buildings on top of the existing industrial sheds, this transformation is less feasible due to construction difficulties and high costs.

36
Each resident uses 60 m² (based on the size of a dwellings of 125 m² with 2.1 people in residence); each office worker uses 30 m² and each industrial worker 60 m². A mix of the two results in 50 m².

The second strategy explored the effects of demolishing parts of the area and introducing different dwelling types to arrive at a balance between working and living. Based on our findings it became clear that 80 per cent of the territory of the mid-rise office environment needed to be re-developed (read: demolished and rebuilt), to reach a goal of a mix of working and living of 1:1. In this case, the work areas were substituted with a large quantity of single-family houses.[37] In the areas along the highway (low-rise small-scale firms), less than 40 per cent of the territory needed to be transformed, and for the low-rise compact industrial environment, 50 per cent would have to be redeveloped. When projecting apartments[38] instead of single-family housing into the mid-rise office environments, the necessary amount of transformation was reduced to less than 50 per cent of the plan area. To arrive at this level of programmatic mix, 85,000 m² of floor area for living (675 dwellings) had to replace 40,000 m² of office floor area, a costly enterprise. The same return, namely one dwelling (125 m²) per 60 m² of demolished office floor area, is achieved by adding single-family housing to the low-rise small-scale industrial environment adjacent to the highway. The results improved (judged in terms of mix) further by adding higher-density building types to this area, such as denser single-family houses or single-family houses in combination with apartment buildings. Hereby a return of one dwelling (125 m²) per 15 m² of demolished office floor area could be achieved, a factor 4 better than in the mid-rise office environments adjacent to the railway tracks.

For the third strategy, reuse of buildings, no changes in FSI would occur. In both of the industrial environments, 50 per cent of the buildings had to be transformed into dwellings. Because offices are more intensely used than dwellings, almost 70 per cent of the office towers had to be transformed into dwellings to arrive at a balance of 1:1 between inhabitants and workers.

RECOMMENDATIONS

Based on these findings, we concluded that the small-scale industrial areas along the highway were the easiest to transform into a mixed urban area. Our argument was that less floor area had to be replaced to achieve a balance between inhabitants and workers of 1:1. All three strategies could be used simultaneously in a slow process of bottom-up transformation. Density guidelines and targets for the functional mix could be described to guide the development in the intended direction. The most realistic scenario for the large-scale industrial environments was the replacement of the large sheds with dwellings and new offices, or smaller-sized businesses. For the areas dominated by office towers, replacing existing buildings with housing would 'cost' too much. For each dwelling 60 m² of office floor area would be demolished. Here, the addition of dwellings seemed to be the most realistic.

We advised the municipality to revise their ambitions based on our conclusions. Instead of realizing a mixed-use metropolitan area (*grootstedelijk wonen-werken*) only along the railway, we proposed that such an environment would be realized along the highway first. The area next to the railway could then later be intensified by adding mid-rise buildings in between the office towers. A new type of living and working environ-

37
The Spacemate density of the additional single-family housing type is: FSI=0.45; GSI=0.18.

38
The Spacemate density of the additional apartment type is: FSI=1.80; GSI=0.35.

The region Leiden-
Alphen aan den Rijn.

ment could be introduced here, similar to Waterstad in Rotterdam, where high-rise apartment buildings are inserted into an existing urban pattern of building blocks. Instead of inserting high-rise, we propose to insert the block type into an existing urban pattern of towers. The large-scale industrial environment of the middle area could in our opinion best be developed by replacing the existing sheds with new building types (offices, small businesses and/or housing).

EXPLORATIVE USE OF SPACEMATE

As discussed in the previous section, plans and locations can be analysed and possible transformations can be monitored, but also explored, by sketching the possible 'routes' a plan can take in the Spacemate. In this section we discuss two projects that use the Spacemate method to explore the spatial and programmatic capacity of an area, or, in other words, to identify the potential that a location offers for urban development. The first project, *OndersteBoven* ('UpsideDown') was commissioned by the Ministry of Housing, Spatial Planning and the Environment (VROM) in the Netherlands, and studies the spatial capacity for further urbanization of the region between Leiden and Alphen aan den Rijn.[39] The second project is located in Alkmaar and concerns the optimization of the financial and spatial output of an existing urban design by manipulating the programmatic and spatial objectives.[40]

EXPLORING SPATIAL CAPACITIES

In the project *OndersteBoven*, the main objective was to make an inventory of the possibilities for low-density developments in the western parts of the Randstad, the region Leiden-Alphen aan den Rijn. ♠ Instead of projecting a programme onto a chosen location, the territory should

39
Permeta architecten, *Project Ondersteboven,* in cooperation with Delft University of Technology, commissioned by VROM/DGR (Amsterdam, 2005).
40
Permeta architecten, *Task Force Ruimtewinst. Assist Alkmaar: Een groeimodel voor de Waterkwekerij*, in cooperation with Rudy Uytenhaak, commissioned by DHV Ruimte en Mobiliteit, (Amsterdam, 2007); Permeta architecten, 'Verdichtingsstudie groeimodel', *TFR-update* 5, (Haarlem: Task Force Ruimtewinst, Provincie Noord-Holland 2007), 8-10.

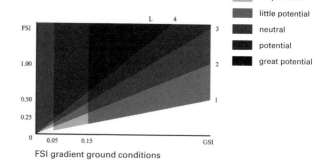

FSI gradient ground conditions

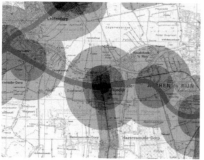

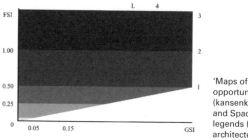

Conditions for car accessibility

FSI gradient car accessibility

no potential
little potential
neutral
potential
great potential

'Maps of opportunity' (kansenkaarten) and Spacemate legends (Permeta architecten 2005).

define the programme, based on its intrinsic properties. An example where existing patterns of urbanization and infrastructure determined the choice for new urban developments is the project Westergouwe (Gouda West). Based on the accessibility and the existing patterns of urbanization, this location seems logical for urban developments, but from the perspective of its ground conditions (water management and soil conditions), the choice for development in this area becomes less self-evident. In the project discussed here, the ground conditions, combined with accessibility and landscape values, dictated the possibilities for further urbanization. The Spacemate method was used to translate the conditions of the territory into density criteria and related possible urban forms.

We distinguished three steps in this study. The first step included the registration of the hard regulations and restrictions which limit further development. Examples are restricted zones along highways and other infrastructure, and areas with protected nature. The second step involved the use of GIS technology to manage the different characteristics of the region such as the ground properties (soil conditions and water levels), accessibility (by car and public transport), and the valuation of the landscape. This resulted in 'maps of opportunity' (kansenkaarten). To be able to relate these to the potential for urban development, the characteristics were in a third step translated into density criteria that can be seen in ⚙. It was beyond the scope of the project to do an exhaustive study of all relevant factors conditioning the potential, so we chose to interview specialists within the Ministry of VROM to arrive at a workable set of assumptions.[41]

41
W. de Visser, R. van Etteger and M. Odijk (VROM); J. Jonkers (Spanbroek, Jonkers en Tiemessen).

Two factors of the ground conditions were defined: first, the consistency and content of the ground itself and the depth of the sand layers and, second, the elevation and water management within the areas. When looking at the composition of the ground, large amounts of sand in both shallow and deep layers do not restrict types of construction. Sand in deep layers, however, implies that piles must be driven, making new developments more expensive. It makes more sense to construct taller buildings and, as elevators become economically viable in buildings of six storeys and higher, these heights are defined as the minimum standard. When there is a large quantity of sand in the top layer only, construction of light buildings is possible without driving deep piles. Light developments of two storeys maximum are then deemed possible.

The second element of the topography considered was the elevation of the land in relation to water management (height of the area in comparison to NAP[42]). Lower areas in the Netherlands are considered at risk for flooding and therefore less suitable for building than higher areas. Sea water is expected to rise over time and, with more rain, more areas are needed to contain the water. Water storage areas should preferably be located in the lower lands. In the current project, all developments were prohibited in areas 5 m below NAP, while no restrictions were placed on developments above NAP. Semi-permanent or water-resistant developments were allowed between these two extremes. Spacious developments, of a maximum of two storeys, were allowed down to a maximum of 2 m below NAP. The ground floor of the building had to be able to resist water so that when the water rises to extreme levels (once in 1,000 years) the buildings remain intact. For the lower areas (ranging from 2 to 5 m below NAP) compact development, behind dykes or on terps (*terpen*), were considered feasible. This implied that at the scale of the fabric, the GSI had to be kept high, while at the district scale it had to be low to keep enough land available for water storage. This resulted in concentrations of compact urban developments in an open landscape.

Accessibility by car and public transport defined the capacity in terms of gross floor area, or FSI. The proximity of a regional highway network determined the score for cars, and the score for public transport was dependent on the distance to a train station. The highest densities could be achieved within a radius of 500 m. At a distance of 4 km, this potential decreased to zero.

The last factor taken into account in this project related to the 'spatial cluttering' (*verrommeling)* of the landscape. This term was used in contrast to an open landscape with no or few constructions. In areas of high spatial and cultural qualities, new developments were prohibited or had to be concentrated to create a clear distinction between the urban development and the open landscape. This could be done by guiding density at two levels: again, at the fabric scale the GSI ought to be relatively high, and at the district scale very low. According to the landscape architects from VROM, in areas where the quality of the landscape is already 'spoilt' by scattered developments, new developments could contribute to improving the situation and should therefore be allowed. The visual chaos could thus be tempered by aesthetically pleasing, higher and more compact developments (relative high L and GSI).

42
Normaal Amsterdams Peil (NAP) or Amsterdam Ordnance Datum is a vertical datum in use in large parts of Western Europe.

	0.0–0.1
	0.1–0.3
	0.3–0.5
	0.5–1.0
	1.0–2.0

FSI on district level

FSI on fabric level

Density maps generated through the juxtaposition of the 'maps of opportunity' and Spacemate criteria (Permeta architecten 2005).

All these characteristics were translated into Spacemate terms using FSI, GSI, OSR and L, and, if necessary, at different scale levels (fabric and district). To calculate the potential for further urban development, the 'maps of opportunity' were projected on top of each other in the last step, resulting in a map that shows all possible combinations. These included, among many other things, areas with a combination of high landscape value and good accessibility, locations above NAP but with nature restrictions, and good accessible areas, above NAP and with few restrictions. Based on the combination of factors, zones were constructed in the Spacemate; the relevant factors overlapped in these zones. Protected areas, even when in close proximity to a train station, were prohibited from any development; areas with a good car and public transport accessibility in combination with a location above NAP were given a high potential. The result was a map that showed the potentials for further urbanization within the region, based on the characteristics of the territory.  The conditions for further urbanization were the best along the Rhine River and the main road between Leiden and Alphen aan den Rijn (N11). Besides developments in low densities, more urban developments were possible on locations in the proximity of existing urban areas (Leiden, Hazerswoude-Rijndijk and Alphen aan den Rijn). In the areas north and south of this axis, densities were lower on the scale of the district, but again relatively high on the scale of the fabric. In other words, concentrated new developments on a small scale were allowed here as it guaranteed an open landscape at the larger scale.

This analysis provided to be a tool to explore the range of programmatic options for and use of space on a regional scale. However, the whole approach is dependent on the content of the smaller scales. The compound effects in the region can only be analysed and understood if the lower levels of scale are engaged with as well, in this case the fabric components. The project is an example of the application of Spacemate in a process where the programmatic potential of an area has yet to be defined. In such circumstances, Spacemate can be used as a pure pre-design application. Combined with the insights concerning fabric types and performance presented in Chapter 4 and 5, this could lead to a more sophisticated tool for regional planning. Further research, including specialist knowledge and efficient computer management of large amounts of data, should be done to develop this further.

400 m

The Alkmaar
project.

OPTIMIZING URBAN DESIGNS

In Alkmaar we worked on a project that was part of a larger programme, financed by the Province of Noord-Holland: the *Task Force Ruimtewinst* (Task Force Space Efficiency).[43] The goal of this programme is to assist municipalities in intensifying their land use. The role of Permeta architecten, in cooperation with 4DStad, DHV group and Rudy Uytenhaak architectenbureau, was to assist in the evaluation of a design by GroupA of the redevelopment of a sewage treatment area in Alkmaar.[44] (● left) The design comprised 500 dwellings (260 single-family houses and 240 apartments) and 25,000 m² of office space, resulting in a plan with an average density of 45 dwellings per hectare, or FSI 0.85. The plan was € 40 million over budget. It was estimated that at least 620 extra dwellings were needed to make the plan financially feasible, and thus a density of 100 dwellings per hectare, or FSI 1.60, was needed. The assignment was to explore the intensification opportunities and to provide insight into the programmatic, spatial and financial effects of this intensification.

The Spacemate method was used to explore the extent to which intensification could take place in the area and by which means. The following four strategies were used ●:

1   Enlargement of the plan area (more A);
2   Increase in the number of apartments (higher FSI_f and/or GSI_f);
3   Increase in the density of the building types already part of the design (higher FSI_i and/or GSI_i);
4   Decrease in the amount of non-built (public) space (less T_f and T_d).

The first strategy involved a simple increase in base land area. For these additional plan areas, the same densities were used as in GroupA's plan, resulting in an increase in the number of dwellings and the amount of

43
Permeta architecten, *Task Force Ruimtewinst*, op. cit. (note 40); Permeta architecten, 'Verdichtingsstudie groeimodel', op. cit. (note 40).
44
The design was made by GroupA, an architecture office situated in Rotterdam.

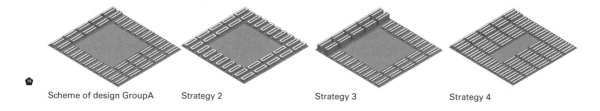

Scheme of design GroupA   Strategy 2   Strategy 3   Strategy 4

Three strategies for intensification (Permeta architecten 2007).

office space. In other words, the design was copied to available locations nearby. A park adjacent to the plan area, used partly as a municipal nursery, was available for this extension. This provided, however, locations for only 100 dwellings; six more parks of similar size were needed to accommodate the dwellings required to achieve the requested financial target.

Using the second strategy, we attempted to find the appropriate balance between the less dense, low-rise developments (FSI_i=2.0), and the more dense, mid-rise developments (FSI_i=3.6). This option, even when all single-family housing was replaced by apartments, provided us with half of the intensification needed (330 more dwellings).

The third strategy, which involved increasing the density of the different building types, was only possible for the apartment buildings. The low-rise buildings that GroupA had proposed were patio houses with relatively high densities (FSI_i=2.0; GSI_i=0.7). To provide greater intensification of the apartments suggested by GroupA, the building height was increased. The 5.5 storeys were doubled, reaching 11 storeys, resulting in 240 extra dwellings.

The fourth strategy focused on the public space surrounding the islands. Decreasing the amount of water, greenery and infrastructure – the tare space of the plan – provided more space for construction. This implied that the density was not increased at the level of the islands, but at the level of the fabric and district. The design by GroupA consisted of an extraordinary amount of tare space, 65 per cent to be precise, leaving only 35 per cent for privately issued land. In comparison, the average fabric tare space of the Amsterdam samples used in this research is under 40 per cent. By reducing the tare areas for water, greenery and infrastructure to 40 per cent, 425 additional dwellings could be developed.

Combining the different strategies made it possible to improve on GroupA's design. The result was a schematic proposal that defined the new programme with other spatial qualities than those proposed by GroupA. (right) The density increased from 0.85 to 1.40, resulting in an estimated budget shortage of 20 million euros. Under more optimal circumstances, the design process could have been improved by altering the sequence of activities. The key starting points of the design should have been defined with the stakeholders first, using the Spacemate method. This would have resulted in a spatial framework with density guidelines that could then be used for commissioning the designer to make an urban design.

EFFECTIVENESS OF SPACEMATE IN PRACTICE

This chapter demonstrates that the Spacemate method can be used to analyse and describe urban areas, to depict their transformation over

FSI / GSI

0.7 / 0.2

1.4 / 0.4

1.4 / 0.2

2.8 / 0.4

3.5 / 0.4

Urban design by
GroupA (left) and
alternative plan
based on density
guidelines (right)
(Permeta architecten
2007).

time, explore the quantitative and qualitative nature of possible futures, prescribe densities to differentiate living environments, urban form and types of open space, and evaluate these density guidelines during the urban design process.

From the experiences in the Western Garden Cities in Amsterdam, the conclusion is twofold. The first conclusion concerns the Spacemate method itself, the second the organization of the planning and design process in relation to the method. Concerning the method, we can conclude that the scale at which density guidelines are defined is crucial for the level of success. In a first phase, the scale had not been defined clearly, with the result that density guidelines were merely programmatic checks afterwards and not, as was intended, a standard to guide urban form on the level of the urban fabric. Besides clear definitions concerning scale and demarcation of the plan area, it showed that it is important to construct the environmental zones in the Spacemate graph with care. Too much overlapping of zones resulted in little variation between different environments. These issues were improved largely by explicitly defining the scale and the accompanying demarcations of plan areas. The constructed zones in the Spacemate graph were revised, this time without any overlap. Besides, the addition of network density to Spacemate, as discussed in Chapter 3, would most probably have improved the description of urban form and performance and would have been helpful in defining the environments in the Western Garden City with even more precision. On the other hand, the complexity of the method could in such a case have become counterproductive.

The second conclusion that can be drawn is that the lack of an assessment procedure of the agreed upon guidelines within the design process was a problem. However, the method in itself cannot be blamed for this. If Saunders is correct when he sketches the future role of governments in defining intelligent and flexible guidelines, these governments need to become aware of their responsibility to not only define them, but also to assess whether the design solutions meet the requirements.[45]

The project in Alkmaar proves that using Spacemate to explore the spatial possibilities before a design is made could have prevented a time-consuming design experiment as that carried out by GroupA. If a plan would have been made after the Spacemate explorations, the programme of requirements could have been defined more precisely (densities and tare space at different scales), and the outcome would have been more in line with the feasibility expectations. A general conclusion based on this experience is that the Spacemate method can best be used at an early stage in the planning and design process. It is a powerful tool to explore possibilities, discuss both quantitative and qualitative objectives with all actors within the process, and then define the guidelines for the urban design. In the projects *Ondersteboven* and *ZuidoostLob* the moment of implementation of the method was therefore the most appropriate and successful in defining the capacity of a plan area in terms of programme and urban form.

Although we categorized the Spacemate method in this chapter as being more concerned with describing urban from, prescribing density and exploring possible futures, all projects actually used a mix of description, prescription and exploration. Prior to defining density guidelines, existing urban patterns or a plan area were analysed, followed by a process of optimization. Where monitoring, exploring and optimizing the relation between urban density, form and performance occurred simultaneously, the method became rather complex. Often, one or two of the aspects of the method were less developed and, especially in the Parkstad project, a great opportunity to relate the micro scale to the macro scale was not made use of. In 2001, density guidelines were defined for all living environments. Based on the spatial ambitions of Bureau Parkstad, the intensification target (plus 11,000 dwellings) should have been confronted with the spatial ambitions defined with the ten living environments. This was done, but not until 2005, when the first phase of the renewal plan was evaluated. Only then were we able to conclude that, based on the spatial ambitions, many more dwellings than 11,000 could be realized. The spatial map was adjusted to meet the programme, resulting in lower densities in the northern part of the Western Garden Cities. This area was planned to be transformed in the period between 2005 and 2011. Whether this will have severe consequences for the amount of amenities in these areas – something that the sub-municipality very much fears – remains to be seen. This could have been prevented by simultaneously analysing the existing situation, prescribing future densities and monitoring the urban designs during the process of realization. In addition, different scales should have been addressed simultaneously to understand how small-scale developments relate to large-scale ambitions and vice versa. Customized software could assist a process like this.

45
Saunders, 'Cappuccino', op. cit. (note 11).

Finally, there has been little discussion of network density as part of the projects in the present chapter. The effectiveness of this third variable in practical city development still has to be demonstrated. We are convinced that the use of network density could have improved the definition of the living environments in the Western Garden City and could have aided the analysis of Zuidoostlob. The same can be said about the performances discussed in Chapter 5. A real performance-based design method can be developed if more attention is given to performance in relation to density early in the process. In the case of the Alkmaar project, a pre-design discussion among stakeholders could have taken place concerning the mix of dwelling types, mix of functions, walkability in the area, and energy efficiency. Based on these discussions, density guidelines could have been defined on different scales which could have been used as a programme of requirements for the urban designer. Now the urban designer was set to work with a vague set of ambitions. Attractive images and engaging visions can be made based on vague ambitions, but in a situation where space is scarce and ambitions are high, and often conflicting, it is wise to discuss the performances first and then make a brilliant design that meets those goals.

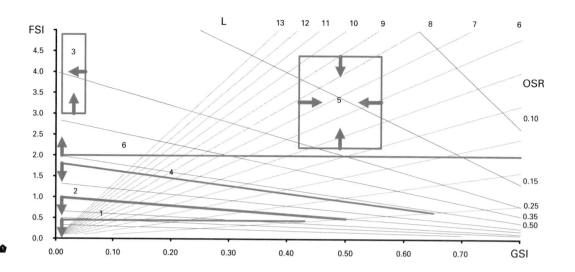

Doctrines which
have been argued
for through history,
polemically
translated into
density thresholds
in the Spacemate.
1
Unwin (1912)
2
Hoenig (1920s)
3
le Corbusier (1920s)
4
Gropius (1930)
5
Jacobs (1961)
6
Lozano (1990)

7
QUALITIES OF DENSITY

This book started off with a critical examination of the history of existing concepts of density and different measuring methods. As shown in Chapters 2 and 3, density was already present in early twentieth-century city building, and was used both to diagnose an ailing city and to prescribe solutions to the problems. Density was often used as part of the ideological agenda of urban professionals, ranging from Raymond Unwin, Reinhard Baumeister and the Garden City Movement at the beginning of the twentieth century, striving for a more healthy and social city, through to the modernist planners of CIAM and their preference for high-rise developments in a green and functionally organized city, via Jane Jacobs's advocacy for a compact city of medium height in the 1960s, to the late twentieth-century pursuit of urbanity and 'parallel revaluating of the [dense] city as the site of desirable middle-class lifestyles'.[1] All are examples of very different doctrines, relying on different applications of density to make their argument. These doctrinal shifts can be charted in the Spacemate. ◖

Serving as one of the instruments of modernist planning, density has lost much of its shine since the 1970s. At the same time, rather simplistic density measurements have continued to be used to formulate policies, plan ambitions and draw up contracts. Both these facts have been to the detriment of the notion: on the one hand, there is an association with the missionary zeal of a technocratic functionalism, and on the other, a lack of precision in its pragmatic use in current practice.

The development of the *Spacematrix method* to measure density and identify a series of associated properties is the main result of our research. We have redefined density as a multivariable and multi-scalar phenomenon to counter the existing Babel-like confusion in the terminology currently being used by those working in the urban field. Furthermore, through the use of this multivariable and multi-scalar approach, density can be related to urban form and other performances as has been shown in Chapters 4 and 5. This makes it possible to reposition the concept of density in the field of urban design and research. From an instrument to prescribe the programme of a given area, density can become a tool to guide both quantitative and qualitative ambitions in the urban planning and design process.

A MULTIVARIABLE AND MULTI-SCALAR DEFINITION OF DENSITY
Instead of expressing density through the number of dwellings per hectare, which is still dominant in the Dutch practice, we have demonstrated that density has to be treated as a *multivariable* phenomenon. The difference between high, spacious and compact, low developments with one and the same building bulk can only be made when density is viewed as a *composite of indicators*. Furthermore, we have argued for the integration of network density within the multivariable definition of density. This is, as far as we are aware, a unique addition to density research. By adding network density, an indicative size of the mesh of the urban fabric, its islands and street profile can be integrated in the definition of

1
Sorkin, M., 'The End(s) of Urban Design', *Harvard Design Magazine* fall 2006/winter 2007, 5–18, 10.

density. The combination of indicators proved to be adequate in defining fabric types and their performance in terms of parking, daylight, connectivity, exposure, etcetera.

In addition to being defined as a multivariable phenomenon, density should also be approached as a *multi-scalar* phenomenon. Knowledge of how density behaves through the scales generates important information about the distribution of built and open spaces. Adding a large park or a piece of large-scale infrastructure on the scale of a district reduces the density within that district, or, when this is unfeasible, necessitates compensation through higher densities on the lower scales. On the other hand, small-scale decisions and developments add up and result in a compound spatial claim on the scale of a city and region. Architecture and urban design on the micro scale must thus be related to urban space consumption and the associated spatial, environmental, economic and social consequences on the macro scale. And vice versa.

The creation of consensus concerning the Spacematrix method could ensure a certain objectivity that can dispel much of the confusion and subjectivity that surrounds the current application of density. Our research provides urbanists, be they researchers or planners and designers, with the definition of scales, the way boundaries on each level of scale are drawn and a method to calculate and compare different densities. Most important here is that the different actors use the same set of definitions, preferably published in an international or a Dutch standard such as the NEN 2580 standard used in architecture for measuring gross and net floor area. In December 2007, we initiated a process in collaboration with the NEN institute to arrive at a Dutch Standard for measuring urban density (NEN 9300). Delft University of Technology, PBL, NEPROM, BVR adviseurs, NVB, Aedes, and the municipalities of Rotterdam (dS+V) and Amsterdam (dRO/OGA) participate in the committee responsible for the creation of the new standard.

The last couple of years, the use of the Spacemate by a wide range of practitioners and researchers in urban planning and design has increased significantly, as was discussed in Chapter 6. Not only urban designers, architects, planners and students from the Netherlands and abroad have registered for the open source database SpaceCalculator, also consultants in the field of urbanism, developers, municipalities and researchers from other fields. This shows that our research has already contributed to the acceptance of density as a multivariable and multi-scalar phenomenon, and proves that the method is thought of as effective for the urban practice.

PERFORMANCE-BASED DESCRIPTION OF URBAN FABRICS

The 110 empirical samples that have been analysed in this research show that fabric types cluster in different positions in the Spacemate diagram ◑. These types do not have rigid borders, but slowly transform from one density position to another. What is most important to understand is that the conditions set by density very much influence the performance of a built environment. We suggest that performance-based descriptions of fabrics could become more important than the traditional image- or activity-based descriptions. Instead of naming low-rise block types or high-rise strip types, the fabric type could be described

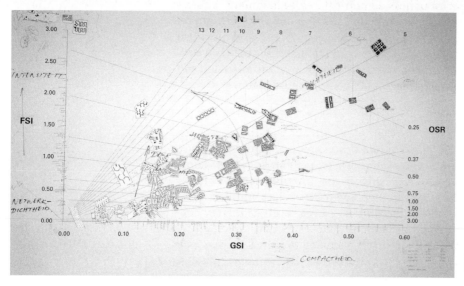

Emprirical samples
in the Spacemate.

❷

and prescribed solely by its Spacematrix density and the performance characteristics embedded in this density. The results of our research can hereby also be of great value to more traditional typomorphological research, as it relates urban form to density and performances other than form.

In Chapter 5 we discussed the performance of parking, daylight access and urbanity under different density conditions. Many more performances of urban fabrics could, and in our opinion should be researched and related to density in the same manner, contributing to a better underpinning of urban plans and designs. Instead of creating images, urban professionals will then be more involved with defining the conditions under which specific qualities (positive and negative) are most likely to be realized. This is especially the case for higher densities. In the light of the problems of increased urban space consumption, intensification will frequently become unavoidable. Understanding the capacity of space and the effects that density has on the performance and quality of the built landscape then becomes even more important.

We recommend that a distinction be made between *hard* and *soft* performances. Hard performances are more closely related to the geometry and the physics of the built environment and can be approached quantitatively through explorative research. Examples of such hard performances include parking and daylight access, which have been treated in Chapter 5, but also aspects such as traffic capacity, energy use, wind, noise and air quality. Examples of soft performances are urbanity, attractiveness and privacy. They are in many ways conditioned by the density and geometry of the built environment (distance, potential user intensity in open space, etcetera), but can only realistically be calibrated if collective and individual valuation are taken into account. In addition to explorative research, the correlation between soft performances and built density must be explored through more qualitative surveys. Besides the addition of other performances, empirical research on the subject should be done to further underpin and develop our results. More research on fabrics from an array of cultural, geographical and historical contexts can improve the understanding of the dialectics between density conditions and all sorts of constraints (physical, cultural, social) and the role they play in the emergence and transformation of cities.

SUSTAINABLE DENSITIES

As shown in Chapter 2 with the example of Amsterdam, there has been an exponential increase in per capita urban space consumption since the end of the nineteenth century. The causes and effects of this 'demo-spatial' development are the subject of intense debate among academics and experts. However, there seems to be a general consensus that sprawling cities, private mobility and high levels of energy consumption go hand in hand. Car mobility makes suburbia possible, and suburbia demands private mobility. Decreasing densities further contribute to car dependency, CO_2 production and climate change. Certainly, high-density alternatives to sprawling cities do not provide an instant solution to the problems of energy consumption and CO_2 production caused by car mobility, but they are prerequisites for other policies to combat climate change such as fiscal incentives, carbon rationing, investments in public transport, and so forth. These will be largely incompatible with low densities. The idea to densify our cities is more and more regarded as the key solution to arrive at a more sustainable city form. However, in the recently published *Concept Structuurvisie Almere 2.0*, only 20 per cent of the foreseen 60,000 new dwellings that are planned between now and 2030 are to be realized within the existing city.[2] In other words, more than 45,000 will be built on agricultural land or on new islands in the IJmeer. Of those, 60 per cent will be in low densities, similar to the extension areas built in the time of Vinex (<45 dwellings per hectare or FSI 0.7). Likewise, in the *Structuurvisie Randstad 2040*, 60 per cent of the envisioned new dwellings will be realized outside existing cities.[3] And in Rotterdam the ambition to intensify the city will for 60 per cent be realized by adding low-rise environments, consuming large amounts of tare space.[4] In our opinion, such developments are deeply in contradiction not only with much of the consensus among scientists and critics, but also with the guiding ambitions concerning energy, pollution and carbon reduction of the state and municipalities themselves. Sometimes intensification achieves real results, but very often it is offset by the continuing growth of (semi-urban) sprawl.

Knowledge about the consequences of micro-scale developments (for instance, consumers eager to live in ever-larger single-family homes) on the meso- and macro-scale (sprawling of people and activities, increased loss of arable land, ecosystem fragmentation, increase of car transportation, resulting in an increase in energy consumption, CO_2 production and air pollution), is needed to help informed debate and justify political decisions. Investigations also on micro-scale characteristics of (un)sustainable settlement patterns can help stimulate a general revaluation of high-density developments and the exploration of specific qualities of such high-density urban environments. The Spacematrix method can assist urban professionals and researchers in such investigations.

2
Municipality of Almere, *Concept Structuurvisie Almere 2.0* (Almere: Municipality of Almere and MVRDV, 2009).
3
VROM, *Structuurvisie Randstad 2040: Naar een duurzame en concurrerende Europese topregio* (The Hague: Ministry of Housing, Spatial Planning and the Environment, 2008), presented by the Dutch cabinet on 5 September 2008.
4
Municipality of Rotterdam, *Stadsvisie Rotterdam: Spatial Development Strategy 2030* (Rotterdam: dS+V, 2007).

On many fronts in society, an awareness of energy efficiency and conservation is manifest. In the area of spatial planning and design, more attention should be given to what could be called space economy. Space should be regarded as a scarce product. Not because it is really scarce in itself–the Netherlands could theoretically house the whole population in densities comparable to Los Angeles without any great spatial problem–but because an increased consumption of it corresponds to a larger consumption of other finite resources, and the increased production of waste and emissions. Studying the capacity of space and exposing the negative impacts of dispersed settlements can contribute to a larger awareness of the spatial dimension of the present crises.

Viewing urban density as a multivariable and multi-scalar phenomenon can at an early stage in decision making and urban planning contribute to more sustainable ways of city development. Knowledge of the relationship between density, urban space consumption and the environmental consequences of urbanization should be central to both policymaking and the planning and design practice.

THE PROFESSIONAL CHALLENGE

Other crucial challenges facing urban professionals have been described in this book. They are very much related to the all-encompassing neoliberalization of society of the last three decades. The privatization of spatial developments has led to a project-based planning approach where earlier public initiation and guidance (more or less centralized and publicly generated) has been scattered into localized particularities. Furthermore, globalization, the associated intensified competition between cities and regions, and the strengthening of an economic growth paradigm have contributed to a continuous increase of urban space consumption. All these processes have conditioned the present practice of city development and very much defined the task of the urban professional. For urbanism, this has meant that all actors are forced to negotiate quantitative goals and qualitative ambitions very early in the process of city development. Furthermore, the dynamics of the market makes programmes accidental and necessitates an open-ended and flexible planning and design process. The same market dynamics also fosters the use of imagery to attract investments, businesses, skilled employees, tourists, etcetera, and as such promotes a scattered project-based approach where 'seduction and inspiration' are prime effects, resulting in a kind of inverted blueprint planning. The end goal in such a situation is no longer a programme, but an image quality of a plan.

Both economic stagnation and environmental deprivation on a global scale at the beginning of the twenty-first century will have their repercussions on the nature of urban landscapes, existing as well as new ones. The trickledown effects of these developments will most certainly also be visible in spatial matters. As the state has regained some of its influence in the wake of current crises, the knowledge and instruments necessary to translate political goals into spatial results should become very important. This might result in a stronger emphasis on regulations and guidelines. To formulate such guidelines, the performance of different urban environments on many fronts–spatial, environmental, economic–will become central to decision making.

In this book a method has been presented that neither focuses specifically on the image nor on the programme for the city. The Spacematrix method provides urban professionals with an instrument that can simultaneously address quantity and quality, content and image, flexibility and precision. It can be used to make pre-designs in which the main programmatic and spatial qualities are described. Based on these, the feasibility of the project and other performances can be estimated. At the same time, the method allows for enough flexibility to incorporate changes during the process of realization. Chapter 6 has given some examples of initial applications of the method in practice.

An important contribution could be made to the national planning reports, such as the *Structuurvisie Randstad 2040* or structural visions on lower scale levels such as those in Amsterdam, Almere or Rotterdam.[5] *Structuurvisie Randstad 2040* states the ambition to realize 500,000 new homes in the Randstad, of which 40 per cent should be realized within existing cities. If the other 60 per cent (300,000 dwellings) were to be realized in suburban areas dominated by detached housing types (FSI_f=0.5), almost two times the area of Amsterdam would be required.[6] If this spatial claim is judged to be too large, and the addition has to take place on only half of this area (thus the size of Amsterdam), then density has to increase, be it on the scale of the fabric (requiring other fabric types) or the district and city (less green, working areas, etcetera). The Spacematrix method could be effective in understanding the relationship between such national plans mainly concerned with programme, the need for certain types of living environments and their effects in terms of space consumption, micro-scale options and energy efficiency. Changes in the demands for one of these components will affect all the others. Evaluating the result could lead to changes in other components, which will then again affect the parts and the whole. Such an iterative approach should profit from a simultaneous understanding of the quantitative and qualitative consequences on different levels of scale, and thus make better underpinned decisions possible.

Furthermore, truly flexible plans could be made using the Spacematrix method. Neither the image nor the programme are predetermined through the method, but density and performances are conditions under which the plan can be developed further by individuals, either in a competitive, self-organizing process, or by urban professionals in a more publicly guided process. Such a performance-based design is regarded by many as the new way to make urban plans, leaving blueprint planning – both image and programme driven – behind.

THE SCIENCE OF URBAN DENSITY

Density has the capacity to facilitate the communication between many different disciplines. Architecture, urban planning, traffic engineering, building physics, environmental sciences, social sciences, geography and economics; to those, density can act as a catalyst for a truly interdisciplinary branch of research: the science of urban density. We see three important fields of research for the future. First, the exploration of the relation between density and its performances on the scale levels of island and fabric should be continued and deepened. More research into the different soft and hard performances in relation to density is essential.

5
VROM, *Structuurvisie*, op. cit. (note 3); Municipality of Amsterdam, *Structuurplan Amsterdam: Kiezen voor stedelijkheid* (Amsterdam: dRO, 2003); Municipality of Almere, *Concept Structuurvisie*, op. cit. (note 2); Municipality of Rotterdam, *Stadsvisie Rotterdam*, op. cit. (note 4).
6
Based on 150 m² of floor space per dwelling, an FSI_f of 0.50, and needed tare space between fabrics and urbanized land comparable to the Amsterdam case (50 per cent).

Performances such as energy use, the valuation of different urban fabrics by (different groups of) the public, health issues in relation to density (such as walkability, stress and air quality) have a great potential to be further researched and instrumentalized for practical use. The GIS maps of Amsterdam that represent the Spacemate density and the functional mix in the city, available on the Internet since 2009, are an example of such a combined approach.[7] The expansion of the database SpaceCalculator with more international examples and more additional statistics (functional mix, house prices, socioeconomic figures and historical developments) could be used for further empirical research and would enable other disciplines to relate spatial and non-spatial issues to density. An open editing database, modelled on Wikipedia, would make it possible to collect and manage samples from all over the world. To be able to satisfy multiple, and often conflicting, performances in a design process, computation could be used to reach the most suitable densities and spatial solutions that fulfil the preferences of planners, developers or politicians.

Secondly, research into the relation between our multivariable approach to density to characterize a specific place, and the network analyses undertaken to understand the spatial interrelatedness of streets in a city, would enhance two fields of research that are currently separate. A first step in this research would be to relate the findings in this book to the work done by the research community of Space Syntax.

Finally, the extension of the approach presented in this book to the scale of the city and the region is of great importance. At these scales, the notion of tare space becomes central. The way the urban fabrics are distributed within a city or region is decisive for the spatial qualities that can be achieved. The focus on the relation between architecture and urbanism, which has been dominant until now, would then shift to urbanism, landscape architecture and planning. These scales are, in the light of the scarcity of land and other finite resources, necessary to address, and could lead to new distribution patterns of tare space within cities and regions. Local and regional population shrinkage might also contribute to the introduction of new tare spaces within cities.

A contribution to the science of density would be the initiation of a still to be formulated research project under the name of *ScarCity*. The engagement with *ScarCity* does not need to be a curse. On the contrary, it might stimulate a trans-disciplinary search for new qualities and the extraction of more out of less, using the Spacematrix method as one of its guiding tools.

7
www.gisdro.nl/functiemix.

LIST OF REFERENCES

Abrahamse, J.A., 'De ruimtelijke ontwikkeling van Amsterdam in de zeventiende eeuw en de opkomst van de stedebouw als wetenschap', in: B. Bakker and E. Schmitz (eds.), *Het aanzien van Amsterdam: Panorama's, plattegronden en profielen uit de Gouden Eeuw* (Bussum: Uitgeverij THOTH, 2007), 24-41.

Alexander, C., et al., *A Pattern Language: Towns, Buildings, Construction* (New York: Oxford University Press, 1977).

Alexander, E.R., 'Density Measures: A Review and Analysis', *Journal of Architectural and Planning Research* 10 (3) 1993, 181-202.

Angenot, L.H.J., *Verhandelingen over het vraagstuk van de dichtheid van bebouwing* (Alphen aan den Rijn: N. Samsom NV, 1954).

Anonymous, 'Nota tegen rommelig bouwen', *NRC Handelsblad* 28 June 2008.

ANP, 'CDA wil 5 miljoen extra parkeerplaatsen', *de Volkskrant* 1 July 2008.

Ashworth, G.J. and H. Voogd, 'Public Sector Market Planning: An Approach to Urban Revitalisation', paper presented at the conference *European Cities: Growth and Decline* (The Hague, April 1992).

Bach, B., et al., *Urban Design and Traffic; A Selection from Bach's Toolbox/Stedebouw en verkeer; een selectie uit de gereedschapskist van Bach* (Ede: Crow, 2006).

Barnett, J., 'Omaha by Design – All of It: New Prospects in Urban Planning and Design', *Harvard Design Magazine* Spring/Summer 2005, 44-49.

Barnett, J., *An Introduction to Urban Design* (New York: Harper and Row, 1982).

Barré, F., 'The Desire for Urbanity', *Architectural Design* 11/12 (1980), 4-7.

Berghauser Pont, M. and P. Haupt, *Space, Density and Urban Form* (Dissertation Delft University of Technology, 2009).

Berghauser Pont, M. and P. Haupt, *Spacemate: The Spatial Logic of Urban Density* (Delft: DUP Science, 2004).

Berman, M., *All That Is Solid Melts into Air: The Experience of Modernity* (New York: Penguin Books, 1988, first published in the USA by Simon & Schuster in 1982).

Bik, M. and D. Linders, *Factsheet – prognose: Bevolkingsontwikkeling Rotterdam 2003-2017* (Rotterdam: Centrum voor Onderzoek en Statistiek, 2003).

Brenner, N., *New State Spaces: Urban Governance and the Rescaling of Statehood* (Oxford: Oxford University Press, 2004).

Brenner, N. and N. Theodore, *Spaces of Neoliberalism: Urban Restructuring in North America and Western Europe* (Oxford: Blackwell Publishing, 2002).

Brenner, R., *The Economics of Global Turbulence: The Advanced Capitalist Economies from Long Boom to Long Downturn, 1945-2005* (London: Verso, 2006).

Bruegmann, R., *Sprawl: A Compact History* (Chicago: University of Chicago Press, 2005).

Brunner, C., *Densité et formes urbaines dans la métropole marseillaise* (Marseilles: Edition Imbernon, 2005).

Buchanan, C.D., *Mixed Blessing: The Motor in Britain* (London: Leonard Hill, 1958).

Bureau Parkstad, *Een blik vooruit: Vijf jaar vernieuwingsoperaties in Amsterdam Nieuw West: evaluatie en keuzerichtingen* (Amsterdam, 2005).

Bureau Parkstad, *Ruimtelijke kwaliteitskader ParkStad: Toetsingskader, instrumentarium en handvat voor ontwerpers*, second concept (Amsterdam, May 2001).

Bureau Parkstad, *Richting ParkStad 2015: Ontwikkelingsplan voor de vernieuwing. Samenvatting*, concept (Amsterdam, February 2001).

Bureau Parkstad, *Leefmilieus ParkStad: Bijlage 5 – Richting Parkstad 2015*, concept (Amsterdam, February 2001).

Burg, A.J. van der and B.L. Vink, 'Randstad Holland towards 2040 – Perspectives from National Government', 44th ISOCARP Congress (Dalian, China 16-19 September 2008).

Busquets, J., *Barcelona, the Urban Evolution of a Compact City* (Rovereto: Nicolodi, 2005).

Calabrese, L.M., *Reweaving UMA: Urbanism, Mobility, Architecture* (Rotterdam: Optima Grafische Communicatie, 2004).

Cammen, H. van der, and L. de Klerk, *Ruimtelijke Ordening: Van grachtengordel tot Vinex-wijk* (Utrecht: Het Spectrum, 2003).

Campoli, J. and A.S. MacLean, *Visualizing Density* (Cambridge, MA: Lincoln Institute of Land Policy, 2007).

Carbonell, A. and R. Yaro, 'American Spatial Development and the New Megalopolis', *Land Lines*, 17 (2) 2005.

Castex, J., J-C. Depaule and P. Panerai, *De rationele stad: Van bouwblok tot wooneenheid* (Amsterdam: SUN, 2003), originally published in 1977 as *Formes urbaines: de l'ilot a la barre.*

CBS, *Historie bouwnijverheid vanaf 1899* (The Hague: Statistics Netherlands, 2008).

CBS, *Kerncijfers postcodegebied 2004* (The Hague: Statistics Netherlands, 2006).

CETAT, *Indicateurs morphologiques pour l'amenagement: Analyse de 50 périmetres batis situes sur le canton de Geneve* (Geneva: Departement des traveaux publics, 1986).

Churchman, A., 'Disentangling the Concept of Density', *Journal of Planning Literature*, 13 (4) 1999, 389–411.

City of New York, *Zoning Handbook* (New York, 1990).

Claessens, F. and E. van Velzen, 'De actualiteit van het stedelijk project', *Stedebouw & Ruimtelijke Ordening*, 87 (4) 2006, 32–37.

Conzen, M.R.G., *Alnwick, Northumberland: A Study in Town-Plan Analysis,* series: The Institute of British Geographers, publication 27 (London: Philip, 1960).

Couch, C., L. Leontidou and G. Petschel-Held, *Urban Sprawl in Europe: Landscapes, Land-Use Change & Policy* (Oxford: Blackwell Publishing, 2007).

Crimson, *Too Blessed to Be Depressed: Crimson Architectural Historians 1994–2002* (Rotterdam: 010 Publishers, 2002).

Davis, M., *Planet of Slums* (London/New York: Verso, 2006).

Davis, M. and D.B. Monk (eds.), *Evil Paradises: Dreamworlds of Neoliberalism* (New York: The New Press, 2007).

Dijkstra, C., M. Reitsma and A. Rommerts, *Atlas Amsterdam* (Bussum: Uitgeverij THOTH, 1999).

Duivesteijn, A., *Notie van ruimte: Op weg naar de vijfde nota ruimtelijke ordening*, Parlementaire werkgroep vijfde nota ruimtelijke ordening (The Hague: Sdu uitgevers, 2000).

Elliott, D.L., *A Better Way to Zone: Ten Principles to Create More Livable Cities* (Washington, DC: Island Press, 2008).

Engel, H., 'Randstad Holland in kaart', in: F. Claessens and H. Engel (eds.), *OverHolland 2* (Amsterdam: SUN, 2005), 22–44.

Engel, H. and E. van Velzen, 'De vorm van de stad: Nederland na 1945', in: E. Taverne and I. Visser (eds.), *Stedebouw: De geschiedenis van de stad in de Nederlanden van 1500 tot heden* (Nijmegen: SUN, 1993), 276–282.

Faludi, A. and A. van der Valk, *Rule and Order: Dutch Planning Doctrine in the Twentieth Century* (Dordrecht: Kluwer Academic Publishers, 1994).

Fernandez Per, A., and J. Mozas, *DBOOK: Density, Data, Diagrams, Dwellings* (Vitoria-Gasteiz: a+t ediciones, 2007).

Fernandez Per, A., and J. Mozas, *Densidad/Density* (Vitoria-Gasteiz: a+t ediciones, 2004).

Floet, W.W. and E. Gramsbergen, *Zakboek voor de woonomgeving* (Rotterdam: 010 Publishers, 2001).

Florida, R., *Cities and the Creative Class* (New York: Routledge, 2005).

Forsyth, A., 'Measuring Density: Working Definitions for Residential Density and Building Density', *Design Brief*, 8 2003, Design Center for American Urban Landscape, University of Minesota.

Hajer, M., 'Rekenen of tekenen?', *Staatscourant*, 11 October 2000, 3.

Hajer, M., *De stad als publiek domein* (Amsterdam: Wiardi Beckman Stichting, 1989).

Hall, P., *Cities in Civilization* (London: Phoenix, 1999).

Hall, P., *Cities of Tomorrow* (Oxford: Blackwell Publishers, 1996).

Hameleers, M. (ed.), *Kaarten van Amsterdam 1866-2000* (Bussum: Uitgeverij THOTH, 2002).

Harvey, D., *A Brief History of Neoliberalism* (Oxford: Oxford University Press, 2005).

Harvey, D., 'New Urbanism and the Communitarian Trap', in: W.S. Saunders (ed.), *Sprawl and Suburbia, A Harvard Design Magazine Reader* (Minneapolis: University of Minnesota Press, 2005).

Harvey, D., 'From Managerialism to Entrepreneurialism: The Transformation in Urban Governance in Late Capitalism', *Geografiska Annaler* 71B 1989, 3-17.

Harvey, D., *The Urbanization of Capital* (Baltimore: John Hopkins University Press, 1985).

Haupt, P., 'Adriaan Geuze, Rem Koolhaas och staden som inte längre finns', *Arkitektur*, 1 1996, 68-73.

Haupt, P. and M. van Esch, 'Daylight and Urban Density', in: H. Bekkering et al. (eds.), *The Architectural Annual 2005-2006*, Delft University of Technology (Rotterdam: 010 Publishers, 2007), 86-91.

Heeling, J., H. Meyer and J. Westrik, *Het ontwerp van de stadsplattegrond* (Amsterdam: SUN, 2002).

Heimans, A., *Bebouwingsdichtheid en grondgebruik voor de woningbouw in stadsuitbreidingen* (The Hague: Ten Hagen, 1965).

Hellinga, H. and P. de Ruijter, *Algemeen Uitbreidingsplan Amsterdam 50 jaar* (Amsterdam: Amsterdamse Raad voor de Stedebouw, 1985).

Hereijgers, A. and E. van Velzen, *De naoorlogse stad, een hedendaagse ontwerpopgave* (Rotterdam: NAi Publishers, 2001).

Hobma, F., De verwevenheid van publiekrechtelijk en privaatrechtelijk handelen. In: I. Bruil et al. (eds.), *Integrale gebiedsontwikkeling: Het stationsgebied 's-Hertogenbosch* (Amsterdam: SUN, 2004), 280-293.

Hobsbawm, E., *The Age of Extremes: 1914-1991* (London: Michael Joseph, 1994).

Hobsbawm, E., *The Age of Empire: 1875-1914* (London: Weidenfeld and Nicholson, 1987).

Hobsbawm, E., *The Age of Capital: 1848-1875* (London: Weidenfeld and Nicholson, 1975).

Hobsbawm, E., *The Age of Revolution: 1789-1848* (London: Weidenfeld and Nicholson, 1962).

Hoenig, A., 'Baudichte und Weitraumigkeit', *Baugilde* 10 1928, 713-715.

Hulsman, B., 'Die domme steden', NRC *Handelsblad* 28 February/1 March 2009, 4-5.

Jacobs, J., *The Death and Life of Great American Cities* (New York: Random House, 1992), originally published in 1961.

Jameson, F., *Postmodernism, or, the Cultural Logic of Late Capitalism* (London: Verso, 1991).

Jenks, M., E. Burton and K. Williams (eds.), *The Compact City: A Sustainable Urban Form?* (London: E&FN Spoon, 1996).

Jong, T. de, et al., *Sun Wind Water Earth Life and Living: Legends for Design* (Delft: Publicatiebureau Bouwkunde, 2004).

Jong, T. de and H. Engel, 'Typological Research', in: T.M. de Jong and D.J.M. van der Voordt (eds.), *Ways to Study and Research Urban, Architectural and Technical Design* (Delft: DUP Science, 2002), 103-106.

Jong, T. de and D.J.M. van der Voordt, 'Criteria for Scientific Study and Design', in: T.M. de Jong and D.J.M. van der Voordt (eds.), *Ways to Study and Research Urban, Architectural and Technical Design* (Delft: DUP Science, 2002), 19-30.

Jong, T. de and D.J.M. van der Voordt (eds.), *Ways to Study and Research Urban, Architectural and Technical Design* (Delft: DUP Science, 2002)

Kann, F. van and W. Leduc, 'Synergy between regional planning and energy as a contribution to a carbon neutral society – energy cascading as a new principle for mixed land-use'. Paper presented at the SCUPAD conference (Salzburg, Austria, 2008).

Kendig, L., *Performance Zoning* (Washington, DC: Planners Press, APA, 1980).

Klerk, L. de, *De modernisering van de stad 1850-1914: De opkomst van de planmatige stadsontwikkeling in Nederland* (Rotterdam: NAi Publishers, 2008).

Klerk, L. de, *Particuliere plannen: Denkbeelden en initiatieven van de stedelijke elite inzake volkswoningbouw en de stedebouw in Rotterdam, 1860-1950* (Rotterdam: NAi Publishers, 1998).

Kloos, M. and D. Wendt, *Formats for Living: Contemporary Floor Plans in Amsterdam* (Amsterdam: ARCAM/Architectura & Natura Press, 2000).

Koolhaas, R., *S,M,L,XL* (Rotterdam: 010 Publishers, 1995).

Koolhaas, R., *Delirious New York* (Rotterdam: 010 Publishers, 1994).

Kuenzli, P. and A. Lengkeek, *Urban jazz: Pleidooi voor de zelfgebouwde stad* (Rotterdam: 010 Publishers, 2004).

Kunstler, J., 'Review of Sprawl: A Compact History', *Salmagundi* 152 (Fall 2006), 175–183.

Kusumo, C., *Railway Stations, Centres and Markets: Change and Stability in Patterns of Urban Centrality* (Dissertation Delft University of Technology, 2007).

Laloli, H.M., 'Beter wonen? Woningmarkt en residentiële segregatie in Amsterdam 1850–1940', in: O.W.A. Boonstra et al. (eds.), *Twee eeuwen Nederland geteld: Onderzoek met de digitale volks-, beroeps- en woningtellingen 1795–2001* (The Hague: DANS and CBS, 2007).

Larice, M. and E. Macdonald (eds.), *The Urban Design Reader* (Oxon: Routledge, 2007).

Le Corbusier, *Towards a New Architecture* (Los Angeles: Getty Research Institute, 2007), originally published in 1923 as *Vers une architecture*.

Leeuwen, H. van, 'Geef bouwgrond niet aan speculanten', *NRC Handelsblad* 18 August 2008.

Lengkeek, A., *Stedelijkheid als rendement: Privaat initiatief voor publieke ruimte* (Haarlem: Trancity, 2007).

Loon, P.P. van, E. Heurkens and S. Bronkhorst, *Urban Decision Room: An Urban Management Instrument* (Amsterdam: IOS Press, 2008).

Lörzing, H., W. Klemm, M. van Leeuwen and S. Soekimin, *Vinex! Een morfologische verkenning* (Rotterdam: NAi Publishers, 2006).

Lozano, E., 'Density in Communities, or the Most Important Factor in Building Urbanity', in: M. Larice and E. Macdonald (eds.), *The Urban Design Reader* (Oxon: Routledge, 2007), 312–327.

Lynch, K., *A Theory of Good City Form* (Cambridge, MA: MIT Press, 1981).

Maarse, A., 'Wetten en regels', *Rooilijn* 41 (3) 2008, 155.

Marshall, S., *Streets & Patterns* (Oxon: Spon Press, 2005).

Martin, L. and L. March (eds.), *Urban Space and Structures* (Cambridge: Cambridge University Press, 1972).

Martin, M. and C. Wagenaar, 'Stadsverfraaing en stadsuitbreiding', in: E. Taverne and I. Visser (eds.), *Stedebouw: De geschiedenis van de stad in de Nederlanden van 1500 tot heden* (Nijmegen: SUN, 1993), 124–129.

Meer, A.J. van der, *Gemeentegrenzen Nederland 1795 – heden* (Dissertation, Delft University of Technology, 2007).

Meijsmans, N., 'The Urban Project on a Regional Scale?', paper presented at the conference *The Urban Project* (Delft, the Netherlands 4–7 June 2008).

Metz, T. and M. Pflug, *Atlas van Nederland in 2005: De Nieuwe Kaart* (Rotterdam: NAi Publishers, 1997).

Meyer, H. et al., *Ruimtelijke transformaties in kleine nederzettingen: West-Nederland: 1850–2000* (Delft: Delft University of Technology, Faculty of Architecture, 2006).

Meyer, H., F. de Josselin de Jong and M.J. Hoekstra (eds.), *Het ontwerp van de openbare ruimte* (Amsterdam: SUN, 2006).

Meyer, H., 'In dienst van de stad onder postmoderne condities/Working for the City under Post-modern Conditions', in: H. Meyer and L. van den Burg (eds.), *In dienst van de stad/Working for the City* (Amsterdam: SUN, 2005), 64–68.

Meyer, H., 'Plan Analysis', in: T.M. de Jong and D.J.M. van der Voordt (eds.), *Ways to Study and Research Urban, Architectural and Technical Design* (Delft: DUP Science, 2002), 125–136.

Meyer, H., *City and Port: Transformation of Port Cities London, Barcelona, New York, Rotterdam* (Utrecht: International Books, 1999).

Moll, H., 'Vuile teringstad: Vijf eeuwen besmettelijke ziekten in Amsterdam', *NRC Handelsblad* 31 January 2001.

Moudon, A.V., 'Getting to Know the Built Landscape: Typomorphology', in: K. Franck and L. Schneekloth (eds.), *Ordering Space: Types in Architecture and Design* (New York: Van Nostrand Reinhold, 1994), 289–311.

Mulder, B. de, 'Old Dispersions and Scenes for the Production of Public Space. The Constructive Margins of Secondarity', *Architectural Design* 78 (1) 2008, 28–33.

Mumford, L., *The City in History: Its Origins, Its Transformations, and Its Prospects* (New York: Harcourt, Brace and World, 1961).

Municipality of Almere, *Concept Structuurvisie Almere 2.0* (Almere: Municipality of Almere and MVRDV, 2009).

Municipality of Amersfoort, *Amersfoort in cijfers* (Amersfoort: Onderzoek en statistiek, 2006).

Municipality of Amsterdam, *Uitwerkingsplan kerngebied Reimerswaalbuurt* (Amsterdam: Neighbourhood Council Osdorp/Ymere, 2005).

Municipality of Amsterdam, *Studie hoogbouw in Amsterdam-Noord* (Amsterdam: Neighbourhood Council Amsterdam-Noord, R&EB, 2003).

Municipality of Amsterdam, *Structuurplan Amsterdam: Kiezen voor stedelijkheid* (Amsterdam: dRO, 2003).

Municipality of Amsterdam, *Meten met twee maten: Referentieplannen bebouwingsintensiteit* (Amsterdam: dRO, coördinatieteam Optimalisering Grondgebruik, 2001).

Municipality of Amsterdam, *Midwest: Differentiatie en intensivering in de Westelijke Tuinsteden* (Amsterdam: dRO, 1999).

Municipality of Amsterdam, *Algemeen Uitbreidingsplan van Amsterdam (AUP): Nota van toelichting* (Amsterdam: Stadsdrukkerij Amsterdam, 1934).

Municipality of den Haag, *Haagse referentie projecten: Achtergronddocument: Uitwerking structuurvisie den Haag 2020* (The Hague: DSO-ROMZ, 2006).

Municipality of Rotterdam, *Stadsvisie Rotterdam: Spatial Development Strategy 2030* (Rotterdam: dS+V, 2007).

Municipality of Rotterdam, *De Rotterdamse woonmilieuprofielen-atlas* (Rotterdam: dS+V, afdeling Wonen, 2003).

Municipality of Tilburg, *Ontwikkelingsvisie Piushavengebied* (Tilburg, 2002).

Musch, M., 'Polder Ground', OASE 52 (1999), 16–31.

MVRDV, *Metacity/Datatown* (Rotterdam: 010 Publishers, 1999).

MVRDV, *Farmax* (Rotterdam: 010 Publishers, 1998).

Neighbourhood Council Slotervaart, *Stedebouwkundig Plan Sloterweg Zuid West*, (Amsterdam, 2006).

NEN, *NEN 2580: Areas and Volumes of Buildings – Terms, Definitions and Methods of Determination* (Delft: NEN, 2007).

NEN, *NEN 12464–1:2002: Light and Lighting – Light of Workplaces – Part 1: Indoor Workplaces* (Delft: NEN, 2003).

Netherlands Institute for Spatial Research, *Demographic Decline and Spatial Development: Planning for the Consequences of Population Changes, Summary* (The Hague: RPB, 2006).

Neuman, M., 'The Compact City Fallacy', *Journal of Planning Education and Research* 25 (2005), 11–26.

Newman, P. and J. Kenworthy, *Sustainability and Cities: Overcoming Automobile Dependence* (Chicago: University of Chicago Press, 1999).

Nozzi, D., *Road to Ruin: An Introduction to Sprawl and How to Cure It* (Westport: Praeger Publishers, 2003).

Nycolaas, J., *Volkshuisvesting: Een bijdrage tot de geschiedenis van woningbouw en woningbeleid in Nederland, met name sedert 1945* (Nijmegen: SUN, 1974).

O+S, Statistics available on www.os.amsterdam.nl.

Ottens, E., 'De aanloop naar de Woningwet: "de holen der mensen..."', in: J. Keesom (ed.), *Wonen. Woning. Wet. Wij wonen – 100 jaar Woningwet* (Amsterdam: Stedelijke Woningdienst Amsterdam, 2000), 9–40.

Panerai, P., 'De schaal van het bouwblok', in: S. Komossa et al., *Atlas van het Hollandse bouwblok* (Bussum: Uitgeverij THOTH, 2002), 11–14.

Permeta architecten, *Task Force Ruimtewinst. Assist Alkmaar: Een groeimodel voor de Waterkwekerij*, in cooperation with Rudy Uytenhaak, commissioned by DHV Ruimte en Mobiliteit (Amsterdam, 2007).

Permeta architecten, 'Verdichtingsstudie groeimodel', *TFR-update* 5, (Haarlem: Task Force Ruimtewinst Provincie Noord-Holland 2007), 8-10.

Permeta architecten, *Project Ondersteboven*, in cooperation with Delft University of Technology, commissioned by VROM/DGR (Amsterdam, 2005).

Permeta architecten, *Spacemate – Zuidoostlob: Kwantitatieve analyse van dichtheden en transformaties*, in cooperation with Delft University of Technology, commissioned by dRO (Amsterdam, 2004).

Permeta architecten, *FSI-GSI-OSR als instrumentarium voor verdichting en verdunning: Case study Nieuw West*, commissioned by Bureau Parkstad (Amsterdam, 2002).

Permeta architecten, *FSI-GSI-OSR: Atlas Westelijke Tuinsteden, instrumentarium voor verdichting en verdunning*, commissioned by Bureau Parkstad (Amsterdam, 2001).

Permeta architecten, *FSI-GSI-OSR als instrumentarium voor verdichting en verdunning: Case study Nieuw West*, commissioned by Bureau Parkstad (Amsterdam, 2000).

Plas, G. van der, 'Amsterdam 1750–1850: van stadsstaat naar hoofdstad', in: E. Taverne and I. Visser (eds.), *Stedebouw: De geschiedenis van de stad in de Nederlanden van 1500 tot heden* (Nijmegen: SUN, 1993), 148-159.

Poulantzas, N., *State, Power, Socialism* (London: Verso, 2000), originally published in 1978 as *L'Etat, le Pouvoir, le Socialisme*.

Province of North-Holland, *Bouwen voor Waterland 2020* (Haarlem, 2004).

Punter, J., 'Design Guidelines in American Cities: Conclusions', in: M. Larice and E. Macdonald (eds.), *The Urban Design Reader* (Oxon: Routledge, 2007), 500-516.

RACM, *Nota Belvedere* (The Hague: The National Service for Archaeology, Cultural Landscape and Built Heritage, 1999).

Rådberg, J., *Doktrin och täthet i svenskt stadsbyggande 1875-1975* (Stockholm: Statens råd för byggnadsforskning, 1988).

Rapaport, A., 'Toward a Redefinition of Density', *Environment and Behaviour* 7 (2) 1975, 7-32.

Rees, W., 'Ecological Footprint and Appreciated Carrying Capacity: What Urban Economics Leave Out', *Environment and Urbanisation* 4 (2) 1992, 121-130.

Roding, J., 'Vande oirdeningh der Steden', in: E. Taverne and I. Visser (eds.), *Stedebouw: De geschiedenis van de stad in de Nederlanden van 1500 tot heden* (Nijmegen: SUN, 1993), 51-56.

Rofé, Y., 'Space and Community: The Spatial Foundations of Urban Neighborhoods', *Berkeley Planning Journal* 10 (1995), 107-125.

Rosenberg, C.E., *The Cholera Years: The United States in 1832, 1849 and 1866* (Chicago: The University of Chicago Press, 1987).

Rowe, C. and F. Koetter, *Collage City* (Cambridge, MA: MIT Press, 1978).

Ruijter, P. de, *Voor volkshuisvesting en stedebouw* (Utrecht: Matrijs, 1987).

Rutte, R., *A Landscape of Towns: Urbanization in the Netherlands from the 11th to the 19th Centuries* (Delft: Delft University of Technology, Faculty of Architecture, 2004).

Sandercock, L., 'Anatomy of Civic Ambition in Vancouver: Toward Humane Density', in: W.S. Saunders (ed.), *Urban Planning Today* (Minneapolis: University of Minnesota Press, 2006), 48-62.

Sassen, S., 'Too Big to Save: The End of Financial Capitalism'. Available online at http://www.opendemocracy.net (accessed 24 November 2009).

Saunders, W.S., 'Cappuccino Urbanism, and Beyond', *Harvard Design Magazine* fall 2006/winter 2007, 3.

Schreuder, A., 'Wat goed in Breda past, past niet overal in de Randstad', *NRC Handelsblad* 13/14 September 2008, 5.

Schuit, J. van der, H. Van Amsterdam, M. Breedijk and A. Hendriks, *Ruimte in cijfers 2006* (The Hague: Netherlands Institute for Spatial Research, 2006).

Segeren, A., *De grondmarkt voor woningbouwlocaties* (Rotterdam: NAi Publishers, 2007).

Sennet, R., *The Fall of Public Man* (New York: Knopf, 1977).

Sert, J.L., *Can Our Cities Survive? An ABC of Urban Problems, Their Analysis, Their Solutions Based on Proposals Formulated by the CIAM* (Boston: Harvard University Press, 1942).

Siksna, A., 'The Effects of Block Size and Form in North American and Australian City Centres', *Urban Morphology* 1 (1997), 19–33.

Sola-Morales, M. de, 'Towards a Definition: Analysis of Urban Growth in the Nineteenth Century', *Lotus*, 19 June 1978, 28–36.

Sommer, R.M., 'Beyond Centers, "Fabrics," and the Culture of Congestion: Urban Design as a Metropolitan Enterprise', *Harvard Design Magazine* fall 2006/winter 2007, 50–59.

Sorkin, M., 'The End(s) of Urban Design', *Harvard Design Magazine* fall 2006/winter 2007, 5–18.

Sorkin, M. (ed.), *A Theme Park: The New American City and the End of Public Space* (New York: Hill and Wang, 1992).

Stichting Architectuur Research, *Deciding on Density: An Investigation into High Density Allotments with a View to the Waldeck Area, The Hague* (Eindhoven, 1977).

Ståhle, A., *Compact Sprawl: Exploring Public Open Space and Contradictions in Urban Density* (Stockholm: KTH, 2008).

Taverne, E., 'Kan de erfgoed de ruimtelijke ordening redden?', in: F. Claessens and H. Engel (eds.), *OverHolland 2* (Amsterdam: SUN, 2005), 107–110.

Taverne, E., *De wortels van de contemporaine stad*, Reader Architectuur- en Stedenbouwgeschiedenis (Groningen: Rijksuniversiteit Groningen, 2000).

Terlouw, E., 'A House of One's Own', *OASE* 52 (1999), 32–77.

Tummers, L.J.M. and J.M. Tummers-Zuurmond, *Het land in de stad: De stedebouw van de grote agglomeratie* (Bussum: Uitgeverij THOTH, 1997).

UN, National Statistical Offices/UN/Euromonitor International, 2009.

Unwin, R., *Nothing Gained by Overcrowding! How the Garden City Type of Development May Benefit Both Owner and Occupier* (Westminster: P.S. King & Son, 1912).

Unwin, R., *Town Planning in Practice* (London: T.Fisher Unwin, 1909).

Urhahn, G.B. and M. Bobic, *Strategie voor stedelijkheid* (Bussum: Uitgeverij THOTH, 1996).

Urhahn, G.B. and M. Bobic, *A Pattern Image* (Bussum: Uitgeverij THOTH, 1994).

Urhahn Urban Design, *De woonwijk van de toekomst*, Idea book for the Bouwfonds Award, organized by the NIROV, 2000.

Uytenhaak, R., *Cities Full of Space: Qualities of Density* (Rotterdam: 010 Publishers, 2008).

Venema, H., 'Bos en Lommer', in: S. Komossa et al. (eds.), *Atlas van het Hollandse bouwblok* (Bussum: Uitgeverij THOTH, 2002), 112–123.

VROM, *Structuurvisie Randstad 2040: Naar een duurzame en concurrerende Europese topregio* (The Hague: Ministry of Housing, Spatial Planning and the Environment, 2008), presented by the Dutch cabinet on 5 September 2008.

VROM, *Standaard vergelijkbare bestemmingsplannen 2006* (The Hague: Ministry of Housing, Spatial Planning and the Environment, Directoraat-Generaal Ruimte, 2006).

VROM, *Nota ruimte – ruimte voor ontwikkeling* (The Hague: Ministry of Housing, Spatial Planning and the Environment, 2004).

VROM, *Vijfde nota over de ruimtelijke ordening* (The Hague: Ministry of Housing, Spatial Planning and the Environment, 2001).

VROM, *Nota wonen: Mensen, wensen, wonen* (The Hague: Ministry of Housing, Spatial Planning and the Environment, 2000).

VROM, *Vierde nota over de ruimtelijke ordening extra* (The Hague: Ministry of Housing, Spatial Planning and the Environment, 1994).

VROM, *Vierde nota over de ruimtelijke ordening* (The Hague: Ministry of Housing, Spatial Planning and the Environment, 1988).

VROM, *Structuurschets stedelijke gebieden* (The Hague: Ministry of Housing, Spatial Planning and the Environment, 1983).

VROM, *Derde nota over de ruimtelijke ordening* (The Hague: Ministry of Housing, Spatial Planning and the Environment, 1973-1983).

VROM, *Verstedelijkingsnota* (The Hague: Ministry of Housing, Spatial Planning and the Environment, 1976).

VROM, *Tweede nota over de ruimtelijke ordening* (The Hague: Ministry of Housing, Spatial Planning and the Environment, 1966).

VROM, *Wet op de ruimtelijke ordening* (The Hague: Ministry of Housing, Spatial Planning and the Environment, 1965).

VROM, *Nota inzake de ruimtelijke ordening* (The Hague: Ministry of Public Housing and Construction Industry, 1960).

Wagenaar, M., 'Amsterdam 1860-1940: Een bedrijvige stad', in: E. Taverne and I. Visser (eds.), *Stedebouw: De geschiedenis van de stad in de Nederlanden van 1500 tot heden* (Nijmegen: SUN, 1993), 218-234.

Webber, M., 'The Urban Place and the Non-Place Urban Realm', in: M. Webber et al., *Explorations in Urban Structure* (Philadelphia: University of Pennsylvania, 1964).

Wigmans, G., 'Maatschappelijke trends en gebiedsontwikkeling: Een probleemschets', in: I. Bruil et al. (eds.), *Integrale gebiedsontwikkeling: Het stationsgebied 's-Hertogenbosch* (Amsterdam: SUN, 2004), 30-49.

Wintershoven, L., *Demografisch eeuwboek Amsterdam: Ontwikkelingen tussen 1900 en 2000* (Amsterdam: dRO, 2000).

Wouden, R. van der (ed.) *De stad op straat: De openbare ruimte in perspectief* (The Hague: Sociaal en Cultureel Planbureau, 1999).

Wright, F.L., *The Disappearing City* (New York: W.F. Payson, 1932).

Yoshida, H. and M. Omae, 'An approach for analysis of urban morphology: methods to derive morphological properties of city blocks by using an urban model and their interpretations', *Computers, Environments and Urban Systems*, 29 (2005), 223-247.

Zijderveld, A.C., *Steden zonder stedelijkheid: Cultuurhistorische verkenning van een beleidsprobleem* (Deventer: van Loghum Slaterus, 1983).

Zimmerman, A.L., *Ruimtegebruik in de stedebouw* (Amsterdam: Woningstichting Eigen Haard, 2007).

This book was made possible in part by the generous support of the Department of Urbanism, Faculty of Architecture, Delft University of Technology; The Ministry of Housing, Spatial Planning and the Environment (VROM); The Spatial Planning Department – City of Amsterdam (DRO); and Van Eesteren-Fluck & Van Lohuizen Foundation

Authors: Meta Berghauser Pont and
    Per Haupt
Copy editor: D'Laine Camp
Book design: Studio Joost Grootens /
    Joost Grootens, Tine van Wel
Paper: Munken Lynx, 120 grs
Printing: Lecturis, Eindhoven
Production: Marcel Witvoet, NAi Publishers,
    Rotterdam
Publisher: Eelco van Welie, NAi Publishers,
    Rotterdam

Although every effort was made to find the copyright holders for the illustrations used, it has not been possible to trace them all. Interested parties are requested to contact NAi Publishers, Mauritsweg 23, 3012 JR Rotterdam, The Netherlands.

NAi Publishers is an internationally orientated publisher specialized in developing, producing and distributing books on architecture, visual arts and related disciplines. www.naipublishers.nl

Available in North, South and Central America through D.A.P./Distributed Art Publishers Inc, 155 Sixth Avenue 2nd Floor, New York, NY 10013–1507, tel +1 212 627 1999, fax +1 212 627 9484, dap@dapinc.com

Available in the United Kingdom and Ireland through Art Data, 12 Bell Industrial Estate, 50 Cunnington Street, London W4 5HB, tel +44 208 747 1061, fax +44 208 742 2319, orders@artdata.co.uk

Printed and bound in the Netherlands
ISBN 978–90–5662–742–3

www.spacematrix.nl